MOUNTAIN LION

MOUNTAIN LION
An Unnatural History of
Pumas and People

Chris Bolgiano

STACKPOLE
BOOKS

Published by
STACKPOLE BOOKS
5067 Ritter Road
Mechanicsburg, PA 17055

Printed in the United States of America

Jacket art by Heiner Hertling
Cover typography by Mark Olszewski with Tina Hill

First Edition

10   9   8   7   6   5   4   3   2   1

Portions of several chapters appeared in different form in *Wilderness, Buzzworm,*
and *Defenders* magazines, and in the travel section of *The Washington Post*.

Page 209 constitutes a continuation of the copyright page.

Library of Congress Cataloging-in-Publication Data

Bolgiano, Chris.
     Mountain lion : an unnatural history of North America's big cat / Chris Bolgiano.
  — 1st ed.
      p.   cm.
     ISBN 0-8117-1044-0
  1. Pumas—United States—History.   2. Indians of North America—Ethnozoology.
  I. Title.
QL737.C23B645   1995
599.74′428—dc20
                                                                              95-10063
                                                                                  CIP

For Ralph

CONTENTS

ACKNOWLEDGMENTS

MANY PEOPLE HAVE BEEN ASTONISHINGLY KIND AND GENEROUS IN helping me research this book. For inviting a total stranger into their homes, I heartily thank Kathleen McCoy and Pat Ryan, who shared their love and knowledge of the Navajo Way; Harley and Patty Shaw, who settled me in their Treetops room; and Kerry and Sue Murphy, who allowed me to stay longer than expected as carefully laid plans crumbled. Leigh Jenkins of the Hopi Tribe, Henry and Ambrose Wallace and Albert and Maria Sagina of the Navajo Nation, and officers in several Pueblos made me feel welcome. Kenny Logan and Linda Sweanor changed their research schedule to come down from the mountains and talk with me. More people than I can conveniently name in state and federal wildlife agencies gave unstintingly of their time and knowledge, particularly in Florida, California, and Texas. Steve Croy and John Coleman of the George Washington National Forest in Virginia; Chip Clark, Bob Fisher, and Claudia Angle of the Smithsonian; and the McIlwee family of the Shenandoah Valley took pains to acquaint me with local knowledge about cougars. Kevin Hansen, Sue Morse, Jay Tischendorf, Ted Reed, John Lutz, Beverly Fronk, Bob and Pat Downing, Scott Ryder, Mark Palmer, and many other individuals shared their passion for mountain lions with me. Richard Greenwell of the International Society of Cryptozoology in Tucson, Arizona, shared his knowledge of cryptic animals around the world and the human reactions to them.

Without the remarkable electronic expertise of the reference and interlibrary loan personnel at the James Madison University Library, I could not have proceeded.

The Virginia Foundation for the Humanities and Public Policy awarded me a delicious summer at the University of Virginia, when I needed to do nothing but research. That's when the idea for this book originated.

Thanks to the faith of my editor, Sally Atwater, who wrote to me out of the blue to ask about a book, the idea turned into reality.

My dear friend Janet Wright read my drafts and made invaluable comments.

Most of all, I owe a debt of gratitude to my husband, Ralph, who argued or agreed as my rantings required, bought bicycles and a canoe to lure me into taking breaks, wired my fax and installed my programs, and—last but hardly least—has supported me all these years when I could have been earning a decent salary instead of writing. A simple thanks seems a poor return.

PREFACE

MOUNTAIN LIONS, ALSO KNOWN ACROSS THE UNITED STATES AS COUGARS, pumas, and panthers, intrigue me in various ways. On a superficial level, I'm a cat person. Give me an aloof gaze over slobbery kisses anytime. On another level, because I'm a first-generation immigrant from the Old World, never quite at home here or there, I envy mountain lions their ability to be at home throughout the New World, from Canada to Patagonia. Then there is the matter of their sleekness and agility, the quintessence of feline grace, and their shy mystery. These qualities are deeply feminine, but mountain lions couple them with a sinewy strength that is savagely masculine. It is a powerful combination, one that powerfully affects the people and cultures that encounter the animals.

Some of the people I met while exploring these encounters have decided preferences among the names. It *would* eliminate a lot of confusion to settle on just one, but I have come to love all the names because they express nuances of a complex creature. My favorites are cougar and puma, which derive from Native names rather than Old World carryovers. Puma now has the cachet of being the genus name (changed by the American Society of Mammalogists in 1993, although not widely accepted). Mountain lion has the positive side of what writer Edward Hoagland called the "immense mythic force of the great cats of the Old World," but is misleading because the cats can live in many other habitats besides mountains. Another Old World term, panther, has connotations of blackness like the devil's beast. I have used the local term in each area I explored, and I've enjoyed not having to repeat the same name over and over.

NATIVE AMERICANS
AND AMERICAN LIONS

THE SPIRITUAL CENTER OF THE UNIVERSE IS LOCATED ON A HIGH, DRY plateau in northeastern Arizona, where land stretches out in a vast meditation of mind, and mountains ring the far horizon with surrealistic shapes of desire. This is Hopi Land. For nearly a thousand years the Hopi people have raised corn, squash, and beans without irrigation in a place where rainfall averages eight to twelve inches a year. Their success points to the power of Hopi ceremonials. Today, as they always have, Hopis focus their lives on communication with the spiritual world. Throughout the year they dance and pray in ritual celebrations. Hopi culture is one of the most intact Native lifeways left in North America, and mountain lions play a strong symbolic role in it. Hopi Land was the first place I visited to try to understand how the force of the sacred guides the routine of everyday life. I wondered how real mountain lions fared in the secular world of human ego.

Mountain lions are not the largest predators in temperate North America, being far outweighed by grizzly and black bears, but bears are omnivores and rely more on plants than on meat. In this, and in the way they use their hands and feet, bears are like humans. Mountain lions are true carnivores, living almost exclusively on animals—preferably deer—that they themselves kill. Wolves have a similar diet, but they procure it through family cooperation in a way that is easily observed and appreciated by humans. Lions live and hunt alone, except for mothers with young.

They seem magically elusive, able to remain invisible even when the landscape is clearly imprinted with signs of their passing. They are agile enough to traverse the roughest country, and strong enough to kill animals much larger than themselves. When Europeans arrived in the Americas, mountain lions ranged from Canada to Tierra del Fuego, from the coasts of both oceans to the peaks of the Appalachians, Rockies, and Andes. The only large mammals more widely distributed throughout the western hemisphere were humans, so every Native culture except those in the Arctic encountered lions—a fact that contributed to the long list of names by which the animal became known to European settlers. Coping with a creature so alien to humans, so physically powerful and potentially threatening, and above all so mysterious must have been a serious exercise for the human psyche.

Not all Natives revered mountain lions. Thousands of cultures have come and gone in the Western Hemisphere, each with its own language, myths, traditions, and beliefs. Only in stereotypes is there a universal American Indian and a standard, nature-loving religion. Indians of the Pacific Northwest, for example, disliked the mountain lion. A Nootka Indian from that area, interviewed in 1955, called the lion the one animal the Indians did not understand. Lions are still relatively numerous today in Washington State and British Columbia and it's likely they have always thrived there, but they are largely absent from local Native imagery. When they do appear, it's usually for a disreputable performance, as in the story of how the whale's body came to have slits from chin to breastbone— a mountain lion clawed him.

To the south, toward the Plains, mountain lions kept Indians in a constant state of uneasiness. Charles A. Eastman, a mixed-blood Lakota from Minnesota who graduated from Dartmouth around the turn of the twentieth century, called the great cats "unsociable, queer people. Their speech has no charm. They are very bashful and yet dangerous, for no animal can tell what they are up to. If one sees you first, he will not give you a chance to see so much as the tip of his tail. He never makes any noise, for he has the right sort of moccasins."

Tribes from the Great Lakes southward feared the Underwater Panther, a composite monster with the body and tail of a mountain lion, antlers of a deer, scales of a snake, feathers of birds of prey, and parts from other animals as well. It lived beneath bodies of water. Water monsters appear in various guises the world over, but in North America the Native images tended to merge the traits of the mountain lion, or in some cases the lynx, with those of snakes. Mountain lions can swim but rarely choose to, and it's curious that they came to be so intimately associated with water. A friend who is part Potawatomi, (a people indigenous to the Great Lakes region) suggested that the mystery of the animal's hidden life became associated with the unknown underwater world. Potawatomis wove the image of the Underwater Panther, master of underworld forces, into one side of the fiber bags that held medicine objects, and the Thunderbird, master of the powers above, into the other. At least as late as the 1950s, the Prairie Band of Potawatomi Indians performed their traditional ceremony to placate the Underwater Panther and maintain balance with the Thunderbird.

The Underwater Panther was often a malevolent creature that punished human transgressions by calling up fierce storms to swamp canoes and flood towns, but it could be beneficent as well, leaving nuggets of shining copper on the shoreline to reward good behavior. East of the Great Lakes, Algonquian peoples believed the Underwater Panther had the power to heal. Its tail was covered by copper scales, and copper was used in curing rituals. When the first Europeans offered smelted copper alloys in trade for furs, Iroquoian tribes worked them into spirals and hoops that invoked the panther's long curving tail. Skillfully fashioned and beautiful in their simplicity, these ornaments are among the earliest objects made by Natives from European materials. Never was there greater need for help in battling illness than when Europeans arrived, bringing devastating new diseases.

The ancestry of the Underwater Panther can be traced, dimly, to Central America. Artisans from Oklahoma to South Carolina and from Illinois to Florida began to incise horned cats on shell cups and pottery around 800 A.D. That was when the revolutionary technique of growing maize reached the vast Mississippian drainage at the heart of North America. Agriculture meant a whole new way of looking at the world. It apparently began in Mexico, where a feathered and horned serpent and a jaguar with bird's eye and serpent's tongue were fundamental religious images. Their complex meanings embraced both good and evil. The Anasazi, ancestors of the Hopis and of Pueblo peoples, whose language is distantly related to Aztec, seem to have come from the south. The Anasazi painted horned snakes on canyon walls throughout the Southwest. These creatures were rulers of water and could make ponds puddle or dry up with their presence or absence. Mountain lions, too, were scratched and painted into the rocks of the Southwest by Anasazi and other Native tribes. Feet and claws are often exaggerated, but the bodies are long and lean, true to life. The tail curves up and backward to run parallel to the backbone. Sometimes the face is grinning fiercely, as all cats do when they engage an organ in the roof of the mouth to sense chemical odors.

As far as lion symbolism goes, the Hopis achieved a classic statement of reverence for nature. "The mountain lion," said Leigh Jenkins, the Hopi cultural preservation officer, "is very sacred to the Hopi. He is a deity, a guardian of the tribe, to whom Hopis look for guidance during certain ceremonies. He is regarded as the strongest and most fearless animal and the greatest of hunters. His name, *tuhu,* also refers to the black clays used to decorate particular kinds of prayer sticks. Black represents strength in delivering the prayer stick's message to the homes of the rain gods."

Leigh was a short, stocky man with lustrous black hair cut just below the collar of his blue shirt. His office was in Tribal Hall at dusty Kykotsmovi, down in the hot, windowless basement. I went there to ask his help in entering a foreign country. He was the only access for someone like me, an easterner with no contacts in Indian country. I was nervous and sweating in my wool shirt. Once it was land that whites pirated from Indians; now it's ideas, and on the basis of past experience you can't blame Natives for being cautious about what they give away. And of all Natives, the Hopis are the most secretive. They believe that knowledge is power. To prevent the draining away of their knowledge and their power, Hopis zealously guard the details of their lives. In the Hopi Museum I was asked to stop taking notes on a display based on a *Wall Street Journal* article about Louis Tewanima, a famous Hopi athlete. Photographs are prohibited everywhere in Hopi Land.

Hopis are very popular with certain kinds of non-Hopis, and such precautions don't always work. In August 1987 one of the various contingents of New Age believers who gathered around the world for a global hum-in, a harmonic convergence to save the world from destruction, decided to tap the spiritual force of Hopi Land. They neglected to communicate their plans to any Hopis, who ask that visitors stay on main roads. A Hopi farmer out weeding his corn one morning came upon a group of disheveled white people dancing slowly through his field, chanting, beating drums, planting traditional Hopi prayer sticks, and waving feathers. *Hopi* means "people of peace." The farmer did not confront the trespassers but called Leigh, whose job is to mediate contact with outsiders.

That was the first story Leigh told me. He was a natural teller of tales. Gruff at first, he slowly loosened up and came to life, smiling, moving his hands in strong descriptive gestures. I could see the billowing scarves of the New Agers and the exasperated shrug of the Hopi farmer. For two hours I sat in Leigh's office and listened to his stories. I had not expected such generosity. Through his stories, he invited me into his world. He opened a window into a different way of thinking and put mountain lions into a rich and living context of ideas. I responded in the most polite way I knew, by listening intently and gazing at the glowing computer screen, the laser jet printer, the framed certificate of appreciation from Harvard Medical School, the piled-up desk, the pictures of his children on shelves crowded with books on Indian art and history—in short, by resting my eyes on everything except Leigh's face. Indians consider it rude and confrontative to stare eye to eye.

Lions were probably always sparse on Hopi Land, and there were few tales to tell about them—Leigh hadn't heard of any sightings since his grandfather's time. There is some cover lions might like along the ragged, boulder-strewn edges of the three long mesas and around a few small, truncated pyramids that look like Aztec temples. But there simply isn't much for deer to eat, and land without deer is poor lion country. A wide flat desert of sage and brittle, scattered shrubs unfurls endlessly from the foot of the mesas. The country is so spare that there isn't, actually, much wildlife of any kind. Around the turn of the century, one of Arizona's last jaguars wandered onto Hopi Land. A 1908 photograph of his spotted skin is reproduced in a book, and as far as I could tell, the author's assertion that there were no punctures was true. Hopis and other tribes have traditions of ceremonial killing, in which the skin of the animal cannot be broken. Deer and even antelopes were run down and smothered with sacred corn pollen. No motive for the jaguar's death was given other than to show the bravery and skill of Second Mesa hunters.

A few years ago a black bear meandered onto Hopi Land. She was young and naive and probably had just left her mother to find her own home ground. Someone called the Anglo wildlife biologist who worked for the Navajos, and he arrived to find a small crowd, some carrying rifles but without serious intent to use them, near a den in some rocks where the bear was hiding. The biologist jabbed the bear with an immobilizing drug, and several Hopi helped carry her two miles to the car. As they went they prayed, sprinkled sacred corn meal, and tied turkey fathers to the bear's fur. The next day, as the biologist prepared to release the bear in suitable habitat on the Navajo Reservation, the Hopi Bear Clan leader made a visit and performed similar rituals.

What Hopi Land does support, presumably with rodents and small game, is the undauntable coyote. Leigh told several stories about coyotes, who love melons. Just when the fruit is round and luscious, on the day before Leigh means to set out traps, coyotes come and devour them all.

"I trap and shoot them," Leigh said, "and so do most Hopis that have been damaged by them. Some people bury the carcass with an offering, honoring the spirit even when it has harmed them, but others just leave the body lie. It's very individual. Dry farming is hard, and I'm proud of my crops. When it comes to protecting them, I'm a human being first and a Hopi second."

The Hopi male ego, Leigh said, is closely tied to being the provider of corn and vegetables. The produce is given to women for storage and preparation, in a reciprocal arrangement. Farming is the link to the past. Hopi Way, the plan for a moral life, depends upon agriculture and reverent, ritual supplication for rain. Leigh still dry-farmed more than ten acres of corn and raised traditional squash and melons for his family.

His father and grandfather were shepherds as well as farmers. "My grandfather," Leigh said, "could recognize his five hundred sheep by their individual faces. I'll never reach that level of intensity because I don't depend utterly on sheep and land for survival. I have my checkbook," he said, patting his back pocket, "and a job, a savings account."

The grandfather couldn't participate much in ceremonies because he had to stay out with his herd. "But I pray just like you do," he told Leigh. "And I will tell you what is the greatest tranquility in life. On the very hottest day in summer, when the sheep are too hot to walk and lie panting on the sand, when the dogs crawl under the tiniest bush that offers a speck of shade and hang their tongues out, then I sit and feel the serenity of the whole earth."

Heat waves shimmered against the adobe brick wall of the office and the panting of animals filled the room.

"It strikes me that the white way would be to curse the heat," I said, thinking how unpleasant a truly hot day in that landscape would be.

"You know, it's just like the weather reports lately," Leigh said. "The announcers complain about the rainy spell we're having and say, hold on, good weather is coming. But to us Hopis, rain is the best weather. The more drizzly days the better. Just the opposite of the white way of thinking."

Leigh's grandfather was the last Hopi to ride a burro to herd sheep; when he stopped in 1979, that was the end of a tradition that had started with the Spaniards, who introduced livestock in the 1500s. Nowadays Hopis use pickup trucks. Cultures are dynamic, changing in response to the world around them, but change in Native American cultures has for five hundred years mostly been inflicted by the arrogance of outsiders. The story I remember most vividly, because it was so painful to listen to, was about four Hopi elders who traveled to Washington, D.C., in 1890. Invited by Bureau of Indian Affairs bureaucrats who wanted to intimidate them into sending Hopi children to a new government school on the reservation, the elders hoped to plead for justice against persistent tres-passing by Navajos. The trip was engineered to terrorize people who had never before left their own remote world. A train carried the Hopis through Kansas where thousands of acres of wheat amazed them. They toured Leavenworth Prison, and as Leigh spoke I saw the ugly block walls, the thick black bars across the windows. St. Louis was the first city the Hopis had ever seen. At a naval base near Washington, troops paraded before them and ships fired canon shots. When they returned to Hopi Land, the elders met with their people in the kiva, the underground ceremonial chamber.

"How many whites are there?" the spokesman for the travelers asked his people rhetorically, then answered by scooping handful after handful of sand from the ground. I watched the grains stream from Leigh's palm. "How many Hopis are there?" he asked, and he bent down for a tiny pinch of sand. "I have learned that the white man has two ways he treats people who don't do what he wants. He puts them in cages, or he shoots them. I don't want that for my people." The elder picked up two strands of cotton; they floated from Leigh's outstretched hands. "Never forget Hopi Way, but also take the best of the white man's way," the elder said, and Leigh twisted the strands together. From that time on the Hopis were divided, as most Native societies inevitably became, into often bitterly opposed factions. Progressives advocate cooperation with whites and are often propped up through white influence on tribal governments. Traditionals seek to maintain the old ways.

"How do you choose what's best in white culture?" I asked.

"It's hard," Leigh said. "It's very individual. For me it's a tractor to weed the corn with. But I still plant the old way, with a planting stick."

Tractors stood among the cars and four-wheel-drives parked outside the homes in Hopi villages. There were few yards; houses opened right onto the one-lane rutted roads that wound through, but there were flowerpots and flowered curtains in the windows. One- and two-story houses were built of cut and uncut stone, some of them plastered over, some not. In Old Oraibi, the oldest continuously inhabited village in North America, where ground has been packed by bare feet since 1150 A.D., TV antennas rose from the most ancient-looking homes. Wooden doors were splintered by weather. Occasionally a bit of aluminum guttering coursed along the edge of a flat roof. Scattered on the ground were ceramic shards, corncobs, and broken glass winking in the sun. Firewood lay stacked here and there; at the back of the village was a heap of coal, and an acrid smell wafted on the air. A breeze blew up now and then, flapping the plastic sheets anchored by rocks and tires on some of the roofs and blowing up dust devils in the road. A small boy played with a puppy. In Old Oraibi, in 1947, after atomic bombs had exploded in the region and on the other side of the world, clan leaders revealed prophecies they had been taught to keep "until a gourd of ashes fell from the sky." Their desperate energy helped spark a slow renaissance of Indian thought and art, which continues to accelerate.

From Old Oraibi the snow-capped San Francisco peaks gleamed pure and alluring across the desert. On those beckoning summits lived the kachinas, the myriad supernatural beings whom the Hopi called on for help from mid-July to the winter solstice. For the other half of the year, the kachinas lived in Hopi villages and manifested themselves as masked dancers. The mountain lion kachina wore a green face mask, a red hair shirt, and yellow body paint.

For a couple of days I stayed at the Hopi Hotel on Second Mesa, ate piki bread and bean and hominy soup and blue corn pancakes at the restaurant, and drove desultorily through the Hopi Reservation. I eavesdropped on conversations in gift shops and poked around after mountain lion curios. Mostly I wanted to turn my thoughts loose into that simultaneously demanding and quieting landscape, to search for meaning that transcends culture. In a jewelry shop a black-haired woman wore a sweatshirt that offered, at least for her, a resolution for cultural Angst. It said, "Don't Worry, Be Hopi."

One of the Hopis' long-standing worries is the neighbor that completely surrounds them: the Navajo Nation. Navajos (and their relatives, the Apaches) traveled down from western Canada around 1200 to 1500 A.D., just before the Spanish arrived to give another spin to the cultural mix. By then the Anasazi had been building and abandoning villages throughout the Southwest for millennia. They were fundamentally different from the Navajos and became traditional enemies, although trade was always an important dimension of their relationship. Agriculture was the basis for every aspect of Anasazi life and the lives of their Hopi and Pueblo descendants. The Navajos were hunters and gatherers, although they soon learned to grow corn from the Pueblos. Pueblos live together in communities of hundreds of people of various clans, with formal authority vested in the heads of religious societies. Navajo houses are scattered in family clusters, and authority is informally dispersed among many clans; elders give advice but there were historically no chiefs as whites defined them. This caused no end of trouble to Anglos who thought they had made a treaty with the Navajo tribe rather than with one small, autonomous band. Pueblos were generally nonaggressive; Navajos raided the Pueblos for women and slaves. The growing Navajo population—at 260,000 the Navajos are now by far the largest Indian tribe in America—continually pushed onto Pueblo lands, causing a still ongoing dispute with the Hopis. Pueblos regularly reach outward to the spirits for community blessings. Navajos, too, communicate with the spirit world, but spontaneously, for the inward purpose of healing an individual's illness.

For Navajos, sickness reflects a disruption of the harmony and balance that constitute the normal order among all components in the universe. Every element in creation has evil as well as good aspects, and when evil becomes dominant—usually through improper conduct by humans—it takes the correct application of mystical knowledge to control it and restore right order. For their curing ceremonies the Navajos adopted and adapted many Hopi and Pueblo practices.

Navajos adapted just as readily to the horses, goats, and sheep brought by the Spanish. Before Columbus the Natives of the Southwest had domesticated turkeys for feathers used in prayers, and they and others throughout North America had domesticated dogs to pull baggage and perhaps to flush small game. But no North American Natives tended livestock; thus this crucial source of conflict with mountain lions and all other predators did not exist. Sheep assumed enormous importance to Navajos after 1868, when the tribe was allowed to return to its homeland after Colonel Kit Carson had shot livestock, pillaged orchards and cornfields, and herded all the Navajos he could find to Fort Sumner in New Mexico. So deeply scarring was that experience that even today in casual conversation, the "Long Walk" is likely to come up. In partial recompense, the U.S. government issued thirty-thousand sheep to the remaining nine thousand Navajos. As they worked to rebuild their lives, Navajos counted the number of sheep they owned, regardless of how scrawny or parasitic, as a status symbol. The range was overgrazed and serious erosion resulted, which continues today. And since the mountainous portions of the seventeen-million acre Navajo Reservation offer good bear, lion, and wolf habitat, conflicts with predators became a factor in Navajo life. Wolves and grizzly bears were exterminated by whites early on, but lions and black bears remained.

In Navajo thought some creatures have particularly dangerous potential for evil, and among them the bear is prominent. His Navajo name should not even be whispered, lest his spirit be called. But the bear also has potential for great good and was once a lovely and kind sister to the first people. In remembrance the Navajo traditionally used bears for food only in direst famine and killed them only in a ceremonial way, although bears lost such protection if they killed livestock. A number of Navajos told me that mountain lions, too, were in the same sacred category as bears, but there was no traditional requirement for ritual hunting as for bears.

To cope with the physical power of these spiritual beings, the Navajo Nation in 1956 borrowed a wildlife manager from the U.S. Fish & Wildlife Service to set up a tribal wildlife department—the first such entity on any reservation. Its major aim was to reduce the number of predators. In 1961, for the first time, a Navajo was paid a bounty for killing a mountain lion. On the whole, though, the Navajo have historically suffered few sheep losses to lions. In part this was probably because lion numbers ebbed as deer declined from overhunting. Game seems to have been fairly plentiful until about 1900, after which unrestrained hunting to supply inns along the Santa Fe trail reduced the deer herd to less than one hundred head on the entire reservation. One of the first projects of the new Navajo wildlife office was to restock deer.

Navajo shepherds usually penned their sheep at night, which deterred the few lions still around. Bears didn't mind climbing into corrals for sheep, though. Bears love the small Navajo fields of corn, too, not just to eat but, for some inscrutable reason, to roll in. To traditional Navajos, once a bear has walked into a corn field, he has claimed it, and they may no longer harvest it for their own use.

The new head of the Navajo Fish & Wildlife department trained whites as well as Navajos (who called themselves renegade wildlife agents) to trap bears. Over the next couple of decades, these trappers averaged about ten bears a year. Then it began to seem that bears weren't so plentiful as before. It wasn't simply a matter of overtrapping: Navajo population doubled in the 1960s and 1970s, logging as well as coal mining accelerated in the Navajo Nation Forest, and explorations for oil and uranium opened up previously wild areas to human intrusion. The trappers voiced their concern to tribal officials, who hired a young white wildlife biologist named Pat Ryan to assess bear populations on the Reservation.

When I met Pat, he had been working in various capacities for the Navajo wildlife department for nearly fifteen years. The girlfriend he had met in college, Kathleen McCoy, followed him to the reservation and was hired as the big game manager. Together they had somehow survived innumerable purges, periodic campaign promises to replace all belaganas (whites) in tribal jobs with Navajos, and other assorted political whirlwinds. Pat once returned from a ten-day stint in the field to find all new people in his office. Nevertheless, the Navajo commitment to preserve bears was solid. Pat spent ten years tracking bears he had captured with foot snares and collared with radio transmitters and responding to calls from Navajo families about problem bears. It was Pat who answered the Hopis' call to come get the bear on their land. His stories, like Leigh's, helped to put mountain lions in the context of a different way of thinking about animals. Pat's narrow, mustached face was topped by a camouflage hat from which unruly curls escaped around the sides. He was very fond of beer but also of skiing, bicycling, and backpacking, which kept him lean and wiry enough to scramble up rocky slopes and crawl into bear dens. He loved the fieldwork except when a Navajo colleague kept him up all night guarding against skinwalkers, the human witches who assume animal disguise. Pat found that many sheep killings blamed on bears were actually due to dogs, and of those bears that did eat sheep, many were old or crippled.

"I learned to pretty well predict where bear problems will come up," he said, "and that's at the worst overgrazed areas. Bears like to eat a lot of grass, and some of the old ones seem to learn that they don't have enough because of the sheep, so they eat grass by way of sheep." When I asked him how Navajos reacted to bears, Pat shook his head. "It's so varied I couldn't characterize it," he said. "Some would blast a bear on sight. Some would call us out to set traps when they had only seen bear tracks in the area. One family wanted us to kill a problem bear, but when we did, they refused to help load it on the truck because they didn't want to touch it. They were afraid of spiritual retribution. The older people tend to be most traditional. One grandma said to me, 'The bear came last night and ate three sheep. I just hope he doesn't want any more.' She called her brother, a medicine man, who did a horn blowing ceremony, and it worked. I guess it's just a matter of time until the old ideas fade away."

Even as they fade, the old ideas still sparkle with intermittent force. Because the mythical hero Changing Woman named the mountain lion as one of the guardians of the first Navajo clans, lions are considered protectors. When Gloria Notah moved back home to the reservation after working for a federal predator-control agency in New Mexico, she brought with her a mounted lion head. "My knowledge of Navajo culture is limited," she said, "because my parents didn't feel it important for me to learn about it. But when my father saw that lion mount, we got into a tug of war. He wanted it for his house to guard against bad spirits."

Gloria wanted it because she thought it was beautiful. "I have this dream of a stone fireplace with the lion head above it," she said. Gloria was director of the Navajo wildlife section and Kathleen McCoy's boss. When I interviewed her at tribal headquarters in Window Rock, she was working through lunch. Phones were ringing, people were hurrying in and out, the entrance door had kickmarks from people with their hands full, and boxes of supplies were stacked in corners because there was no other room for them. Except for the posters celebrating Navajo heritage, the place looked just like every wildlife management office I've ever been in. Gloria had short hair and a broad, attractive face. As a female and member of a minority, she had her pick of jobs when she graduated in wildlife science from the University of Arizona, but she chose to work for the Navajo Nation for a couple of years, until she couldn't stand the politics anymore. Then, after five years in New Mexico, she grew homesick.

"I've been here a year now," she said, "and if they don't run me out, my first priority is to put wildlife on the same level as grazing, logging, strip mining, oil and gas exploration, and all the other development now going on. Planning for fish and wildlife has always lagged behind. An interdisciplinary team has just developed a management plan for the Navajo Nation Forest—that was a milestone for wildlife. With careful planning we can have all those land uses." Use of wildlife was paramount in Gloria's mind. "I'm a strong advocate of consumptive use rather than preservation," she said. "We need to be practical and address both human and animal needs. Like with endangered species—yes, we need to preserve them in some cases, but in others, do we need to save what little is left of a species and cause great human dislocation?"

Mountain lions are not officially listed as endangered anywhere in the West, and I wondered what their future might be on the reservation. "There's no lion hunting allowed now," she said. "We know we have lions but we don't know much about lion populations. I'd like to see a research project to determine whether we could have a sport hunting season, which would bring income from licenses."

Sport hunting was scorned as a disgustingly wasteful white habit by most of the Indians I met, but there is money to be made from it: the White Mountain Apache manage their elk herd for trophy bulls and charge white hunters $10,000 a week for guiding and camp services (permits are also sold to white guides for lions and bears). "Navajo are meat hunters," a ponytailed man said during one of the periodic public meetings that Gloria and Kathleen host to discuss hunting regulations on the reservation. "We can't eat antlers." And yet, at a similar meeting a few years ago, several young Navajo hunters requested a bear sport hunting season. One had been opened in the 1960s but was closed when traditional Navajos protested. Kathleen was amazed when the tribal council passed her proposal for the bear season without opposition. Three permits had been purchased the first year; only one in the current year.

As big game manager, Kathleen was responsible for monitoring the health of the deer herd, now at eight thousand to ten thousand, and for keeping track of elk, wild turkey, and bear populations. She liked to hunt at least every few years for the meat but wasn't avid about it. Kathleen was tall and well proportioned, with large but very feminine hands. Her blue eyes were just a bit lighter than her navy sweater, and in the sun her brown hair shone a burnished red—the effect of iron in her well water. She and Pat Ryan had in common not just an Irish Catholic background but a quiet, reclusive rejection of most things connected with it. Supplying animal parts for use in Navajo ceremonies was a major part of her job. She liked being able to fulfill the requests, because she figured it helped keep poaching down. The biggest demand was for eagle feathers because the eagle was viewed as master of the upper world by many tribes, but federal regulations complicated the dispensing of any feathers Kathleen was occasionally able to obtain from captive birds or birds found dead. Turkey feathers were the next most frequently requested item; the turkey hunting permits she mailed out asked for donation of the plumage. Deer hides were also popular, and she confiscated them from the few poachers caught (Kathleen estimated that deer poaching amounted to roughly five times the legal yearly kill of four hundred to five hundred).

I was in Kathleen's office, just down the hall from Gloria's, when Maria Sagina came in to request parts. An herbalist, Maria is a stout, jolly woman who seems always ready to laugh. She wanted badger grease to rub on the hands and feet of children to toughen them against falls. "I want a badger skin to throw babies onto," she said, "because badgers are so hard to kill"—and she made motions of clubbing a badger many times. She also wanted lion urine, skin, and claws to use against dizziness, fainting, and other evidences of witchcraft. Like the Pueblo peoples, Navajos believe that evil arises not from nature but from human witches who use spiritual powers for destructive purposes. Maria worked in concert with her husband, a gentle, kindly man named Albert. When I met Albert, later, he searched through his wallet to give me an elegant if battered business card that read, "Medicine Man." There was no phone number. Albert was self-conscious about his broken English and spoke mostly in Navajo, with Maria translating. He described a stone he had found, in the shape of a cat's paw, which he like to rub on the palms and soles of children to enable them to keep hold of a basketball and leap with agility for the basket. Natural stones in the shape of animals have long been thought to have special powers.

"That's how it works with us," Maria would interject. "That's how it is."

When people saw lion paw prints and were afraid for themselves and their livestock, they might ask Albert to come over. "When we get a problem animal, we talk to it, pray to it, tell it to go away, and it will," he said. "That's how it works. Sometimes when an animal comes around, it wants help from you, just like it sometimes gives you help."

"If you see a bear around, talk to it, tell it not to bother you," Maria added on her own. "Like a child. Sometimes we leave honey on a log for him—not often, he would forget how to take care of himself, get spoiled like a child. But we want to keep him around to guard against the bad spirits.

"People that lose sheep or cattle," she went on, "it's because they are negative. They bring it on themselves. Maybe something is bothering the person, or witchcraft is being done."

"Some bears are bad, they don't listen," Albert said. "Then we call Kathleen. It's like we had a bank robber, who did it a second time. There is no way but to execute him."

"But we try to talk to them first," Maria said. "Like with the buzzard, he owns cancer—you go to his home, tell him to take back the cancer, then we give the patient herbs."

"It works," ventured Albert in heavily accented English, "if you believe."

Many Navajos do believe in medicine men. If a medicine man could prescribe and sing precisely the right songs, perform exactly the right dry-painting, he could bring raging forces under control and defeat sickness. This took a lifetime of learning. Although there were fewer and fewer disciples, there were, still, quite a few medicine men, even an association (though it was, not surprisingly, an ephemeral sort of group). Kathleen and Pat directed me to several medicine men they knew. It was Pat who had first met Henry Wallace. Henry had called Pat some years ago about a bear that was eating his corn. The two men stayed up all night, sitting in Pat's tribal truck with a spotlight, but the bear decided to move over to a neighbor's field, where Pat eventually scared him away through the use of a solar-powered electric fence smeared with bacon grease.

No one was home the first time I pulled off the main road into the Wallace compound—several trailers, a small house, a larger house under construction, various outbuildings, and a large unfinished hogan, the traditional seven-sided log house that reflects the circular nature of the cosmic process. From Tony Hillerman novels I knew that I should wait by my car for a while, giving anyone who wanted to a chance to come out, but only the five horses grazing around the yard came over to investigate. The next time, a lanky young man came out as I leaned against my rental car. I looked away as I explained who I was and what I wanted, and I noticed he did, too.

"My father's not home," he said. "Come back tomorrow afternoon." Worried by the stories I had heard about Indian time, I mentioned a specific hour, and he nodded so readily my worry wasn't much alleviated. But the next afternoon he was there, although his father wasn't. "He's at sheep camp," the young man said. "Can your car handle some ruts? I'll take you there." He doubled his long skinny frame into the car, and we took off.

Ambrose had a pencil-thin mustache, a slightly pocked skin, and warm brown eyes. He loved Navajo lore and knew a lot of it. "I won't tell you the lion's ceremonial name in Navajo," he said, "because that wouldn't be proper. But it translates as Walking Silently among the Rocks."

This name, and the fact that Ambrose had volunteered it, made me happy. As we drove across a high plateau, past stands of young pines interspersed with taller trees and stumps and past the sign that read "Navajo Nation Forest," Ambrose talked freely and earnestly about Navajo life. He mourned lost traditions and the decline of medicine men, scolded the younger generation for drinking while hunting, and condemned the violence on TV. Most of all, he was concerned that his young daughter grow up learning to speak Navajo. When I said that I appreciated his friendliness and openness, he said simply, "We like to have company from outside."

We turned off the pavement onto a good dirt road. Pinyon pines grew more stunted and juniper and sagebrush became more common. The land was gently rolling, and the distant horizon blended into long gray clouds and thin blue strips of sky. Miles passed. Occasional green street signs seemed incongruous in the middle of that huge plain, especially since they were lacking in downtown Gallup. Canyons that you couldn't see until you began to descend into them sliced across our route. The road to Henry Wallace's place had by now become deeply rutted. It led down into a red-walled canyon, crossed a wide, rushing creek, and started up the other side. Tucked into big old pines just above the canyon wall was the sheep camp. A small band of sheep grazed around an old woman in wide skirts and a scarf like a Russian babushka, whom Ambrose identified as his grandmother. We pulled into a yard with a hogan and a small, rectangular log-and-mud house. I followed Ambrose in, noting how he bent his long body to duck under the low doorway. Carefully, to avoid looking like a clumsy greenhorn, I did the same. The house had a single room. It reminded me of houses I've visited in Appalachia except it was cleaner, neater, and sweeter smelling. Along the left wall was the kitchen, with a new gas stove, a counter and a sink, although I wasn't sure about running water. In the center of the room was a small round wood stove that radiated warmth. It was early spring and still very cool; a good time for my purposes, because Navajos believe that animals should be discussed only after first frost and before first thunder, during their winter quiescence.

Two iron bedsteads stood at right angles to each other, with an arm-chair between them. In this sat Henry Wallace. Ambrose settled on one of the beds. His mother, a large woman in a skirt and print blouse, with dark-framed glasses and long hair pulled back into a bun, sat on a couch doing needlework. Ambrose motioned for me to pull up a chair from the dining table. The room was full but there was a comfortable, even a spacious sense of a living room. A shelf above one of the beds held spools of sewing thread and a radio, which was playing pop music. Henry turned it off.

He looked at me and made a motion of writing. Clearly others had sought him out, and I could understand why. He made an extremely impressive appearance. He had white hair in a buzz cut and bristling eyebrows of pepper and salt. His features conveyed strength and deter-mination. His skin was neither dark nor red but golden. His eyes didn't seem brown like Ambrose's; there was something else glinting there, but in the shadows of the house and with only the quick glances I allowed myself, I couldn't quite tell what. He wore jeans and a heavy red sweat-shirt with a hood.

"It starts with the big one, the main one," he began, in hesitant English, "what you call the boss." He touched his chest and shoulders. "Then it goes down from there," and he moved one hand in a step motion, implying levels of cat. "Leopard with spots, tiger with stripes, panther is black. All cats are the same, from mountain lion down to—" and he pointed at a white cat sleeping on top of a neatly folded stack of quilts. Then he changed to Navajo, and Ambrose translated. It was a pleasant language to listen to, alternately guttural and sibilant.

When Mother Earth was first created, Ambrose said, each animal was told what he would be used for. "The mountain lion was told his skin would be used for ceremonies, and for quivers," Ambrose said. "The gall bladder is used against evil, if a person is witching against another person. Lion claws are used to tear yucca leaves for making ceremonial arrows."

Quivers seem to have been one of the most widespread uses of the mountain lion in North America. Maybe Natives hoped to convey the strength and silence of the lion to the arrow. The Lakota of the northern Plains also made saddle blankets from lion skin. Southeastern Indians wrapped male infants in lion skins and female babies in the skins of deer or bison, the lion's prey. Natives along the Mississippi tapped thin sheets of copper around the lower jaws of cougars to use as headdresses. Lion claws were strung into necklaces, and tails decorated clothing. The ultimate use of mountain lions was to eat them, which some cultures did in both Americas.

Lion skins, claws, and gall bladders were passed down from generation to generation, Ambrose said. A Navajo can't just go out and shoot a lion for parts whenever he wants, he added emphatically. "To kill for no reason is against our ways," Henry said in English. Then he described, in Navajo, how lion fat, mixed with eagle, bear, and bobcat fat and with the ashes from dead branches of the most venerable juniper trees, would be smeared on human bodies. "What you would call war paint," Ambrose added.

Fat was not something that could be handed down through the ages, and I wondered how it was obtained. The only reason for a Navajo to hunt a lion is for his own ceremonial uses, Ambrose said, but few if any Navajo did that anymore. "We buy from sport hunters off the reservation," he said. "All they want is the head."

Henry began to speak about the four cardinal directions and the colors—black, blue, yellow, white—associated with them. As he spoke he moved his hands in a dignified, expansive way toward the east, west, north, and south. Each direction was marked by a sacred mountain. In some way, mountain lions in each of these colors and on each of these mountains had a role in ceremonies. "It's because lions are used in cere-monies," Ambrose said, "that we consider them sacred. If you don't want them to bother you, if you find a track, put turquoise and shells on the foot tracks and pray, 'Leave us alone.' The lion might be sick and wants to be cured."

I asked what happened if a lion didn't go away.

"We call Kathleen or Pat," Ambrose said. "We get other nationalities to kill them for us."

So guilt for killing was avoided. In Navajo mythology, as in the myths of many hunting cultures around the world, there was a time long ago when humans and animals were essentially the same. People became animals, and animals turned into people, and all spoke the same language. They married and had children. Hunting, then, meant killing relatives. A solution to the problem of guilt was to identify with predators who, like humans, needed to kill to live. Ambrose explained one way in which Navajo linked themselves to hunter animals. "We hunt the Wolf Way," he said. "It depends on what clan you're born into. We have a separate prayer and chant. When I make a kill, I put my right foot on the deer and howl—all the coyotes will hear and come. It's like saying, 'Come eat,' because we leave the entrails for them. Then we share with our family, like the wolf. One who hunts in the Mountain Lion Way uses his own prayers, and when he kills, he sniffs the blood. The lion is stingy, so the hunter will eat the meat by himself." The Mountain Lion Way of hunting was also known as the Tiptoe Way or the Deer Way, and aimed to bring down deer and sometimes antelope. The hunter kept his arrows on the bowstring ready to shoot, and walked against the wind on tiptoe along game trails.

Occasionally Ambrose's mother added to the conversation; her English was a bit more confident than Henry's. She nodded when Henry said they didn't see many lions around, but sometimes they noticed one passing through.

"Are there enough lions?" I asked. "Would you want more around?"

"No!" she said, her eyes widening. After a while she asked me, "What do you think of this zoo?"

I had been to the Navajo Zoo, an attractive, well-run cluster of cages set into the spectacular monoliths at the escarpment where Window Rock was located. It held a variety of native species, including bears, lions, wolves, and coyotes. The staff often found cornmeal by the bear's cage, a sign of praying. Once in a while it looked as if someone was praying by the lion's cage. The director routinely received requests for body parts—a lion's whisker, rattlesnake blood, particular hawk feathers—and filled those that weren't too physically intrusive. More than thirty-thousand people a year visited, most of them Navajo, but after fifteen years of operation, the zoo's budget had just been slashed by a member of the tribal government who held the traditional view that wild animals should never be caged. It was a view I could sympathize with. "But it's the only way the young kids are going to learn about the animals," Ambrose said. "It's good to have for the younger generation."

A car drove into the yard, and a couple with two small boys knocked and came in. I assumed these were relatives. Each one went around the room to each of us and shook hands—an Indian kind of handshake, just barely touching palms, because a firm grip shows assertiveness, a trait not highly valued. Something Pat had mentioned came to mind. "The Navajo love to shake hands," he had said. "When I have two meetings in a row with the same people, they'll come up again to shake even though we've just done it." The newcomers sat down; the little boys were still and quiet, while their father joined in the conversation.

After a short while, Henry said to me, "That's all. Not many stories of lions." It was clearly time for me to go. Ambrose planned to stay. I went around and shook hands with everyone, highly pleased with my cultural sensitivity. On the way out I hit my head on the low door frame.

The clouds had knit together into a gray weave that nestled over the long green plain. It wouldn't be the kind of blustery, pounding storm that brings what the Navajos call male rain, but rather the soft, gentle patter of female rain.

Long blades of ice sheathed the trail up the canyon wall, and I watched my footing carefully. I was backpacking alone and did not care to trip. Although it wasn't sheer, the cliff on my right fell off several hundred feet. There were tussocks of stunted oaks and gnarly pines among the boulders that probably would have broken my fall, but the thought was not comforting. Elk and deer droppings absorbed the heat of the morning sun and rotted the ice around them, the larger elk apples making deeper wells, so that's where I stepped. This part of New Mexico has more than enough deer and growing numbers of elk. It has cliffs with rimrock overviews, jumbled talus slopes, forests of pines and junipers for cover, and innumerable natural caves for dens. Some streams even run year-round. It is great mountain lion country.

It has been great lion country for a long, long time, and that fact has shaped the culture of the Natives who lived there. On some ledge of mind below the reach of words, the Southwest is the home of lion spirit. Maybe in the clear air and sparse vegetation, lions were glimpsed more often than in lusher, denser landscapes. Maybe those more frequent sightings revealed the agility and grace that are the essence of lion beauty. Other Native cultures besides those in the Southwest have found beauty in mountain lions. A century before the Spanish arrived in Florida, a Calusa Indian carved an elegant wooden figurine with a small head, large round eyes, delicate nostrils, and sinuous limbs arranged in a human posture. Eastern Woodland Indians carved many stone and clay-fired pipes with fluid features of naturalistic lions. But in New Mexico, Pueblo peoples honored lions in a way unique in North America: they sculpted a pair of life-sized lion figures from bedrock and enclosed them in a ring of stone. It was to the Shrine of the Stone Lions that I was headed.

Actually, there were two such shrines within a few miles of each other, each consisting of a pair of lions that had been chipped and rubbed with stone and bone tools from the compressed volcanic ash that forms the local rock. By 1880, one of the shrines had already been blasted by treasure hunters who thought, mistakenly, that something might be buried underneath. It was no longer an active shrine. The one to which I was hiking, accessible because the mesa on which it sits is now within a federal wilderness area, was created between 1200 and 1500 A.D. and is still visited by Indians from many miles away. As late as the 1950s, local hunters from nearby pueblos (villages) were still anointing the eyes and toes of the Stone Lions with red ocher (oxide of iron) to transfer to themselves the vision and strength of the lion. "We're planning to start taking groups of our schoolchildren there," a tribal officer for the nearest pueblo told me. "It will be a good way to teach them the traditions, especially the young boys." While at that pueblo I passed the reservation school, where a marquee proclaimed, "Home of the Cougars."

It was the distant ancestors of those very schoolchildren who had most likely made the Stone Lions. Their pueblo had been in the same place for more than five hundred years, but that was its fifth or sixth site. Periodic drought, warfare, expanding populations that killed off the game and cut all the timber within easy reach, exhaustion of the small pockets of good soil—some or all of these factors forced the ancestral

Anasazi to move, and move again. (Hopi mesas, on the other hand, have a different geology that holds water, and a coal seam that was worked by Stone Age strip-mining reduced the need for wood, so Hopis didn't need to move.) Today's nineteen New Mexico pueblos descend from thousands of sites through the Southwest, most of them still unexcavated. Toward the end of my hike I came upon one called Yapashi, linked in oral tradition to the pueblo village that was Home of the Cougars and believed to be home of the Stone Lion sculptors. Mounds of earth and stone rubble formed an irregular circle from which stretched arms of cholla cactuses. Here and there a corner wall of stone cut from the light volcanic rock still stood upright. Five hundred people may have lived here. I stood in the middle of the central plaza, where dances and games were held, and heard voices singing in the wind. They were bluebirds, flashing like little pieces of sky. Without them I would have felt so alone in that dead city. The earthen roofs of the kivas had collapsed, and pines had seized the advantage of extra soil. In those pits with painted walls and fire hearths, ceremonies and social events took place, and the men slept.

Yapashi commanded a 360-degree view. Mountains far and near, the higher ones still mantled with snow, circled the entire horizon. Just beyond view, some hundred and fifty miles east of Hopi Land, was the Puebloan Center of the World, a shrine made of a rock cairn atop a high peak that contains obsidian for arrows. Like many other Native peoples, the Pueblos venerated various natural features as shrines. And like most other tribes, they felt themselves to be the focus of the living world.

The Stone Lions lay a short walk to the northwest from Yapashi. The shrine was very inconspicuous. Squat junipers, bushy pinyon pines, and Gambel oaks still thick with the dead leaves of winter screened my view. Needles and leaves had built up under trees, but between them was bare dirt, visibly eroding in a continuing legacy of overgrazing. The first sign of the shrine was a jumble of rectangular boulders. Some were three or four feet tall and standing upright; others were smaller and had tumbled over, or perhaps there had been some sort of wall built outside the ring of monoliths. One pinyon pine, present in photographs from 1890, grew through the rocks. The ring was broken on the east side with an entrance way paved in stone. Inside, the lions lay off-center, side by side and apparently identical, stretched out in what has been variously interpreted as a crouching or reposing posture. They might have been resting their heads on their paws or getting ready to spring. Their expressions might have clarified their intention, but bored shepherds had battered the heads and obliterated the faces in the late nineteenth century. All that remains is the body shape—a hint of massive shoulders, distinct haunches, and broad, flat tails extended straight out. Someone had placed a single deer antler in front of them.

I have seen pictures of the Stone Lions wreathed in white antlers, a very pretty effect and seemingly appropriate. The local Pueblos, however, didn't think so. They complained to the federal superintendent about foreign objects at the shrine, and in the early 1990s the religious leader of the closest pueblo held a ceremony at the Stone Lions to burn everything found near the sculptures. Federal rangers agreed to clear out whatever they found at the shrine on their rounds. The next summer the superintendent received a Freedom-of-Information Act request for all records relating to the shrine. The letter read, in part:

> On August 8th we led a group of hikers to the Shrine of the Stone Lions. It was the third time I had been there in as many years. The stone circle at that Shrine has much in common with ancient sacred stone circles throughout Europe, and much of the worship of the Native Americans is common to our ancestors also . . . When we arrived at the Shrine, we were greatly disappointed to find that the Shrine had apparently been stripped of many of the sacred objects that had formerly been used in religious worship there . . .

Below the signature was the title, "Priest of Wicca." The superintendent replied, in part:

> Early photographs taken at the turn of the century and again in the 1920s, 1940s, and 1950s show that the Shrine was completely clean; no ring of antlers and no objects of worship were historically nor prehistorically (according to

oral history) left within the Shrine . . . the ring of deer antlers and the addition of worship items did not appear until the 1960s . . . The leaving of "foreign objects" no matter how good the intentions, within the Shrine . . . compromises the Shrine for Puebloan people . . . The Pueblo elders and religious leaders inform us that they do not leave things within the Shrine . . .

There was no further correspondence. The foreign offerings had included beads, bullets, potsherds, and hawk and owl feathers. In Puebloan tradition, owl feathers tied to bags of human excrement are the most vile implements of witchcraft.

I sat on stones around the circle and peered at the lions from various angles, looking for red ocher, but couldn't see any. Local Natives ask that visitors do not enter the stone ring, but the bare dirt was trampled by many footprints. I felt an active desire not to walk in, although I did, after a long time, step quickly in to toss away the antler. After a while a chill breeze drove me downslope to scout for a place to camp. I wanted a reasonably flat site that I could restore from the impress of my tent and its stakes. Unfortunately every such place was sprinkled with prickly pear cactuses, and eventually I uprooted two of them. Maybe that's why I didn't see a lion, but then I hardly expected to. Nonetheless, I put up the tent where I could see across the little canyon that ran behind the Stone Lions. There was a good sitting rock next to my tent. For hours I sat. I've never been good at meditation. I didn't even try to clear my mind. I let it wander over the canyon wall, between several huge boulders that framed my view. On the left, one was patterned with green lichen into a sad frog face. On the right, two rocks formed a lowercase, dotted *i* five stories high. Between them lay several arrangements of beige rocks that looked invitingly like lion dens. I kept hoping a lion would stick her head out of one, yawn, stretch, and call out her kittens. Or leap from rock to rock in a display of feline grace. Nothing of the kind happened. The life of the canyon simply went on. Birds sang and sometimes winged by. The sun slowly sank. Trees transpired. Spirit flowed.

Spirit is a human concept, like justice, and equality. The people of Yapashi believed that lion spirit was strong enough to fend off evil, especially from the west, the direction that the lion represented. One of the functions of the Stone Lions was to guard Yapashi. Another was to serve as a hunting fetish. Like the Hopis, the Pueblos saw the lion as the greatest hunter of all, and the master of other predatory animals. There doesn't seem to be the least hint of human competitiveness for deer; on the contrary, the Pueblos gloried in the lion's hunting prowess. The leaders of some Pueblo hunting societies were called Cougar Men. Hunters gave the cry of the lion to intimidate deer and carried small fetishes of natural or carved stone, shell, or wood. Without these, in which the power of the lion lived for a time and favored the hunter with increased skill, hunting would have been useless. When the hunter made a kill, he smeared blood on the mouth of the fetish to feed it. Properly treated, the lion acted as a protector and could advocate human interests among the other powers in the world.

At the same time, the lion was an enemy. Killing a lion (or a bear or an eagle) was the same as killing an enemy Navajo and admitted a Pueblo man into the Warrior's Society as fully as if he had taken a human scalp. When a lion was killed, the hunter built a fire and the other men of the Pueblo, alerted by the smoke, crept up to the skin and attacked it with clubs or bows and arrows or guns. The skull was ritually buried. Lion meat was apparently not eaten, although lion bones have been found in archaeological digs in the region. The skin and claws were used for ceremonies, but killing lions to obtain parts doesn't seem to have been any more routine for Pueblos than for Navajos. Lions that died from illness or the hooves of an escaping deer must have been found sometimes. Occasionally a hunter would come upon a lion by surprise and take advantage of the opportunity. And sometimes, in the communal drives of deer and rabbits that were a common method of hunting, lions or bears would be caught in a circle of hunters. Any animal that failed to break through was killed.

These "surrounds" faintly echo the enormous drives of Inca kings in Peru, where thirty thousand men formed a circle dozens of miles in diameter and slowly cinched themselves closed. Tens of thousands of guanacos and vicuñas were captured and shorn; the females were released, as were the best and largest males, while the rest were killed for meat. Lions and all other predators were killed. Animals were tallied and the hunted areas were rotated. This practice, described by the son of an Inca princess and a Spanish conquistador, has been called the earliest game management in the Western Hemisphere.

And yet, despite their enmity to the mountain lion as predator, Incas relied heavily on the cat for cultural symbolism. Lions were associated with transitions—in time, as in initiation rites for young boys, and in space, as in marking borders—hinting at a biological relationship with edges: lions are most active on the brink of night and day and often seek out the prey-rich margins where different habitats abut each other. Lion symbolism and biology entwine inextricably in other Native histories. The Indians of southern California were said to venerate the lion above all animals because, when they saw buzzards gathering, they sought out and feasted upon the lion's kill. The lion's success as a hunter meant their own survival. Cheyenne mythology went even further: their women suckled panther cubs like children, and in turn the panthers killed deer for them. Early humans in Africa probably appropriated leopard kills, and Bushmen have been known to persuade lions to relinquish a freshly killed dinner. Maybe it was the use of mountain lion food by people that generated a body of lore, prominent in parts of Central and South America, of the lion as a friend and even loving helper of humankind.

Enemy, guardian, friend—facets of mountain lion glint and flash through myriad Native beliefs, but underlying them all is a single vein. Natives see the world as a whole in which every entity, animate and inanimate, plays a part. Every part is intimately involved in an unending, mysterious cycle of life and death, and any feature of nature—plants, animals, mountains, waterfalls—might be addressed in terms of kinship. The lives of nonhumans have importance and power. Nonhuman life sustains human life. This fact generated a deeply felt need for reciprocity, which is expressed in mystic rituals and codes of behavior. From the tension between exploiting and worshipping the environment grew a desire for harmony and a tolerance of ambiguity. Ambivalence was recognized and accepted as the most rational response to the beauty and pain, the delight and terror of the natural world. Mountain lions are as fierce as bloodshed but gentle as a mother with kittens, as strong as death yet vulnerable to accidents and age. American Indians were able to reconcile the extremes, and the emotional result was respect. It is a way of knowing through balance.

"What kind of animal is the lion?" I asked an Indian at one of the pueblos, expecting a western-style description of physical traits or perceived behavior.

"Why, there's only one kind of animal, the kind that demands respect!" he said in astonishment.

Much of the sacredness in Native American thought about animals in general and lions in particular may have been wrenched away by half a millennium of disruption, but there's still an embarrassingly simple lesson at the core: live and let live. "Lions should just be left alone," Hopis and Navajos and Pueblos said to me over and over. In the history of white relationships with lions, that's been the last thing to occur to anyone.

European
Impact Statement

THE SKELETON, DISJOINTED AND HEAPED ON A CLINICAL WHITE TRAY, IS weathered in yellow streaks but still can only be called bone colored. Ribs clack together when I lift the wire that cords them. A shoulder bone flares out. At the ends of all the long bones, where the epiphyses are not yet fused, the bones are still growing.

The panther is young and strong and has never been hungry, so the snow is still a plaything to him. He licks and chews it, bats at it, rolls in it, with the abandon of adolescence. But he is not so inexperienced that he does not recognize danger in the sound of human approach. He raises his head and stares down the white slope of Paddy Mountain. Footsteps are oddly muffled by the snow but unmistakable nonetheless. The panther makes a birdlike chirp to his sister, and she stops licking the rib bones of a deer carcass. They move away heavily through the deep snow up the ridge toward the long, undulating crest of the mountain, the brother plowing through the snow like a horse and his sister behind him, bounding from step to step in the trail he breaks. In the few months since they left their mother, they have explored all of Paddy Mountain, and they know exactly where they are going.

Adam Rudolph is a big man and the snow, reaching above his knees, makes hard going for him, too. He tries to breathe regularly, evenly, to the rhythm of his pumping legs. His breath is faintly visible in the cold air. The moccasins he finished stitching last night are already wet and will soon be sodden, and his deer hunt has only just begun. He sloughs up the ridge, peering down over each side, where the deer have their trails. The tracks he finds are not deer, though. He bends over, muzzling his breath in his blue-jean hunting shirt, and puzzles a while. Then he straightens up.

"Hallo!" he yells toward the northeastern arm of Paddy Mountain, where massive trees prickle like beard stubble against the snowy white face of the slope. "Hallo!" he yells again, this time toward the southwest, where another arm of the mountain is glinting in the morning sun. His cousins William and Henry will hear him and leave their own searching to join him. Adam surveys the roiling tracks again, squints against the glare, sets his long rifle down against his side and rubs his hands together.

"Wahrscheinlich Baer," he mutters, frowning. Probably bear.

I have followed Bob Fisher down long, dim, silent hallways lined with metal-clad wooden cases stacked one upon the other and tagged with signs that say Ursidae. Down one passage heads of moose and elk lolled along the tops of cases, their racks vaulting over the narrowed way like arches. The floor of dull marble flagstones absorbed the clatter of our footsteps like old snow. We wended through a maze of corridors past cases marked Canidae until we came to a curving hall. The inside wall of the curve was blocked by cases that reached over my head so I couldn't look down to the lobby below, but I could see the tile ceiling of the Rotunda gleaming in suffused sunlight from high encircling windows. A hum of human voices seemed to rise up and well against it like clouds of vapor. In my mind I saw the elephant that lives in perpetual greeting below the dome and the crowds of schoolchildren, disgorged from buses on the Mall outside, that mill perpetually around him.

Here the cases are marked Felidae. Bob unlocks one and folds down the door. Dozens of empty eye sockets gape at us from neatly stacked trays full of skulls. Bob slides out two trays, a small one with a skull and a larger one with the remainder of the skeleton, and balances them securely in his arms. He is a slight, bearded man with a graceful walk, and leads me carefully back through the maze to the lab prep room.

This was a men's toilet once, but all that remains is an old porcelain sink with a dripping faucet. A table runs the length of the small room, and at one end a wolf skin is bundled in brown paper. All skins that have not been field dressed are prepared here for the National Museum of Natural History, a unit of the Smithsonian Institution in Washington, D.C. There is not a molecule of odor.

Bob sets the trays of bones down on the table, and I reach out to touch them. Some are smooth, some rough. Tags on the larger bones read, "U.S. National Museum. Felis concolor couguar. Capon Springs, Virginia," and on the backs, "C. B. Kennerly, catalogued 1850." On many of the bones themselves, in spidery black ink, is the number 848. Human arrogance, Victorian style, emanates from the pitiless, elegant curl of the 8s.

They will long remember, thinks Adam Rudolph, the winter of 1850. The snow is deadly deep. It is heaped up even under the huge oaks along Cedar Creek, oaks whose thick limbs with their late clinging leaves usually deflect snow, and whose massive dark trunks soak up sun and usually melt an oval around themselves. Hunting under such conditions is hard, as hard as any of the land-clearing and house-building tasks Adam has tackled in his sixty years on the Virginia frontier, but they must hunt if they want to eat meat. In Adam's mind is a hungry wife and assorted relatives in a two-story brick house within earshot of the whispering of Cedar Creek. He dug the clay for the bricks from its banks.

In the middle of the autumn a bear killed both of Adam's pigs as they fattened on chestnuts in the forest. Like people, bears have a decided taste for bacon. Adam wonders now if he is following the bear that killed his pigs. Why would a bear be out in such snow instead of denned up somewhere? Perhaps the bear is returning to a den in the rock outcrops that crenellate the top of Paddy Mountain, thinks Adam. He can see that jumble of rocks from his own backyard. He lets his mind drift to stories of Patrick Blake, the Irishman who left his nickname to the mountain. Adam does not want to think about mountain lions, which he calls panthers, and neither do William and Henry. "Ja, ja," they agree as they study the signs. "It must be a bear," they say, younger than Adam and more comfortable in English than German. They all want it to be a bear.

All his life Adam has heard about panthers. They loom large but indistinct in his mind, their character vague, their habits known only by hearsay. His father, who with a few other Germans pioneered this small, pretty valley tucked into the eastern front of the Alleghenies, had feared them more than any other wild beast. The wizened old people of Adam's youth spoke of panthers with lowered voices as if merely to mention them could invoke an evil presence. Adam's forebears had come to America armed with millennia of experience in dealing with wolves. Bears still rambled through Europe, too, and like wolves inhabited the mythology and folklore that settlers brought with them to interpret America. Even the European wildcat and lynx still secreted themselves throughout northern European forests and rendered the American bobcat easily comprehensible. But the big sleek tawny cat that stalked the woods as silently as a shadow was terrifyingly unknown.

Christopher Columbus, first in so many wrongful ways, seems to have been the second European to name lions as inhabitants of the lands he claimed to discover. In 1500, two years before Columbus wrote of "leones," Amerigo Vespucci recorded such animals along the coast of Central America. Subsequent explorers added panthers and pards (a variety of leopard), ounces (a term for snow leopard), leopards, and tigers to the roster of catlike creatures glimpsed or rumored on the new shores, but lions continued to head the list. By the 1580s, when the English attempted their first permanent colony on Roanoke Island off the coast of North Carolina, they expected to find lions, and so they did. Among this group of settlers were Thomas Harriot, a brilliant mathematician who made precise notes about his observations in the newfound land, and John White, an artist whose drawings became the first published illustrations of the New World. Harriot's text with engravings made from White's drawings appeared in Europe in 1590. "The inhabitants sometimes kill the lion, and eat him," Harriot wrote. One of the accompanying pictures featured an Indian clothed in an animal skin with a long, tufted tail dangling down. Too long for a bison, too slim for anything else, it could only be a lion's tail. But unlike the African lion, the American mountain lion's tail has no tassel at the end. With the few brush strokes that tufted that tail, John White projected an entire cosmos of Old World imagery onto a uniquely American animal.

In our beginning was the lion. Images of leonine power are as ancient as Western culture. Nearly twenty-five thousand years before Christ, someone shaped the head of a lioness in clay and fired it on a hearth in eastern Europe. For thousands of years thereafter, lions were scratched onto cave walls. Greeks sculpted lions from pure white marble to honor the birthplace of Apollo on the island of Delos. Egyptians reposed the sphinx in a lion's body. Lions roam through the Bible, emissaries sometimes of God, sometimes of the devil. Predation may be the earliest Western metaphor for evil, as an animal innocent of sin is struck down by bloody death. Christianity linked this disharmony in the natural world with the fall of man: in Isaiah's vision of paradise regained, "the lion shall eat straw like the ox."

Since the beginning of written history the lion has been acclaimed as the preeminent predator, the king of beasts. Among the earliest influential texts in Western civilization are those of Aristotle, called the father of natural history because he was the first to propose empirical observation instead of age-old lore as the basis of knowledge. In Aristotle's day—the fourth century B.C.—the lions that had once preyed throughout Europe had been reduced (probably through a combination of human hunting and climatic change) to only the northern regions of Aristotle's homeland of Greece. Maybe Aristotle watched lions being hunted there, because he described their gait and habits of eluding pursuers in some detail. He also gave their manner of mating, their fear of fire, even the reasonable explanation that man-killers are too aged and weak to attack other prey. Through this naturalistic portrayal ran the already ancient assessment of lion character. "The lion in his manner of feeding is very cruel," Aristotle wrote, but "in soul he is generous and liberal, proud and ambitious, yet gentle and just and affectionate to his comrades."

Nobility, generosity, courage, mercy, lack of guile, and the utmost ferocity—these dichotomous qualities attributed to the lion persisted, even intensified, as Christianity pervaded the West's view of the world. Christianity changed animals from objects of inquiry to moral allegories. Christ glowed through the guise of a lion in the golden illustrations of many a medieval manuscript; the devil, too, was a roaring, ravenous lion. Resplendent and immensely popular medieval bestiaries evolved from a collection of Greek stories (called the Physiologus) that was roughly contemporaneous with Aristotle but drew on folklore rather than empiricism. In them the chapter on the lion was usually first, longest, and most profusely illustrated. On European shields the rampant lion proclaimed the foremost warriors, those who were invincible yet merciful. Like Native Americans, Europeans made of the lion a powerful symbol, but unlike Natives, Europeans did not have the opportunity to link their symbolism with biology.

English colonists were curious enough about New World lions that they sought skins through friendship or trade with Natives. There was an immediate problem: the animal was so elusive that few skins and less information came to hand. "Lions I will not positively affirm . . . since our people never yet saw any," wrote William Strachey, secretary of the Jamestown colony, in 1612, even though he received assurances from England that the claws he sent there were indeed a lion's. Plymouth Plantation settlers were likewise confused, having never seen a lion but convinced that the mysterious roaring some of them heard in the forest could issue only from lions or devils. As decades passed and no lion with a mane was ever brought forth—though there were a few rumors—it became clear that the long-tailed cat that slunk through the primeval forest was not the lion of fable. John Banister, an English-born minister who came to America in 1678 as the first university-trained naturalist, called the country's large cat exclusively by the name of panther. Confusion continued to spawn many other names elsewhere, but panther was the designation that began to stick in the eastern United States, sometimes corrupted to "painter" by backwoods folk. Curiosity about the true nature of the animal withered as the thin, short-haired pelts proved of little value in the fur trade. The attitude toward wild creatures is clear from a 1676 petition of some Virginia landowners, who wanted to repeal the bounties (supported by taxes) on wolves, bears, wild cats, and other such beasts, "since no man but will, for his own good and security, indeavour to the utmost to destroy all possibly he can."

Busy wresting comfort and profit from the frontier, Americans were too preoccupied to do much more about their mysterious not-a-lion than substitute one mythical image for another. Panthers were vague concepts that for centuries had been inextricably mixed with leopards. There was little ambivalence in the mythology of either. Apparently using the terms leopard, panther, and pard indiscriminately for the same animal, Aristotle wrote, "In soul [the panther] is mean and thievish, and in a word, a beast of low cunning." Medieval bestiaries portrayed the leopard as the bloodthirsty product of an unnatural mating between a lion and a pard. Panthers were painted with open mouths, surrounded by a herd of other animals, because they exhaled a breath so sweet that other animals were drawn to it. In the text of the bestiaries this quality often symbolized the attraction of Christ for the multitudes, but popular culture saw it as treachery. Like woman, the panther enticed only to destroy. Sexual disgust was explicit in the work of Edward Topsell, an Elizabethan who compiled an early encyclopedia of four-footed beasts. The panther resembles the nature of woman, wrote Topsell, "for it is a fraudulent though beautiful beast . . . wanton, effeminate, outrageous, treacherous, deceitful, fearful and yet bold."

Myths were taken quite literally. Referring to the ancient belief that jackals hunted the lion's prey, New Englander John Josselyn insisted in 1672 that the presence of jackals (wolves, perhaps?) was "a shrewd sign that there are lions upon the continent." John Banister, perhaps the most educated man in America in his day, took pains to refute as "vulgar error" an assertion of Roman naturalist Pliny the Elder. Pliny had said that horses treading in the tracks of wolves would suffer their legs to become numbed. "I have seen a live [wolf] taken out of a pit or trap, dragged at a horses tail, and others following on horseback," Banister wrote, "yet the horses did not at all falter."

The Zeitgeist turned slowly secular and animals once again became objects rather than symbols. A few minds transcended cultural blinders and evoked the Aristotelian tradition of direct observation. John Lawson, a keen-eyed surveyor, published his *History of North Carolina* in 1709, just before Indians burned him at the stake for his trespasses. Of panthers he wrote, "This beast is the greatest enemy to the planter of any vermine in Carolina." His accusation gains some credence from the accuracy of his other observations about the animal: "He climbs trees with the greatest agility imaginable," covers his kill with leaves, preys on pigs and deer or anything he can get, and purrs like a cat. Lawson mentioned "tygers" briefly as very rare and to the westward, raising the specter of jaguars. Of lions he said, "I never saw any in America, neither can I imagine how they should come here."

When Americans recognized that their feline was not the lion of lore, a certain disappointment set in. Virginia gentleman William Byrd II was notable for his sly humor as well as his colonial affluence and influence. He expressed the ludicrous in the tension between myth and reality in 1728, in his account of surveying the border between Virginia and North Carolina, *History of the Dividing Line*. The panther was the "absolute monarch of the woods," Byrd wrote after finding a black bear apparently killed and half devoured by a panther. "However, it must be confessed," he went on, "his voice is a little contemptible for a monarch . . . being not a great deal louder nor more awful than the mewing of a household cat."

Travelers' accounts of the New World proliferated through the eighteenth century. In them ancient myths mixed with a growing body of American mountain lion folklore, which was itself compounded of Indian distrust of the cat's secrecy and bits and pieces of backcountry experience. Wildly improbable creatures sometimes resulted, such as the "carcajou," with a tail three times its length and other features from wolves, wolverines, lynx, panthers, even badgers. That distinctly American folk phenomenon, the tall tale, can be seen a-bornin'. Where American panthers emerge more clearly recognizable, their earliest and most resounding attributes are the mythical qualities of treachery and bloodlust. Deer with their throats torn out and gutted as if by a surgeon's knife; calves and pigs, turned loose to forage in the forest, lying in heaps and hardly touched as if killed merely for a draught of hot blood; an enemy who stalked so soundlessly through the black forest that no one ever knew whence he might spring—these were the images that seared settlers' minds.

Adam Rudolph had held in his trembling hands (for all the Rudolphs honored books and learning) only a few books. Most of them were Bibles and religious tracts, but one was a secular work produced in 1813 at a printery in the brash and bustling Shenandoah Valley town of Harrisonburg. Over the years it passed from hand to eager hand, for not only was it a poem of praise to a true American hero, Daniel Boone, but it was also a testimony to the frontier fortitude of the local girl, from just up the Shenandoah River, whom Boone married. In *The Mountain Muse* the many valorous exploits of Daniel in a ravening wilderness are detailed, but of all the danger and heartbreak the hero faces—savage Indians, frightful hunger, slain loved ones—the murderous, "slaughter hungering panther" is the most dreadful. With rending talons and "teeth sharp as spears along his gory, life destroying snout," his body half buried in the "smoking chasm" he had torn in his pain-maddened prey, this merciless monster is the emblem of the wilderness in which Adam lives.

It is this image that Adam banishes from his mind as he proceeds, with William and Henry behind him, to follow the tracks he has found, and that he tells himself belong to a bear. Before long they discover the remains of a deer, with no flesh left, and both large and small tracks around it. The bear has found a dead deer, they figure, and perhaps brought a cub to it. Panting with effort, stopping often to calm their straining hearts, the men pursue the tracks to the top and along the crest of Paddy Mountain. They trip and stagger from one group of white mounded rocks to another, pointing out to each other where the trail leads in and then out of the honeycomb of dens. The sun is lowering. It never occurs to them to quit the search. In places the crest is nothing more than a slender white ligament binding the knuckles of mountain together. Beyond a bare-branched screen of trees, the whole Shenandoah Valley spreads out to the east, the last sharp rays of sun glinting on its blue-white prairies. To the west, the Appalachians hang like streamers of frozen smoke in the growing dusk. The men stop, not to admire the views. The trail has ended in a deep den beneath a pile of boulders, but it is too near dark for further action. They confer, stomping their feet and squeezing their hands under their arms, and decide to go home and come back tomorrow with the dogs to have some sport. They can easily follow their own trail back up the mountain, but with the habits of a frontiersman Adam looks back to impress the spot on his mind. The jagged rocks all cunningly disguised beneath snow, the dead-looking forest succoring rapacious beasts, the airy emptiness now gloomy with evening—they make for a desperate-looking place, oh, most terrible!

⌐Ⴑ⌐

We are trying to piece the skull together. It is darker than the rest of the skeleton, more mottled with dark stains, and incomplete. The left orbital lobe is missing, and the front of the nose, and a segment of jaw. The part of the jaw that is present is a shattered remnant. Little chips of bone and grains of dirt cling to the corners of the white tray. A few teeth clink in a cork-stoppered glass jar.

"There's no canines," Claudia Angle says. "And no claws. People like to keep them for trophies." Like Bob Fisher, Claudia is a museum specialist in the mammal division. Shoulder-length hair falls around her face as she leans over to finger the small bones of wrist and ankle. Severed from the rest of the skeleton but still bound together by connective tissue, the hollow bones look like panpipes. Just below the sliced ovals of the openings are many hacking marks of a knife.

Claudia has brought with her a brown book lettered on the spine, *Museum Catalog: Mammals 1 to 3,500*. The crabbed entry for No. 848 on a blue-lined page is very early in the book, nearly at the beginning of zoology.

When Columbus arrived in North America, Old World thinkers teetered on the verge of science. The strange American flora and fauna challenged medieval notions about God's creation and galvanized European intellectuals. New philosophies were needed to explain the iconoclastic nature of the New World. Curiosity about New World life was intense, not in the minds of the pioneers actually accosting them, but in the European intelligentsia. Wealthy merchants and aristocrats hired back-woodsmen to send specimens of all kinds. Skins of birds, fish, fowl, mammals, reptiles, and even insects were dried and shipped, and among them were a few that instantly fascinated—the unbelievably tiny humming-bird, the pouched opossum, the noisy rattlesnake. The first task of natural historians was to categorize all these specimens in a systematic way, to impose a humanly graspable order on nature's chaos. Through assiduous study, some European scholars proposed remarkably modern structures of relationships without ever observing a living being. As early as 1693, the English naturalist John Ray, considered the greatest of the pre-Linnaean catalogers, recognized as a unique American species a roe-colored cat he labeled the cuguacuarana of Brazil, a Native name. Let the London fops argue, as they did in the pages of fashionable magazines, that lions of the African sort surely must exist in America. Linnaeus settled the question for science once and for all in 1771 when he defined the species as *Felis concolor:* cat of one color.

On the whole, though, animals were of secondary interest to natural historians. Medicine and the curative properties of plants had long been accepted as one of the few legitimate areas of study outside theology, so botany emerged as the earliest focus of natural history. When Americans began to participate in the European ferment of ideas about the natural world, it was mostly to produce great botanical catalogs and treatises for the Royal Society of London, as did John Clayton of Virginia; or marvelous gardens and lively botanical travelogues, as did John Bartram and his son William. To further advance the accumulation of knowledge at home, urbane Americans like Benjamin Franklin founded scientific societies that debated and published the findings of their countrymen. In the proceedings of these societies, interest in large mammals is conspicuous by its absence, except for fossils. Those relics of the past aroused theological and even a sort of jingoistic debate, because of the Old World assertion that New World animals were smaller and more degenerate than Old World species. This notion may have arisen from the accounts of some travelers who, amazed that they were not attacked by wolves and lions and bears in the raw wilderness, concluded that these beasts must be less ferocious in America than in Europe.

The idea of degeneracy was most arrogantly articulated by the Count de Buffon in his widely circulated and translated encyclopedia, *Natural history, general and particular,* which first appeared in French in 1749. Buffon had seen a living example of the animal he named couguar, and gave a succinct description of it, although his mention of its cruelty and rapacity could hardly have come from personal experience. (In later editions he gave three short chapters on couguars, listing separately the couguar, the couguar of Pennsylvania, and the black couguar.) In the chapter on lions, Buffon mused that animals were larger, stronger, and more ferocious in hot climates, and remarked by way of proof that the American lion was "smaller, weaker, and less courageous than the true lion."

Such slanders mightily pricked Thomas Jefferson's pride. Much of Jefferson's 1784 *Notes on the state of Virginia,* a work that lent his own immense prestige to the emerging mode of scientific inquiry, was devoted to refuting Buffon's contentions of New World degeneracy. (Jefferson, too, listed three types of American lion: the puma, the cougar of South America, and the cougar of North America.) A few years later, while in Europe as a minister of his fledgling government, Jefferson confronted Buffon with a moose skeleton and forced him to admit it was larger than any European elk. Even this did not abate Jefferson's pique: in a 1797 paper submitted to the American Philosophical Society, he argued, a bit feverishly, that the enormous fossil bones and claws of a lion found west of the Blue Ridge Mountains proved that the New World contained lions three times larger than the Old World big cats, and that such

"Great-Claws" probably continued to thrive in the unexplored interior of the continent.

Dispassionate knowledge about America's lions stalled with John Lawson in 1709. A single paragraph in his book contains as much biological fact about the cougar as would be known for more than two centuries. Mark Catesby's better-known *The natural history of Carolina, Florida and the Bahama Islands* of 1731 merely repeated most of what Lawson had said. The naturalists who published books on American quadrupeds in the early nineteenth century—Thomas Bewick, George Ord, Richard Harlan, John Godman—embellished this meager store of fact with the bloodlust themes of folklore.

"Has Zoology, or the history of animals," asked James DeKay in 1826, "been cultivated in the United States with the same success as botany, or geology and mineralogy? The answer must be," he went on to inform his audience at the Lyceum of Natural History in New York, "in the negative . . . It has had to contend against the unjust views which have been taken of its relative importance." DeKay wrote a natural history of New York in 1842, in which he departed from folklore regarding the threat of panthers to people. He called panthers "uniformly cowardly" and averred that most of the tales of their depredations were fictitious. About this time the theory that cougars, wolves, and all wild beasts were much fiercer in the first centuries of settlement, before they came to understand the efficacy of firearms, began to circulate. A self-serving aggrandizement of ancestors? Or a real instance of bioculture, in which animals learn and pass knowledge on to their young?

A few years after DeKay, John James Audubon and his collaborator John Bachman, in their *Viviparous Quadrupeds of North America,* repeated the charge of cougar cowardice. At the same time, they couldn't resist recounting sensational stories of cougar attacks on people. The illustration of the male cougar, which like most representations of that era looks more like a dog than a cat, showed a cougar killing a black heifer. Audubon noted that the cougar was already nearly exterminated in all the Atlantic states. Only three decades later America's drive to the west destroyed sixty million bison. Livestock replaced them, and killing livestock supplanted attacks on people as a reason to hate cougars. Occasionally, a writer acknowledged that livestock and human overhunting had so reduced deer herds that some cougars ate kine of necessity, but this hardly exonerated them. On the contrary: their very preference for deer was another black mark against them. Like all elements of creation, deer belonged to people, to be used solely for human purposes. Whereas Native Americans worshipped cougars for their hunting prowess, white Americans loathed the animals for exactly the same reason.

The ancient prejudice against predators was more subtle but just as tenacious in natural history as in folklore. Ancient myth and modern science came together in the person of Theodore Roosevelt. The twenty-fifth president of the United States was born in 1858 to a wealthy family in New York City. He was a sickly child, gasping with asthma in his father's arms through many anxious nights. Too weak to attend school, he was privately tutored, and an innate curiosity drove him to read omnivorously on his own. The outdoors lured Roosevelt from a very young age, perhaps because of his desperate need for fresh air. He took long, observant walks at home and in the countryside, where he was often sent. He felt an instinctive interest in natural history. While still a small boy, he passed one day through a market on Broadway and saw a dead seal stretched out on a slab of wood. "That seal," he wrote in his autobiography, "filled me with every possible feeling of romance and adventure." He asked where the animal had come from and was told the harbor. Such was the spirit of natural history at the time that it never occurred to Roosevelt to go to the harbor and look for living seals. Instead, he carefully measured the dead seal's physical dimensions and managed to acquire the skull, which became the first specimen in his natural history collection.

Later, after being roughed up by some boys while on a trip to recuperate from an asthma attack, Roosevelt determined to make his body do what his mind willed. Years of a rigorous exercise and boxing regime strengthened him physically and imbued him with the belief that a man could and should make of himself anything he wanted. It was Roosevelt's ambition to make of himself "a scientific man of the Audubon . . . type," but at Harvard he found that biology was purely a laboratory science, a kind of study that did not appeal to him. He began to write (the first of his many books, *The Naval War of 1812,* was published in 1882). He traveled out West (the subject of several subsequent books). And he carried on the tradition of public service inherited from both sides of his family. The fame of Roosevelt's Rough Riders, the volunteer cavalry regiment he helped raise and lead through the Spanish-American War, catapulted him to the governorship of New York. Next came the vice-presidency of the United States, under President McKinley. When McKinley was assassinated in 1901, Roosevelt immediately used his new power to set conservation on the national agenda. For years he had been working behind the scenes to irrigate the West and preserve forests everywhere. During Roosevelt's first, unexpected term and his second, duly elected term, despite intense opposition he increased national forests from 43 million to 194 million acres and created dozens of refuges, preserves, and parks.

Roosevelt hoped these reserves would forestall the indiscriminate murder of wildlife that emptied the country wherever settlers had full sway. The key word is *indiscriminate*. Roosevelt wanted to protect only those creatures that humans deemed desirable. To Roosevelt belongs a large share of credit for preservation of the bison and many kinds of migrating ducks and plumed birds. The Progressive movement, which Roosevelt espoused, aimed to clean up a government corrupted by overweening business interests, and this reformist impulse, infused with missionary zeal, extended to the predators of the natural world. Obsessed with predators in general, Roosevelt found cougars in particular morally disturbing because they seemed to him the deadliest of all foes to the harmless species of wildlife. There was no more than a perfunctory sort of ambivalence in his attitude. With a detachment at odds with the passion in the rest of his writing, he mustered an occasional reference to cougars as "interesting creatures." Otherwise his words condemn them. Even in his acquittal of cougars as man-killers, Roosevelt maligned them as "abject cowards." In one article he called them "a beast of stealth and rapine," and in another, "ferocious and bloodthirsty as they are cowardly." When, during his hunting trips, he looked into a cougar's face he saw "evil yellow eyes." One of his most often quoted descriptions is "the big horse-killing cat, the destroyer of the deer, the lord of stealthy murder. . . with a heart both craven and cruel." When Roosevelt left office in 1909, a group of his intimates known as the Tennis Cabinet presented him as a parting gift a bronze sculpture of a cougar.

It was Roosevelt's administration that formulated an official policy of eradication of predators and started the Bureau of the Biological Survey, which eventually mobilized the force of government to carry it out. Before Roosevelt even left office, tens of thousands of carnivores had been shot, trapped, snared, or poisoned. Canada pursued the same policies. By the time systematic assassination of predators stopped more than half a century later, some sixty-five thousand dead cougars had been tallied throughout western North America. Wolves and grizzly bears had been extirpated from most of the contiguous United States, and all other animals inconvenient to humans had been drastically diminished, except, perhaps, the irrepressible coyote. The trickle of specimens into museums became a flood as the first few generations of natural historians gorged on a way of knowing through death.

"What is the current acquisitions number for the mammal division?" I ask Claudia.

"Nearly six hundred thousand," she says.

The two panthers hear the dogs baying long before there is any immediate danger. They do not want to run through the snow, and they feel safe in the deep darkness of their den. They lie next to each other, sometimes dozing, sometimes grooming, and wait for the strange sounds to pass by.

Adam Rudolph, his cousins, and five dogs left the brick house in time to reach the top of Paddy Mountain—six or seven miles—by sunrise. They saw where the animals had come out and picked their way through the rock fields, looking for a good place to hide. It is tiresome work to track them. The beasts have picked the very roughest places. The rocks stand high with great flat faces, straight as the walls of a house. Where the tracks end, Adam lies down to peer over the edge of a boulder, into the black mouth of a hole.

"Here," he says. Together they hand a dog down into the hole. The dog begins to bark. Later Adam will describe a growl like the loudest thunder beneath him in answer to the dog's barking. Then all the dogs jump down in. "Such a growling and a barking you never heard!" Adam will tell. He can hear the scratching of claws against rocks as the cornered creatures bat the dogs, tearing them up and biting one. If it was bears, he yells above the din, they would come out, but they don't. William climbs down on a jutting corner of rock to hand up the dogs. Then, all is quiet and nothing to be seen.

"Hold my feet," William says, and palms down the rocks for a look. "I see his eyes. They are wide apart and big as a silver dollar." He is breathless; his voice cracks.

"You are scared," says Adam.

"No, I ain't, but I feel sick from hanging this way. Take me up."

Adam takes a turn going down, the two younger men clutching his shins. He sees the eyes and realizes they do not belong to a bear. It must be a panther. With William and Henry watching him, Adam feels he must set an example. He comes up for a few minutes to let the blood clear from his head. A limb on the ground catches his eye. He picks it up and goes down again to pry away a loose rock and widen the crevice. Now he can see the doe color and the tiger head with the great width between the eyes. He recoils and goes back up to consult with William and Henry. They agree to put two men down, one to hold the gun and the other to pull the trigger. Upside down, Adam sights under rather than along the gun. "A little higher, a little more to the right," William calls out. Adam steadies himself, breathes deeply, then holds his breath and pulls the trigger. The shot reverberates like a cannon, hurting his ears, filling the den with the roar of apocalypse.

The male panther feels a horrible pain in his head and twitches around the den in agony. His sister, terrified, scrabbles toward a tiny sliver of daylight at the back of the den. The crack is too small for her and she rakes frantically at a patch of gravel. The two men scramble to get back on top of the rocks. When the noise of the gun subsides they listen to the panther struggling in his blood. The sounds grow fainter. After a while they let down a dog, but there is silence. Adam climbs down and crawls in as far as he can. He steels himself, reaches around a rock and feels the dead panther's face. He jerks his hand back at the touch of fur, but when nothing happens, he keeps groping. He touches the mouth. He will show William and Henry. Adam curls a finger around one of the panther's teeth and tugs, but can't pull the body forward.

"There's one coming out another way!" Henry yells, but the men are in disarray and cannot stop the second animal from escaping. Above ground again, Adam takes his tomahawk from a loop at his belt, cuts some branches, and they all brush snow away to see which rocks can be moved. They rig a pole with a hook at the end, shove it down the widened hole, and pull the dead cat out. He seems to them huge, monstrously huge. The shot caught him in the jaw. He is too heavy to carry back, so they skin him, sundering the paws, and drape the carcass over a tree. In the red brick house and in the houses of neighbors up and down Cedar Creek, over cups of homemade wine, in English and in German, the men tell the story of the ferocious animal they destroyed.

Panthers are uncommon, and the story makes its way out of the little valley. On top of Paddy Mountain, ravens, crows, and other scavengers quickly strip the dead panther. The skeleton collapses in a heap beneath the tree. The skull rolls into a open spot and catches more weather. Next spring some government man comes along and offers Adam five dollars to retrieve the bones. Ten years later, a roving writer from *Harper's Magazine* seeks Adam out to hear his tale.

By then, panthers were prime copy for the popular press. "The American storywriter's best friend, his chief pet, his reliance in every emergency," wrote well-known naturalist William T. Hornaday in the introduction to a volume of panther stories taken from the famous children's magazine *St. Nicholas*. The volume was so popular it was reprinted about a dozen times in the late nineteenth and early twentieth centuries. "Let me give him one more name," Hornaday continued, after listing puma, panther, mountain lion, cougar, California lion, plain lion, painter, and catamount, "and call him the Story Lion!" In the *St. Nicholas* stories that Adam's grandchildren pored over by kerosene lamps, in the pulp novels that sold for a nickel at newsstands, in refined literature, and in natural history accounts, motifs that had been evolving for centuries coalesced into a body of cougar lore. Cougars dropped from trees onto unsuspecting prey, rode on the backs of their frantically galloping victims drinking blood all the while, screamed like a woman being murdered, covered sleeping hunters with leaves for a later attack, and followed people in order to attack from the rear. Clever folk, finding themselves pursued, dropped one by one any bits of food or other distractions they were carrying, to win enough time to reach home and safety. Panthers padded onto porches, clawed through the chinking in log cabin walls, and climbed onto roofs trying to get down chimneys in their eagerness for human flesh, especially children.

On the other hand, cougars could be dispatched in hand-to-hand combat. They were choked by fists thrust down their throats and killed with sticks and stones, even by children. Less frequently, panthers called to lure people closer (echoes of that old sweet breath), patted their tails on the ground prior to leaping, and met up with black bears, usually on a log over a stream. Sometimes the two animals killed each other and other times the cougar won. In a few stories the cougar vanquished even the massive grizzly bear.

Some of the oddest panther stories were described by turn-of-the-century folklorist Charles Skinner in Maine. Much to be dreaded, wrote Skinner, was the ding-ball, a panther whose last tail joint was ball shaped and served as a weapon to crack a victim's skull. Pomoola, an Indian devil, haunted Mount Katahdin in the form of a huge panther with four-foot-long tusks—an evocation of the real but extinct saber-toothed tiger. Accurate biological fact and ancient, universal demands of the human psyche became so entwined as to be impossible to tease apart. Relying on reports from the professional hunters who supplied wild meat to the markets and specimens to scientists, natural historians continued to discount the danger of cougars to humans, but the twentieth century would be well under way before science developed a methodology or a mindset to examine the rest of the garbled biology in these stories.

The American consciousness of cougars was distilled in the short stories of Ambrose Bierce. Bierce was born on an Ohio farm in 1842, when cougars were already scarce because of the animosity of settlers, and cougar lore was well established. Eventually he became a master satirist in San Francisco. Various of his horror stories feature a low, soulless, unearthly laugh or wail reminiscent of a cougar's scream, and several use a cougar—always malignant—as the major antagonist. Most revealing of the cougar image in the eye of the American imagination is "The Damned Thing," a chilling story in which the cougar cannot be seen at all. It is invisible. Only the lacerations of a dead man's throat provide the irrefutable proof. The hero shoots the animal by following the trembling wild oats that mark its progress across an otherwise still field. In those few pages Bierce captured the essence of American fear of the cougar's mystery.

Bierce reflected mainstream thought, but not every writer invariably damned the cougar. A tiny blush of ambivalence began to spread across the face of perception. Mostly it was an ambivalence unconscious of itself. A trace appeared in a novel serialized through 1869 in a New York magazine, The Old Guard. In The Cub of the Panther, author William Gilmore Simms narrated a South Carolina tale of a boy born with a birthmark in the form of a panther on his forehead, a mark that appeared as a murderous panther threatened to kill the mother at the moment of birth. The boy is lithe, graceful, solitary, quick to anger, and a superb hunter—recognizably similar in body and mind to the dreaded panther—and under duress he kills his own father. Yet he is portrayed as a hero, albeit uneasily, as though the author felt forced to that end by the narrative structure. Nickel-and-dime novels excoriated the cougar as a despicable adversary while con-ferring cougar qualities of strength and agility on their heroes. In one of the *St. Nicholas* stories a little girl who has been frightened but not harmed by a panther declares that it's "not hon'rable" to kill the animal, but who pays attention to little girls?

As society adjusted to the Darwinian view of humans as just another species of animal, writers that found intelligence and virtue in animal behavior became immensely popular. Theodore Roosevelt called them "nature fakers." Among the most beloved was Ernest Thompson Seton, a Canadian who gained an international readership with his sentimental stories about wildlife. Seton was one of the first to openly admire the cougar, "this glorious exemplar of the laws that made the world." In *Lives of Game Animals,* first published in 1909, he devoted a hundred pages to the animal. "Our cougar is in all physical respects a cat," he wrote, "simply a cat multiplied by twenty." Cougars were curious, playful, and friendly; they were also monogamous, and it was an "absurd impossibility" that male cougars killed young ones. It was true that cougars loved horsemeat, but Seton cited Biological Survey hunters who estimated the entire cougar damage in the United States at $1,000 a year. The attacks of domestic dogs on humans, fumed Seton, and the depredations of domestic cats on weed-seed-eating birds, sur-passed this by many millions of dollars. "I am smitten with indignation and shame," he wrote about the relentless drive of the Biological Survey to exterminate "one of the most beautiful creatures that ever lived."

Cougar beauty prompted a paean of pure aesthetic ecstasy from a magazine illustrator named Charles Livingston Bull. In a 1913 issue of *The Century Magazine,* Bull drew a full-page picture of a gray lion on a snowy mountain ledge, the muscular body surging upward to swat at two ptarmigan. Next to it, he wrote: "Oh, the beautiful, splendid, supple, graceful, powerful, silent puma! I would rather watch and draw and dream about it than about any other living thing."

A decade later the debacle of Arizona's Kaibab Plateau began. What had been touted as a spectacular example of the success of the government's predator control—the explosion of the deer herd from four thousand to one hundred thousand in less than twenty years as all predators were killed off—turned into a nightmare as sixty thousand deer starved to death after stripping the range bare. The role of predators in the natural world was grudgingly acknowledged as wildlife science emerged, a subdiscipline of natural history. When Aldo Leopold, with the knowledge of a scientist and the language of a poet, described his flash of understanding of "the fierce green fire" in a dying wolf's eyes, acknowledgment grew into popular appreciation.

In the unfolding of his life—1887 to 1948—Aldo Leopold personified a new attitude toward the natural world. Born in Burlington, Iowa, to a father who manufactured fine hardwood furniture and a grandfather who was a landscape architect, he grew up in a mansion on Prospect Hill, overlooking the Mississippi River. His mother was an award-winning figure skater who loved opera as well as gardening. The three-acre estate bloomed with orchards, vegetables patches, and flower beds, and tropical palms graced the greenhouse. His parents commemorated Aldo's birth by planting a red oak sapling. Aldo was a shy boy who much preferred outings on the river to dancing school. By the age of eleven he could identify thirty-nine species of birds; wrens were his favorite. His father loved to hunt but saw the populations of many animals decline from unregulated hunting, and his personal code of sportsmanship included self-imposed bag limits and seasons. Aldo absorbed this code through several years of apprenticeship to his father as a hunter. He became a crack shot, sometimes practicing on the crows, sparrows, and hawks that threatened his beloved songbirds.

Leopold entered the brand new forestry school at Yale University and graduated with a master's degree in 1909. He joined the U.S. Forest Service, also a very young entity, and was posted to the new national forests of the Southwest, where he fell in love with a Hispanic woman and a monumental landscape. Shortly after his marriage, Leopold was soaked and chilled by foul weather while out on the range. His knees swelled so badly from nephritis that he couldn't ride his horse, and the damage was almost fatally compounded by a country doctor who misdiagnosed it. Eighteen months of recuperation was necessary before Leopold could resume fieldwork. Always a voracious reader, he occupied himself with books and magazines, from Thoreau's *Journals* to Theodore Roosevelt's articles. What seemed to affect him most was William T. Hornaday's accounts of vanishing American wildlife. He began to muse over the human obligation to protect and perpetuate game species. Most of the remaining deer and turkey lived on national forest lands, and when he returned to work, Leopold shifted his focus from forestry to their protection. He lost his shyness and developed into a compelling and highly persuasive speaker. One of his major goals was the eradication of predators. In a 1919 issue of *The Pine Cone,* a newsletter he edited for the New Mexico Game Protective Association, Leopold wrote, "Game protection makes the killing of varmints necessary. The fact that lions are getting away with our deer . . . is most emphatically a reason for going out after the last lion scalp, and getting it."

The deer explosion on the Kaibab in the 1920s, the invasion of coyotes into areas where wolves had been killed off, and many other undesirable results of human tinkering slowly undermined Leopold's confidence in the human ability to control nature. There is little evidence that he was influenced by Native thought, but he came to feel the same sense of connection among all things. It was in the Old World that his thinking coalesced. In 1935, a few years after he began to teach game management at the University of Wisconsin, he was invited to Germany to study German methods of forestry and wildlife management. There he saw regimented forests degraded by the browsing of legions of nearly tame deer. Raptors and other animals of prey were almost nonexistent. The absence of wildness profoundly shocked him. He felt it as a pain in his soul. "I never realized before," he wrote, "that the melodies of nature are music only when played against the undertones of evolutionary history . . . In the German forest, one now hears only a dismal fugue." He did not want to hear that fugue in his own beloved countryside. He began teaching a new course called Wildlife Ecology. Wolves figure more prominently in his writings than mountain lions, but in his later working life Leopold advocated stocking lions in Zion National Park to stop deer from destroying the magnificent canyon bottom, and even used his personal prestige to persuade a private rancher to stop killing lions on a vast Texas estate. At the old farm on the Wisconsin River that he used as a retreat, he wrote a series of essays. *A Sand County Almanac,* published the year after he died of a heart attack fighting a fire near the farm, is revered as the manifesto of a new world order:

> All ethics so far evolved rest upon a single premise: that the individual is a member of a community of interdependent parts. The land ethic simply enlarges the boundaries of

the community to include soils, water, plants, and animals, or collectively: the land . . . A land ethic changes the role of *Homo sapiens* from conqueror of the land-community to plain member and citizen of it. It implies respect for his fellow-members, and also respect for the community as such . . . It is only in recent years that we hear the . . . honest argument that predators are members of the community, and that no special interest has the right to exterminate them for the sake of a benefit, real or fancied, to itself . . . Conservation is a state of harmony.

Like wolves and grizzly bears, cougars began to appear benignly in books, on television, and in movies to an urbanizing audience hungry for a link with the natural world. Nowhere have attitudes swung to a greater extreme than on Madison Avenue. From cars to shoes to knives, cougars today sell a fast, sleek, and sexy power, a dangerous strength, a matchless beauty. No tincture of ambivalence darkens the portrait of pumas as the most magnificent animal in the American bestiary. They inhabit a continuum of cultural images from absolute evil to absolute nobility. In the light of the electrified brick house, Adam Rudolph's great-great-grandchildren have their choice of cougars.

As I pass down these avenues of bones, following Bob Fisher on my way out, I am wondering about ghosts. By all rights there should be a fog of ghosts, but Bob shakes his head and smiles. Instead of ghosts, insects haunt the Smithsonian. Small dermestids called odd beetles, fond of flesh, bone, horn, and hair, are permanent residents. The current exhibit in the Rotunda is "The Corn Palace"—a gorgeous foyer for the quincentennial Columbus Day display. The Corn Palace is pillared, corniced and porticoed with red, green, and yellow corn. I can hardly believe how beautiful the corn is. Moth larvae are hatching from it. Moths fly through the building looking for organic material in which to lay their eggs. The Smithsonian is no longer allowed to fumigate because any gas that would kill the insects is too poisonous for the people who administer it. The collections are used frequently—at least one or two people arrive every business day to see how particular specimens fit into the evolutionary sequence. There is increasing interest in studying DNA from tanned hides.

"So," Bob says, "we're about to try glass bubbles where the oxygen can be drained and replaced with carbon dioxide or nitrogen. The idea is to suffocate pests."

"How fast are you getting specimens these days?" I ask.

"The rate of increase has definitely slowed down in the last two decades. There's no current project aimed at collecting mammals," he says. Since the 1960s, the technology of radio collars, which admit humans into the lives of wild animals, has opened a way of knowing through life. As I walk out I sense the weight of blind knowledge and the lightness, the ethereal waft of wisdom.

I slip out a back door, pass the dumpsters, walk across the Mall to the Metro, and take the last Virginia exit. I drive home toward Paddy Mountain, into the beckoning blue cloud banks of the Alleghenies.

LION HUNTING
IN AMERICA

MOUNTAIN LIONS ARE UNIQUE TO THE AMERICAS, AND HUNTING THEM developed into a skill peculiar to Americans. Accustomed to running dogs after foxes and ferrets, European colonists soon learned that, as John Lawson put it in 1709, "the least Cur" could tree a lion. "Hell," echoed Charley Leeder across 287 years, "on fresh sign a goddamn poodle could run a lion up a tree."

The dogs that milled around us, frantic with early morning energy, racing between the legs of our mules and peeing on every manzanita bush that choked the edge of the gravel road, were not poodles, nor was the freshness of sign of immediate concern to them. They were Walkers and Plotts, redbones and bluets, and they were some of the best lion hounds in the country. Some were lean and leggy with jutting, angular hips; others were stumpy. Most had the small, tight feet that are less apt than big feet to spread out and suppurate from scrabbling across miles of granite. One was pure black but most were brindled, and all had their noses to the ground. Charley and his business associate, Karen LeCount, had trained them to sniff out and follow the faintest bouquet of lion scent across the dry desert landscape of southern Utah without being distracted by coyotes smirking behind ponderosa pines, or deer bouncing like Pogo sticks out of thickets. It was the ability of these hounds to pursue and tree lions, rendering them available for shooting by an accompanying trophy hunter, that earned Charley and Karen a living.

In the eleven western states and two Canadian provinces that permit mountain lion hunting, lion guiding is a steady business for dozens, perhaps hundreds of guides—hard numbers are impossible to come by because many guides pursue lions as only one segment of their total outdoor business ventures. Most guides depend on snow. In snow, especially a fresh dusting, lion tracks are as plain as words on a page. Hunters cruise the roads looking for this blatant evidence of a lion's passing. When they find a track, they need to set the dogs in the right direction, because dogs will track backward to where the lion was as happily as they will chase forward to where the lion is. Then the hunters follow on snowmobile or horseback. Once tracks are discovered, snow hunters with reasonably competent hounds will tree a cat nine times out of ten. There are a few stories of cougar cunning—Old Crafty avoided traps and poison for a decade in New Mexico before falling to a couple of hounds, and Big Foot eluded those same hounds for two years before being brought to bay—but on the whole lions are not clever about evading pursuit in general, and dogs in particular. Their long relationship with wolves and other predators has taught them simply to climb trees and wait. Then there is the story about wolves that kept a cougar treed until his feet froze and he fell out, whereupon they ate him.

Karen and Charley performed the kind of dry-ground tracking used by early settlers and predator hunters to eliminate cougars from terrain rarely or never covered by snow. This requires unusually accomplished hounds but allows hunting in any weather. It was mid-April when I arrived in Karen and Charley's hunting range. Karen met me at the airport. She was one of a very small number of professional lion huntresses in American history. A pretty, buxom brunette in her middle forties, she wore tight jeans and a fashionable plaid blouse with matching earrings. Her fingernails were a pearly shade of rose. Born in a small college town in the state of Washington, she had answered "cowgirl" the first time anyone asked her what she wanted to be. Wind flattened her short curls as we stood outside the airport, keeping company with another client who was waiting to be picked up. He was a thin, nattily dressed shoe manufacturer from Milan who spoke accented but perfect English. This was his fifth attempt to shoot an American lion, his second try with Charley.

"Charley's sending Shad," Karen told him. Shad was Charley's son.

The Italian would bunk in Charley's guest cabin and hunt with Shad, while my party would stay with Karen and ride with her and Charley. Skinny, smooth-faced Shad soon collected his man, and Karen headed her pickup out of town, past the stolid Mormon church that is a fixture in every Utah town, past a barber shop pasted with flyers for an upcoming cowboy poetry reading, past the Jolley's western wear store with its window displays of Nocona Boots boxes and their apocryphal scenes of rattlesnakes, scorpions, wolves, grizzlies and lions attacking legs guarded by pointy-toed boots. Karen's house was twenty minutes out of town, across a sagebrush pasture and around the corner of a gravel road from Charley's. The houses hunkered down on a wide plateau between the glowing red upthrusts of Zion National Park and the dark green horizon of Pine Valley Mountain. Karen had a modest house several years old and still unfinished—guiding fees of several thousand dollars per person went toward dogs, mules, and feeding hungry clients. The floors were rough plywood. There was no shower in the upstairs guest bathroom; we shared the one downstairs. Mountain lions were represented on every wall and in every art form except velvet paintings. The downstairs was a large open space, much of it kitchen. A countertop divided the kitchen from the dining room and was lined on both sides by stools welded from tractor seats. In one of these sat Sue Morse, peeling potatoes.

Sue had arranged this hunt. She was a forester and wildlife consultant from Vermont with a firm handshake and a direct, no-nonsense New England air about her. She regularly dressed in dark green overalls and her short blond hair hung in hanks, as if she cut it herself in a quick, no-nonsense way. Quizzical hazel eyes were her most compelling feature. Animals, wild and domestic, were her passion. All through high school she had been on what she called "an African lion kick" and had made an abortive attempt to get to Africa via the Peace Corps. Then she began to study lions native to America and became nationally recognized as an expert. State and federal agencies asked her to testify on environmental impact studies pertaining not just to lions but to other carnivores as well. She had participated in lion research projects in Alberta, Wyoming, California, and Arizona. Once or twice a year she flew in to hunt with Karen, to hone her field skills. She thought of Karen as a sister and brought her little presents, like a chocolate patty in the shape of a cowpie.

I had met Sue while researching lions, and now joined her in the den of a mountain lion guide. We had hired Karen and Charley to take us on a hunt that was to be traditional in every particular except one: we would pack cameras instead of guns.

Karen and Charley were keenly aware of the opprobrium attached to trophy hunting by a large and growing segment of society. Like a small number of other guides, they saw a possible salvation in the application of their skills to the new breed of people who long to see wild animals in a natural setting but wouldn't dream of killing them. Camera hunts offer both guides and clients some distinct advantages. Camera hunters don't need a hunting license, which can cost out-of-state trophy hunters hundreds of dollars. In several states with lotteries, waiting lists, or alternate-year restrictions, licenses are difficult to get. Some states allow a chase-only season after the shooting season closes, which guides can utilize for camera hunters.

Packing a camera along is almost as traditional as the hunt itself. In the 1880s a writer for *Forest and Stream* contrasted the ease of killing wild animals with the great difficulty of getting a decent photograph of them. Shortly after the century turned, another writer for the same magazine advised readers "fond of hunting with a camera" that cougars treed or driven to the brink of precipices generally gave ample time for taking photos—a serious consideration at a time when bulky, heavy equipment required substantial setup time. In the same era, a hunting partner of Theodore Roosevelt carried along a camera and demanded halts in the action at inopportune moments. By the 1930s, motion picture cameras were being strapped to saddles. One guide in Arizona, writing for *Outdoor Life,* coyly divulged his secret for making camera hunters happy: he shot the lion through a muscle in the foreleg to discourage the animal from jumping out of the tree. In those days the camera shot was merely a prelude to the denouement of the bullet.

Camera safaris as a form of ecotourism have long been popular in Africa but have been slower to catch on in the United States. One well-known tour operator I called while canvassing for information knew nothing of them. When I explained that camera hunts of lions relied on the same clamorous intrusion as shooting hunts, she was incredulous. "We don't run tours like that," she said, "nor would we ever consider it." I also spoke with several state wildlife managers who say that some western hunters don't even bother to take pictures but just go out for the fun of the chase. This is the same catch-and-release concept much lauded in fishermen.

The literature of hunting is replete with early morning risings. Our beginnings were no different. Every morning for a working week Karen called us to breakfast around five. It was still dark as she loaded dogs on the truck and mules into the attached trailer and drove us to Charley's house. On the first morning he took us into his office and handed us a contract. Had we stopped to read it, the sun would have been high before we stepped outdoors again. We signed, agreeing, among other things, not to hold him responsible for saddle sores. Charley had his own truck full of dogs and mules, and throughout the week we clients took turns traveling with him and Karen to the trailheads. That first morning, as I rode with him, Charley gave me instructions on handling a mule: "Don't be afraid to use the reins. Pull him the way you want him to go. The only thing I don't want you to do is hit him with your hand. You'll hurt your hand."

Although he didn't smoke and said he hated being drunk, Charley was in other respects a quintessential Marlboro Man, lean and laconic, dressed in black T-shirts and dusty jeans pulled over cowboy boots. His hat was made of the gray beaver felt called silverbelly. It hid his thick black hair and shaded his face down to a closely trimmed beard, flecked with gray. Walking his mule to the head of our procession, whooping to the dogs, mounting and striking out in the direction for the day, he moved with the grace of a man possessed of total unthinking confidence in his physical prowess. On the back of his mule this archenemy of the lion was light and quick and sure, as sure of himself in those ravines that slashed through time and space as any native cat.

The bold and withering landscape of the Southwest produces few trophy lions. Lions with the largest heads tend to live and die in colder climates, such as the spruce groves of the Pacific Northwest and the northern Rockies, where food is more abundant. Trophy status is determined by the length and width of the skull, added together. The skull measurements of the current record holder, a cougar killed in British Columbia in 1979, total $16^4/_{16}$ inches. The idea of recording trophies, and the notion that cougar hunting was a sport to challenge manly men, originated largely in the mind of Theodore Roosevelt. Roosevelt hunted virtually every large species of animal throughout the American West and Africa in the late nineteenth and early twentieth centuries and wrote extensively about his experiences. As a child, allowed into the gilded and mirrored but nonetheless gloomy parlor only on Sunday evenings, Roosevelt admired a Swiss wood carving of a hunter approaching a herd of chamois and agonized over the fate of a small kid forever stationed in the hunter's path. For hours he sat enthralled by his mother's stories of hunting parties pounding across her Georgia plantation home. At the age of thirteen he received his first gun and took lessons in taxidermy from a companion of John James Audubon. At fourteen he collected bird specimens on a trip up the Nile with his parents.

In his twenties he spent several years in the Dakota Territory as a cattle rancher, proving to every new group of cowboys he met that neither his New York City origin nor the spectacles he wore (he was invariably called Four Eyes) signified a weakling. Men who thrived on the outdoor life, who were self-reliant, hardy, capable of split-second decisions; men who were willing and able to stalk and shoot wild animals—these were the kind of men who had what Roosevelt called "the right stuff." Yet bullfights repelled him, despite the skill and bravery of the bullfighters, because of "the torture and death of the wretched horses. Any sport in which the death and torture of animals is made to furnish pleasure to the spectators," he wrote in his autobiography, "is debasing."

During his ranching days in Dakota Territory it was Roosevelt's job to supply meat for the hands. It was a rule of the range that cattle were rarely butchered for food because of the potential for providing cover for rustlers, so Roosevelt hunted wild meat, primarily deer. Unless his outfit's hunger was extreme, Roosevelt killed only bucks. He came to be regarded as the epitome of the sportsman. The first cougar Roosevelt killed—he preferred the name cougar—appeared while Roosevelt lay behind a pile of rotten logs beside a game trail, waiting for deer. After an hour a cougar materialized, without warning of any kind, treading noiselessly down the path. Roosevelt let him pass by, then fired into his ribs. This more or less accidental form of still hunting accounts for a surprising number of lions shot today—up to a third of the annual lion kill in Arizona, for example. Roosevelt's first intentional cougar hunt took place in the snows of northwestern Colorado in 1901. "No animal," he wrote, "is so rarely seen or so difficult to get without dogs. On the other hand, no other wild beast of its size and power is so easy to kill by the aid of dogs." To prove his point, in five weeks his hunting party took fourteen lions; Roosevelt personally killed all but two. On his last day he shot a large male with a total skull measurement of 15^{12}/$_{16}$ inches (227 pounds, and 8 feet from nose to tip of tail), which stood for forty-three years as the record cougar. It was, in fact, the first record of the Boone and Crockett Club, that elite fraternity founded by Roosevelt in 1887 for gentlemen known in their time as hunter-naturalists. In their enthusiasm for the charm of hunting, their combination of field and book knowledge, and their commitment to systematic methods for preserving game (and thereby hunting opportunities), they were the precursors of state wildlife managers.

In the first decade of the twentieth century a bored dentist from Ohio named Zane Grey also went west, not to kill cougars but to lasso them and bring them back alive for zoos. The art of lassoing a lion was a subgenre of the hunt. Zane Grey climbed trees to take pictures before the lions were pulled down, choking and half dead, to have their claws clipped, sticks thrust between their jaws and wire loops tightened around their noses. Grey's lion adventures became part of the canon of images and themes whose accretion, like the sandstone deposits of the ancient ocean now exposed to weathering, formed the landscape of the West. His was the most eloquent treatment of a theme that haunts many hunter-writers involved with lions, that of a lion's eyes:

> Before the men lowered Tom [the lion] from Marc's [the pack mule's] back I stepped closer and put my face within six inches of the lion's. He promptly spat on me. I had to steel my nerve to keep so close. But I wanted to see a wild lion's eyes at close range. They were exquisitely beautiful, their physical properties as wonderful as their expression. Great half globes of tawny amber, streaked with delicate wavy lines of black, surrounding pupils of intense purple fire. Pictures shone and faded in the amber light—the shaggy tipped plateau, the dark pines and smoky canyons, the great dotted downward slopes, the

yellow cliffs and crags. Deep in those live pupils, changing, quickening with a thousand vibrations, quivered the soul of this savage beast, the wildest of all wild nature, unquenchable love of life and freedom, flame of defiance and hate.

The light in a lassoed lion's eyes was often extinguished by the trauma, heat, thirst, or dogs of capture. When this happened, Grey was as sorry as if he had not himself brought the lion to that extremity. He was aware of "a dawning consciousness that we would be perhaps less cruel if we killed the lions outright." Once he mused that "more and more as I lived in the open I grew reluctant to kill," but he continued, like everyone else, to shoot at every movement that caught his eye. His sense of wonder was most profoundly engaged by the bloodthirsty urge of men to hunt and to slay.

Roosevelt and Grey rode with lion hunters renowned in their time—John Goff, Uncle Jimmy Owens, Buffalo Jones—but those names are archaic now. The name of Ben Lilly still clangs through time. Born in Alabama in 1856, raised in Mississippi, as a young man Lilly inherited a farm in Louisiana and slowly sold off bits and pieces of it to sustain his hunting habits in the bayous and forests. At the age of twenty he killed his first black bear with a knife; for the rest of his life, when hunting bears, he preferred his homemade knife to a gun. His first wife went insane, and he left her after the death of their only child. He married for a second time and fathered three children before relinquishing all his assets to his wife in 1901 and striking out for the Southwest. The deserts and mountains there were the last strongholds of the bears and panthers after whom he lusted so deeply, who so possessed him that he was truly unfit for anything but hunting. Wherever he wandered he always wrote to his children. Thirty years later he was still sending money home.

In Arizona and New Mexico, Lilly made his living from stockmen who paid him to rid them of predators. The federal government also hired him for the same work, but Lilly disliked bureaucratic supervision. He felt himself to be a member of the community of the wild, and he pitied other humans because they had not been so accepted. He spoke to animals, and believed they answered him. "You are condemned, you black devil," he once pronounced to a black bear. "I kill you in the name of the law." The bear's defense went unrecorded. Lilly was not so much a hunter as an avenger. Panthers, as he called them, were to him the Cains of the animal world—killers that should be killed in their turn. He refused to hunt on Sunday and read the Bible instead, leaving his dogs to guard overnight any animal they happened to tree. Convinced that the interiors of men and animals were visible to his eyes and that outer coverings were without value, he never kept a single skin.

In 1907 Lilly was called upon to guide Theodore Roosevelt. The hunt was not successful. Although there was mutual respect, the two hunters did not hit it off. Roosevelt described Lilly as a "religious fanatic . . . with mild, gentle, blue eyes and a frame of steel and whip-cord. I never met any other man so indifferent to fatigue and hardship." Lilly was at ease only in open spaces. Scornful of civilization, he was reluctant even to breathe the rancid interior air of a house. Nauseated by riding in an automobile, he condescended to use old tires to sole the boots he wore out in only a matter of weeks. Possessions beyond the tools of his trade were a handicap to him, and he stashed his wages in small banks around the Southwest, occasionally writing checks on bark or wrapping paper or the bleached shoulder bone of a cow. While working over an area, he would establish camps near moving water. There are probably still caves and sheltered niches under rock ledges where sooty lard buckets, hobnail boots, and old clothes attest to Lilly's passing. He ate and slept with his dogs and followed them on foot, careful to walk like a bear, distributing his weight. Deaf in one ear since youth, he sometimes used an old gramophone horn to amplify the sound of his hounds, or tied a dog to his waist to lead him to the pack. He tracked across solid rock. If the trail was too old, he climbed to a high place and surveyed the landscape for the ridges and passes that lions and bears were likely to use, and headed toward them. There was usually a fresh trail awaiting him. Finding a deer killed by a lion, he would cut a haunch and cook it for dinner. He ate lion meat to keep himself supple and used lion oil to temper his homemade knives. He was proud of himself, of his reputation for strength and for marksman-ship. "I never saw a lion," he boasted, "that I did not kill or wound."

Based on tallies submitted to the U.S. Biological Survey and on his own words, Lilly probably killed six hundred panthers and perhaps as many bears. There are few better examples of the darkest expression of ambivalence: to kill what you love and destroy the very thing that gives your life meaning. "Passionately in love with the wild," wrote Frank Dobie, chronicler of western lore, "he went on annihilating it." By the time Dobie met him in 1928, Lilly was seventy-one, a stocky, white-bearded, pink-cheeked patriarch of the mountains whose calm blue eyes retained the clarity of fanaticism. Lilly died in 1936 in a poorhouse in New Mexico. His daughters came to his funeral.

Throughout the first half and more of the twentieth century, as predator control became a national mission of seemingly divine ordination, there was a legion of men less mystical than Lilly but just as committed to hunting cougars. Methods were variations on a theme. Animals freshly killed by cougars were sometimes poisoned by those with the time and skill to seek out such carcasses. Steel traps, often anointed with oil of catnip, were used with considerable success by those canny about cougar choices of travel routes. Most localities had an official mountain lion man, who used whatever means he found successful. Jay Bruce of California followed his fox hounds on foot to take perhaps seven hundred lions over three or four decades. Jack Butler was reputed to have killed more than a thousand lions in Utah and the Southwest, although he sometimes carried a dart gun filled with nicotine salicylate to take them alive. In South Texas, where heat rendered dogs useless, John E. Hearn ran traplines on foot and took 129 lions between 1930 and 1949.

South Texas also hosted perhaps the only woman hired by the U.S. Biological Survey. Bess Kennedy ranked among the top five of all 120 Texas trappers for total numbers of predators killed. She had wanted to be a concert violinist and travel to all the great cities of Europe. Instead, at sixteen, a dark-haired, long-legged beauty, she married a government trapper and moved from a small town to an itinerant life in tents on vast, lonely ranches. Bored, she learned to trap from her husband and caught raccoons and 'possums to sell for their pelts. When her husband came down with typhus, Bess set his traps while he directed her, weakly, from the car. She shot her first trapped lion in a thicket and gingerly ascertained that he was dead. Then, with trembling hands, she lit a cigarette. The intensity of the incident, and its abrupt cessation, reminded her of the pain of childbirth. Her only child was a daughter named Betty Bob, who, with few toys and no playmates, imitated her parents by setting mousetraps in piles of white Texas sand.

In Arizona, the seven Lee brothers, all of them tall, with grey or blue eyes and brown hair of various shades, began to hunt lions and bears for the government in the mid 1920s. The older boys remembered Ben Lilly wandering into their camp in his dotage. Dale was the youngest and, eventually, the most famous. He began hunting lions in his teens, fresh out of high school. On one of their very first hunts, brother Arthur was shot and killed by a friend aiming at a lion. The remaining Lees quit the job, until the next year, when New Mexico offered Clell and Dale jobs in which they could work as partners. They soon found that people who wanted to shoot lions for fun would pay them more than the government, and being shrewd as well as hard working, they elevated their business to a hemispheric sport-hunting empire. Across the West, in Florida and Louisiana, and in Mexico, lions and bears yielded to the Lee brothers' hounds. Hunting jaguars in Central and South America, Dale called them *tigre* in the Spanish way. The dogs became renowned and fetched high prices. Together, the Lees bred life into the bluetick line, and by himself, Dale invented the electric shock collar as a training tool. Clients included brain surgeons, bankers, brokers, oilmen, printing magnates, Coca Cola moguls, opera singers, and movie stars. Clell played guitar and sang in a mellow tenor to entertain them. Dale told them hunting stories in a big booming voice. He had the topographical memory of a frontiersman and, on a hunt in the late 1950s, recognized the pine tree in which he had seen his first mountain lion in 1921. He had thought then that the cat in the tree was the most beautiful sight he'd ever seen.

By the mid 1960s the Lees reckoned they had bagged more than a thousand cougars and as many bears, 124 jaguars, an unspecified number of bobcats and ocelots, one jaguarundi, and one onca. The onca of Mexico, also known as onza, was a strange animal, longer and thinner in the hindquarters than a lion and striped down the back, that left tracks with claw marks, unlike a lion's. For centuries there had been speculation that the onza was a separate species of cat, perhaps representing a transition between pumas and cheetahs. The Lee specimen disappeared, but in the early 1990s a biologist from Arizona obtained a freshly killed onza from a Mexican rancher and submitted tissue samples for genetic analysis. No genetic difference from cougars could be found.

Dale's stories took on the tinny timbre of bygone times. The species he and his brothers hunted became scarce, and regulations began, slowly at first but inexorably, to fence in the Lees' wide-open range. Later than most other states, Arizona stopped paying bounties in 1970 and legislated the mountain lion from shoot-on-sight varmint to big game animal, with requirements for licenses, seasons, and bag limits. Except for Texas—where the frontier yet lives—all other states and provinces regulated sport hunting of mountain lions.

It was from Clell and Dale Lee that Karen learned to hunt lions. She came to Arizona as a bride and met the Lees when her husband, as new district wildlife manager, paid a courtesy call at The Blue, Clell's ranch. It happened that Clell needed help running cattle. Riding after cattle, Karen learned the country. Helping Clell's wife, Katharine, she learned how to care for clients. From Dale, who made an art of avoiding chores, she learned to feed, clean, train, run, and market hounds and mules. A honeymoon couple booked a hunt at The Blue and Clell asked Karen to come along and keep the bride company. Karen had never hunted before. They caught two lions and a bear in eight days. The mournful howl of the hounds, the rose-colored canyons, the wind-filled silence hooked her. She begged to go on other hunts. "I'm not taking any dadburned woman," Dale said, but he was only teasing, as he often did.

Sometimes Karen worked for cowboy wages, meaning a lion or a bear carcass, which she had mounted or made into rugs. "I was city raised and they made a cowgirl out of me," she said. "Then, when we moved away from The Blue, I got to know Bill Workman, like Charley one of the best lion hunters of this generation. I borrowed his dogs and just made mistakes but finally started catching lions on my own. The next thing that entered my mind was I'd better have some lion dogs of my own. About that time Dale came to live with us. He was real sick with emphysema, but he helped me along quite a bit. After that there was just no quitting. I would figure out my week and my whole month, finagle everything around me so I was able to get my hounds out. The whole thrill in lion or bear hunting to me is the performance of the hound. Of course the end of the challenge is seeing the animal caught, but it means much, much more to me if it's after a long hard track and I've watched the hounds work hour after hour."

After she began professional guiding, Karen now and then attracted a woman who was interested in hunting but intimidated by the thought of hunting with a man. Many of her male clients asked her to step out of their trophy pictures. Karen figured they didn't want to have to make explanations to their wives. She made it a habit to arrange things so that she was never alone in her house with a male client. Charley looked out for her like a brother. The maddest Karen ever saw Charley was when a client, crazy to shoot, fired in her direction. Charley jerked the gun out of the man's hand, packed him out, and left him standing at the airport with a dead cougar in his arms.

For most of the week we worked the long, massive bulk of Pine Valley Mountain, which dominated much of this segment of Dixie National Forest. Except for swatches of private land stippling the valley and a great chunk of it to the north, most of the rest of the country was public land. One copy of our contract would go to Dixie National Forest headquarters, and of their gross earnings tallied from all contracts submitted in a year, Charley and Karen would pay 3 percent for their use of federal lands. Charley had been in business for himself since 1969. He began by trapping sheep-eating lions for Animal Damage Control, learning the terrain and the favorite haunts of lions. His reputation in officialdom was good. "He quotes us regulations we've never even read," a state wildlife officer told me. Karen's business was still too new to have a reputation. Divorced after almost two decades of marriage to a biologist working on bears for the Arizona game department, Karen moved to Utah ten years ago when Charley offered her a job as his assistant. But when Shad graduated from high school and wanted to work for his father, Charley couldn't afford two full-time employees. Although he and Karen still collaborated, Karen was advertising on her own now for trail rides and cattle drives and hoped to expand her clientele of camera hunters. She spoke bitterly of the increasing restrictions on horseback and muleback rides in the national parks. "Not everyone can hike in," she said. "We can help people get into the backcountry responsibly."

For the first time in twenty years of backpacking I found myself astride a species of the beasts I had so often cursed for fouling the trail. Within a few hours I was grateful. Mules were ideal for following dogs through the dense green chaparral of manzanita bushes and mountain mahogany and across bare slopes of loose sand and deep, fast streams— they were less skittish and more surefooted than horses. "They're like four-wheel-drives compared to horses," Karen said. My mule was named Cedar. He was old, slow, and eminently respectable, dependably left to pick his own pace and path. Now and then he paused to ruminate on routes around uncomfortably large rocks. Sometimes he would stop and just look around. "They like views," Karen said. On level stretches, his ears flopped with every step. Going downslope you leaned backward until your feet paralleled the mule's ears. Going up, leaning forward, you discovered quickly the unrelenting prominence of the saddle horn and the tendency of anything affixed to the front of you—camera, binoculars, breasts—to jam against it. Each mule took creeks differently, one with a little jump, another with a smart, splashing step, another with hesitant deliberation. None of the mules made any attempt to go under low branches or between closely spaced trunks, but merely passing through the country required concentrated efforts to keep from losing an eye to a dead branch at face level or slashing a hand against sharp branches. Juniper trees spread sideways like plump women. The greatest danger in lion hunting was being gouged by brush. Chaps were essential, though paralyzing on the ground and clearly designed exclusively around male anatomy.

Charley rode a nimble black mule named Smokey and wore spurs "to make a good animal better." He led with the dogs, watching their behavior closely and often dismounting to scrutinize some spot they seemed interested in. Looming ever nearer above us, the mountain was a great castle, palisaded by rows of creamy columnar basalt and crenellated by darker rocks above. There were towers of rocks and dungeons of caves, and over them all ruled the lions. Day after day I imagined their mysterious presence but felt nothing. Each day the light changed from sharp, cold shadows to sweaty glare. Sometimes we followed dirt roads and trails; sometimes we took off cross-country to places Charley and Karen knew were popular with lions. Clumps of red Indian paintbrush, mats of pink phlox, and bunches of yellow bitterbrush made rock gardens of the lower elevations. Manzanita bushes were mounds of small whitish flowers bedecked with shiny green leaves; those that were dead and leafless revealed an impenetrable structure of branches twisted and curled like entwining octopuses. Serviceberry and silk tassel, just leafing out, made a green haze across the slopes. Higher up were stands of Gambel oaks, still silvery gray from winter, and groves of ponderosa pines as thick and stout as prominent citizens. From high ridges the quilted valley came into view, and across it the skyline of Zion National Park, its monoliths and spires the architecture of a meaning beyond human ken.

Sue constantly pointed to tracks where I saw only frost heaves. The little mounds of dirt scratched up by passing lions, called scrapes, were more identifiable and gave indisputable evidence that lions were present. There were no picnics; we ate on muleback, fishing out from saddlebags the sandwiches Karen had packed—whole wheat bread for us, white for Charley.

Periodically Charley and the dogs left us behind to descend into canyons of rippling cliffs swirled like water and hardened by time. Wind rushed down them as hurriedly as the stream. Swifts flashed through sun and shadow. Karen would go off a little ways and talk to Charley by CB. Sometimes Charley sent her up or down a ridge to deflect any lion that might be running ahead of the dogs. Then Sue and I would huddle together like inmates plotting a breakout, and talk furtively about lion hunting.

For her own part, Sue was evolving from acceptance of trophy hunting as a management tool to concern for the interplay of hunting and habitat loss. Management of hunting is based on the belief that animal populations produce a harvestable surplus of individuals. All wild creatures die sooner or later from disease, starvation, accidents and even, occasionally, from old age, contrary to the cherished belief of hunters. Wildlife managers view hunting simply as a substitute for one cause of death over another—a view being challenged for lions and other predators whose slow rate of reproduction cannot always compensate for losses to hunting. At any rate, the purpose of management is to manipulate seasons, bag limits, number of hunters, and numbers of animals killed to keep the sport harvest from so exceeding the natural rate of death that the population of hunted animals declines. Management is not always successful. There are pockets throughout the West where lions are overhunted, but so far these places keep being recolonized with immigrants from elsewhere. This dispersal is the deus ex machina of wildlife managers.

Charley and Karen killed twenty-five to thirty lions every year. "That's a lot," Sue said. "The real question is, where do the replacement animals come from? How long will that habitat be available to produce replacement lions? We know now that the national parks and other tiny refuges from hunting are much too small to maintain their own populations, much less supply the whole West with lions. And every year I see more and more development in lion habitat." Sue was applying for grants to support a project she had named "Keeping Track." Her goal was to pull wildlife specialists from all agencies together into powerful coalitions that would influence land use planning in favor of wildlife.

She was trying to explain how vision and selflessness could triumph over greed and self-interest when the dogs bellowed from a cut in the rocks to our right. Sweet music, some hunters call it. I wondered how it sounded to the lions and suspected something on the order of Nazi sirens to Jews. Sue concentrated on the individual voices, trying to pick out tones of the dogs she knew. "I think that long, low yelp is Dottie," she said. Dottie was Karen's most senior dog, a brown and white Walker, who had given more than a decade of good work. In the course of those years of service Dottie had lost an eye not to the swipe of a paw but to a fall that killed the optic nerves. Lion dogs are best trained by running young ones with veterans like Dottie, and Karen was running her pup Happy for the first time on this hunt. All of her dogs carried radio collars. Hours after the dogs had quieted—another cold trail—one of them hadn't come back, and Karen fetched out her receiver, tuning it to the frequency of the missing dog. This same technology used by wildlife scientists to spy on the movements of their subjects has been available for hunting dogs since the late 1970s. The best receivers can tune in as many as two hundred dogs at a time and pick up signals fifteen miles away if mountains or cliffs don't deflect the pulse. A telemetry outfit costs hundreds of dollars, but replacing a lost dog costs much more.

"We don't use them for finding the lion," Karen said, a bit defensively. Some hunters do. Collars can indicate whether dogs are resting, running, or holding their heads up, as in barking at a treed animal. Even *Outdoor Life* columnists and collar manufacturers concede that collaring dogs makes hunters more efficient. Despite the fact that the Boone and Crockett Club, considered by the hunting community to be the final arbiters of fair chase, has defined the "use of electronic communications for attracting, locating or observing game, or guiding the hunter to such game," as unfair and unsportsmanlike, the temptation to use collars for more than finding lost dogs is, for some, irresistible. Stories abound of hunters waiting in pickups, joking, shooting the breeze, drinking, until their receivers indicate the dogs have treed. Then they track the dogs electronically. These often merge into stories of will-call hunts, a technique that testifies not only to the wonders of technology but also to the busy schedules of affluent trophy hunters. Once a cougar or bear is treed, the guide calls a distant client, who then travels to the site and shoots the trophy with only as much of the time-consuming travail of the trail as is necessary to reach the laden tree. In general this breaks no laws, although in some states keeping an animal in a tree overnight is illegal.

Outright poaching—the illegal trapping or shooting of mountain lions—seems to be growing. Some people will shoot a lion whenever they happen across one, just for the hell of it. Some will pay big money for a trophy-sized head they didn't have to hunt. Some outfitters will purchase illegally trapped lions to release in front of a client who wants a guaranteed chase. Lion gall bladders have apparently entered the Asian medicinal trade, where bear gall bladders fetch more than $500 an ounce. These organs of the two animals appear almost indistinguishable.

With her receiver in hand, Karen took off into the woods after her lost dog while we dozed in the sun. She returned in an hour with the dog in tow. "It might have taken me days to find him without the collar," she said, "and by then he might have been pretty torn up from the brush or maybe met up with a lion on the ground." Neither she nor Charley wanted to risk letting their dogs roam the woods unsupervised, and the danger of losing dogs at night was one major reason that they ended the day's work by midafternoon. Another was the dissipation, as the day progressed, of the fragile aroma of lion under the baking sun.

With nothing doing on Pine Valley Mountain, we spent one day on the other side of the valley, on state land bordering Zion National Park. Huge red boulders, their faces alternately smoothed or pitted by weather, imprisoned the creek we followed up-canyon. Near the top the trail squeezed between barbs of rock and crossed sheets of stone over which we had to walk the mules; their hooves left thick white marks as if on a chalkboard. Charley's grandfather had dynamited and sledgehammered this path. He homesteaded and ran sheep, and this was the fastest way up the mountain. Only later did I learn this. Charley said little, occasionally offering a wry joke, self-deprecating comment, or punchy one-liner. He spoke in a slow, soft drawl littered with expletives. Once, when his mule stumbled to her knees on a slope so steep and loose that a fall would surely injure both of them, Charley poked his hat up with his thumb, crossed his arms, and said, "Well, are we needing to pray today?"

He seemed cool and unflappable, so I was astonished when he took the opportunity, the first time it happened that the two of us rode in his truck alone together, to talk about his divorce. His wife of twenty-six years had left him a couple of years ago. Karen told me later I looked a bit like her, especially with my shoulder-length hair. Charley wouldn't let his wife cut her hair, or wear makeup, or go on trips.

"I liked being married. I'd still be married if it was up to me," he said. "Going back to dating was hell."

"I don't guess you meet a lot of women on the job," I said.

"No."

"How did you meet Peggy?" Peggy had driven over to Karen's house on our first evening there to borrow some Scotch for Shad's Italian, who was asking for it. A pert, fleshy, and quite young woman with a ready laugh that verged engagingly on a giggle, Peggy arrived on Charley's doorstep one day from Provo with friends who came to shoot skeet. After a few months she quit her job and moved in with Charley to cook and tend his clients. She had short hair, wore quite a bit of eye makeup, and was partial to heavy metal rock music. She and Charley planned to do a little traveling. I asked Peggy if she intended to shoot a lion and she answered "Yup" without an instant's hesitation.

"Peggy's a real good girl," Charley said. Like Karen, he was in his mid-forties, but his hands, resting on the steering wheel, looked as if they had worked through three generations.

The seat belt hung slack and unused behind Charley's shoulder. Country songs whined and sobbed as tough mountains and bitter washes moved past the windows. "When did you start doing camera hunts?" I asked.

"Four or five years ago. We don't have a thing against them," he said a little too quickly. He didn't know too many other guides doing camera hunts, but then he didn't associate much with other guides. As far as Charley knew, he and Karen were the only full-time guides in Utah, but there were plenty of part-time lion hunters who called themselves guides. "These damn houndsmen," Charley said. "People see the dogs and cages and trucks spread all over their yards. No wonder they have such a bad image. They do it to themselves. I used to try to work with their organizations but they were so fixated on their own perspective I got disgusted. Now I don't even sit in the same room with them at game board meetings. They go out on their snowmobiles on a weekend and the damn mountains are as crowded as a parking lot. That's the only really dangerous thing for cougar populations, the goddamn easy snow hunting. I've asked the game department to think about eliminating snowmobiles."

"Do you use them?" I asked.

"I can't afford not to, there's too much competition."

"Do you have any political alliances?"

"I used to ally with livestock organizations but they've lost clout and don't help much anymore," he said.

"Do cats have personalities?" I asked once after there had been a long silence.

"Well, sure, they're like anything, they're all different," he said. "Some are runners, some are jumpers, some are real aggressive."

Of Karen he said, "She's the best helper, man or woman, a person could have in this business, but she's obsessed. There's not many like her, thank God. I keep telling her there's other things in life besides lion hunting but she doesn't listen. The only thing is the dogs. She worries about them so much I don't see how she can stand to let them out in the mountains."

By the time we quit every afternoon the dogs would follow with drooping tails behind the mules, who stumbled with fatigue. We returned to what in hunting parlance would be called our base camp, Karen's house. Like Roosevelt on his first cougar hunt, we did not camp out. A compulsive naturalist, Sue would immediately shoulder a heavy pack full of tracking guides and measuring instruments and set out alone for the foothills. Her nose, slightly tilted at the tip, grew increasingly sunburnt. Once she came back to stand on the porch grinning hugely with handfuls of cougar and bobcat turds.

I drove to town for an ice cream sundae, or into the Kolob Canyons for the views. Karen cared for the animals, cooked for us, did laundry and all the other kinds of household chores that Charley didn't have to do because Peggy now did them for him. Sometimes she touched up her nail polish or changed her earrings. Once the two of us went for a walk around her sagebrush neighborhood and found an elk that someone had shot and dragged off the road—Karen easily read the tire marks. Not much was ever said about it.

With the dusk came cocktail hour. Friends often dropped by for a drink, offering in return fresh-picked asparagus or fresh tales from the neighborhood. It was the kind of town where people craned their necks to see who was driving by. The daughter of a psychologist who worked as a college counselor, Karen deftly caught conversational bait and encouraged everyone to talk about themselves. One of her closest friends, a man she referred to as her adopted father, was Darce. Like most of the people born in the area he was Mormon. As a young man he herded sheep on the land where Karen's house now stood, forcing whiskey down the throats of newborn lambs to make them suckle. For many of his sixty-seven years he had hunted lions through all this country.

"Is there a particular season here when lions mate?" I asked him.

"Well," he said, considering. "I guess I've killed kittens in every month of the year."

Sue and I shared the upstairs guest quarters, a single large room with two beds and windows that framed the glowing Kolob Canyons on one side and Pine Valley Mountain, striated with snow, on the other. Saddles straddled the stair railing. A couple of bookshelves held Louis L'Amour paperbacks and natural history guides. Above Sue's bed a stuffed cougar slunk in frozen motion along a stout branch. This was the first of two cougars that Karen had personally killed. It had required several shots; the first only wounded him and sent him flying out of a pinyon pine, leaving a blood trail to a big cottonwood in a canyon bottom, where Karen took a deep breath and steadied herself. She shot the second lion because it threatened her dogs. "I don't care," she said, "if I never kill another lion."

On Friday morning, our last day, we stood in the half darkness at Charley's house waiting while he finished loading his dogs. A female wouldn't stop yapping; he kicked her, hard. She shut up and lay down. We headed back to Pine Valley Mountain. The day was perfect, with the deep, stark clarity of the Southwest that strikes you speechless. As the morning warmed, orange-and-black-and-white butterflies burst from beneath the mules' hooves and zigzagged around us like electrons run amok. By the time the day was well heated, we arrived at the foot of the final rocky outbreak beneath the long chain of peaks. The nearest cliff was fractured into squat hieroglyphic blocks, like Mayan writing. A tendril of mountain flung out from it, and here we waited as Charley went down one last canyon. The breeze came in tufts. The buzz of an oncoming insect sounded for an instant like a dog howling. A raven sailed over me, very close and then closer, almost within reach, circling and looking directly at me with black shining eyes. In many Native cultures the raven is a powerful spirit, creator of the world. Even Theodore Roosevelt welcomed the raven's company in the desolation of the wild. What the hell, I thought, and made a prayer to the raven: Grant us a glimpse of the lion. We mean him no harm. The raven wheeled around my head, black eyes darting, slowly gaining altitude, then floated away.

Ten minutes later the dogs opened. The wind played with the howls until they sounded like Indian war whoops in an old western. We waited, tensing. In twenty minutes they had treed a lion. Although lions can run extremely fast for short distances, they have little stamina or sporting instinct and rarely run far. It took us an hour to reach them, maneuvering through a forest of burned mountain mahogany that arched over us in black and white, then up into thickening bouldery brush on a knuckle of mountain. Finally the scrub was too dense even for the mules. We dismounted to claw frantically through the last hundred yards up to a huge, lone ponderosa pine that stood like a beacon above us. My heart was racing and my lungs were pushed to extremes. This excitement, this frenzied dance to the rhythm of howling dogs, is what lion hunters sing of. "In cougar hunting the shot is usually much the least interesting and important part of the performance," wrote Theodore Roosevelt. Zane Grey hoped for a prolonged chase "because the race was too splendid a thing to cut short." The very language that Charley and Karen and all hunters use affirm this—they never "take" or "shoot" or "kill" or even "harvest" a lion, but always "catch" one.

At the foot of the tree the dogs were barking furiously and Charley lay stretched out against a rock, grinning. The lion lay draped along a sturdy branch forty feet up. She was a mature female and nearly perfect as a picture, her pelage marred only by a nick in her left ear. She was the color of oak leaves bleached by winter. With one hind leg and her tail dangling, she looked nonchalantly down as we emerged one by one from the thicket. Her expression was grave but sleepy. I stood open mouthed, gaping, feeling limp and breathless and bursting, all at once. With binoculars we were eye to eye. Hers were golden and the pupils were medallions of light. She gazed at the dogs, at us, at the mountain, with a sort of absent-minded composure. Along the top of her nose was a line of froth from running hard on this hot, dry day. Forgive me, I said silently. She snarled once at the dogs, her lips lifting to show white canines, then put her head on her paws and blinked her eyes as if she could hardly keep them open. In fact, she couldn't; she closed them to slits, rested her head on her paws, and dozed. This was typical treed lion behavior, Charley said.

Charley's typical client would, at this moment, be fitting a bow with a razor-tipped arrow. Half or more of his customers preferred archery to firearms. "I got to hand it to them," Charley said, "lugging their bow and arrows through this stuff." Many of his customers took the meat, especially the tender backstraps; Charley froze it and shipped it to them. On his Grand Canyon hunt, Roosevelt was glad to eat cougar, the only fresh meat available. If his client didn't care about the meat, Charley fed it to the dogs then and there. Charley was a member of Safari Club International but felt he got along better with customers of less elite standing, the "little guy that saves for years and is glad just to be out here." The clients he liked the least came from New York and New Jersey. "They're too pushy," he said.

Charley did not like to kill cats under two years of age; he would tell a client that any cat without spots was legal, but he would prefer to let the animal grow up. Mothers accompanied by kittens were not legal. This was a paper prescription that blew away in the field. Kittens younger than six months don't usually travel with their mothers, so hunters can't tell from the tracks that the lion has young who will starve unless she returns. Yet mothers with young to feed travel in search of prey more often than usual, leaving many tracks. In heavily hunted areas, nearly half of the female lions killed probably leave behind doomed kittens. Occasionally the dogs will track up to a litter of kittens still too young to climb trees, and tear them apart. This is a serious consideration for camera hunters. It has happened to lion researchers. It happened to Theodore Roosevelt, much to his regret, for he would have liked to keep the kittens, although he didn't say why. Lions that are chased repeatedly by camera hunters may also suffer permanent lung damage. On her last hunt, Sue suspected that the female she treed was pregnant, and felt badly enough about it that she doubted she would hunt much longer.

The lion in the branches above us had been sleeping on a shaded ledge accompanied by her adolescent daughter, who had bolted in the opposite direction and drawn off about half of the dogs. Charley went after them to pull the dogs off, and Karen put the others on leashes. They barked incessantly while the cat blinked. After about fifteen minutes the lion slid down the branches, there was a flash of white belly, and she was gone. The dogs pulled and strained but Karen held them and we waited for a while, to give the cat a chance to move away. Karen was ecstatic that Happy had treed her first lion. On the way out old Dottie lagged farther and farther behind, and Karen stopped frequently to wait for her.

"I'm afraid she'll just lie down and not come out until tomorrow, or maybe not at all," Karen said.

"She'll die happy then," Charley said. He was ready to move on, but Karen decided to carry Dottie out by muleback, and Charley lifted the dog up to her.

It happened that I rode back that day in the truck with Charley. "I could no more have shot that cat," I said, "than I could have flown to the moon."

He nodded his head vigorously, as if he understood. "Well, sure," he said. "That's just fine. But they need to be hunted. It's better for them and for us."

"Why do they need it?" I asked.

"They goddamn well learn not to fool with people," he said.

"The one that gets shot doesn't learn anything," I said.

He glanced over at me. "I guarantee you that when cats hear us coming, they'll take off," he said.

"There's a lot of statistics that show there aren't any more lion attacks in parks and places where they aren't hunted than in places where they are," I said.

"Do you believe that?" Charley said.

I was too surprised to answer. Did he think that biologists and bureaucrats around the country were conspiring against his point of view?

"Besides," Charley continued, "toms kill kittens. When you take out some toms, it means more kittens will grow up." I could have argued against this half-truth, but decided not to. "And anyway, how many goddamn lions do you need? If you don't kill them, they'll spill over into places where you don't want them. You watch what happens in California. You see if they don't have a lot of problems there." He was referring to a permanent ban on mountain lion hunting that had recently been passed in California.

"You may be right, Charley," I said, willing to concede that anything was possible in California.

"Excuse me, ma'am," he said, "but I *know* I'm right."

After a while I asked, "What would you have done with Dottie?"

"Leave her," Charley said, with no more hesitation than Peggy had shown about killing a lion.

Charley and Peggy came over for dinner that night. The Italian had also caught his lion that day, and Karen invited him, too, but he was busy trying to reschedule his plane reservation to fly out first thing in the morning. He wanted to be back in his shoe factory the next Monday morning, and as far as I know he succeeded. After Charley and Peggy left we were watching Sue's home video of her place in Vermont, listening to her coo and cluck to her six German shepherds as they cavorted through the tape, when Peggy drove back to pick me up. Charley wanted to show me a particular photograph he had told me about, one he liked. The picture, which Shad had taken, was of a cougar in midair, leaping through forest sunlight over a pack of hounds. There were other splendid pictures, of cougars peering mildly from trees or spitting furiously in silhouette from ledges of rock, but I found it difficult to enjoy them, knowing that moments after they were snapped the cougar died a violent, bloody death. Charley had albums of color photographs of grinning customers hugging one limp, lifeless cougar after another—blood on the snow, the ground, everyone's hands. I didn't have the stomach to ask to see the Italian's clotted trophy in the freezer.

After a while Peggy went to look after her pet cat, declawed before she met Charley but not allowed in the house. Charley didn't believe in animals' coming into the house. "You have to let them know who's boss," he said. "They'll get away with whatever they can."

"Did you raise your children that way?" I asked.

"No," he said. "Children and wife I spoiled."

I bit my tongue to keep from asking the obvious question.

The next morning Karen drove me to the airport as dusk dissipated and the mountains lit up. Charley and Karen had both said of my leaving that I was "going back to the real world." I wondered what kind of world they thought they lived in. From thirty-seven thousand feet I tried to grasp their world, tried to gain the perspective of distance. The buttes reached out like blunt fingers, and the mountains were as callused and veiny as the back of Charley's hands.

LION SCIENCE: A PAPER

COUGARS IN THE ABSTRACT SUMMON DISTURBING, AMBIVALENT FORCES in the human mind. Scientific method counters those forces with its own definition of objective reality. Lion science has created a small epiphany of biological illumination, in a quiet way a masterpiece of western civilization. Methods and materials for studying cougars employ the sophisticated technologies of radiotelemetry, computer chips, and pharmaceuticals. But just like every other science, lion studies depend, ultimately, upon the human eye, brain, and heart.

Studying lions doesn't usually result in the teasing of rattlesnakes, but this three-rattlesnake day was bringing out the boy in thirty-six-year-old Kerry Murphy. Of moderate height, slim but very strong, with a wide, open, lively face, Kerry looked as Irish as his name implied. Just then he had a prankish grin. He prodded the rattlesnake with his wooden walking stick, and she writhed and rattled gratifyingly in the knee-high grass. We would never have seen her stout yellow and gray body in that high prairie of yellowing grass dotted with gray boulders. Kerry had heard her shake a warning, the third such alarm we received that day, and stopped in astonishment. In the six years that he had been studying mountain lions in Yellowstone National Park, he had encountered rattlesnakes only on the south-facing slope of one particularly rocky mountain, which rose in jagged profile across the Gardiner River from us.

Rattlesnakes aside, Kerry had found this fourteen-hundred-square-mile study area in the northwestern corner of Yellowstone to be excellent country for field research on lions. Expanses of meadow swept across plateaus and mountain slopes, as bucolic as if humans had ranched here for centuries, but totally wild. These meadows were *relatively* easy (the emphasis is mine) to hike across while tracking lions, and reassuringly spacious when scouting for grizzly bears. Forests of pines, firs, and spruces laced the landscape according to subtle patterns of rain, rock, soil, and slope. The knots and runs of conifers tended to have a low understory, again *relatively* easy to see and hike through. It was good country for lions, too. Forests and rock-strewn hillsides afforded plenty of cover and den sites. High and low seasonal pastures of the northern Yellowstone ecosystem seem to have supported plentiful prey in the form of mule deer, bighorn sheep, antelope, bison, and especially elk for at least a millennium. Theodore Roosevelt, who made a presidential visit to the park in 1903, was "literally astounded" at the enormous numbers of elk and deer. Nevertheless, he enthusiastically affirmed the park's prohibition against hunting game animals. "Roosevelt Not to Shoot," a local newspaper headline shouted incredulously, "But to Protect Big Game!"

At that time big game referred only to ungulates, not predators, and park superintendents had authorized the killing of cougars almost since the park's establishment in 1872. The park-owned pack of lion hounds was trotted out for Roosevelt's amusement. It was reported that the president went to Slough Creek to hunt cougars in the company of the park superintendent, and a dispatch credited the president with bagging one. These stories arose from expectation rather than fact. Roosevelt sent the pack back, saying he did not want them. In the face of overwhelming evidence even cougar-hating Theodore Roosevelt, honest as he was, had to concede that cougars could do little harm, and perhaps some good, where elk numbers were so great. "They ought to be left alone," he wrote later about cougars in a letter to the superintendent, but his advice was not heeded. Until predator control in national parks fell into scientific disrepute in the 1930s, periodic pogroms against lions killed well over a hundred throughout Yellowstone. By then, the regional lion population had been bled white, or as Kerry put it, "reduced to ecological insignificance in the park." The same was true for grizzly bears, and wolves were completely exterminated.

Gradually, lions wandered back in, probably from the dark, brooding Montana mountains to the north. A 1986 survey for cougar sign in Yellowstone's northern winter range turned up enough scats, tracks, and actual sightings to prove that at least a few cats inhabited the forested parts of the area. Shortly thereafter, having recently graduated with a master's degree in wildlife science, Kerry began the fieldwork necessary to characterize this new population. He had two goals: to determine age, sex, birth and death rates, and size of home ranges; and to assess the role of lions in Yellowstone by observing how they behaved, where they traveled, and what they ate.

When he began his master's program, Kerry also began keeping his own lion hound, so he did not need to hire houndsmen in Yellowstone—unlike most other mountain lion researchers, who had to ally with local hunters in order to find lions to study. This marriage of science and sport began with the hunter-naturalists in the nineteenth century. Claude Barnes, a self-taught philosopher and naturalist from Utah, inaugurated twentieth-century lion studies by seeking out and riding with famous houndsmen around the West to compile observations about the cats. Four decades of this "fascinating sport . . . invigorating to the highest degree" convinced him that total elimination of lions was neither necessary nor desirable. "Only the workers under the Biological Survey desire the extermination of the puma," he wrote in 1960. "Professional guides with hounds [would be] foolish indeed to destroy the very means of their livelihood. They are really the puma's friends." In the 1930s a budding anthropologist named Frank Hibben accompanied the lion hunters of the New Mexico and Arizona state game departments for a year. Later, when he became prominent enough to be profiled in directories of scholars, Hibben listed hunting as his only avocation. "There is all the excitement of an old English fox hunt in the chase, with the thrill of a big-game hunt at the end," Hibben wrote in his lion report. "The presence of big game in a state is a great attraction for foreign revenue." He wanted to tag some lions with metal ear clips to follow their travels, but "it was feared that this would raise too much opposition with the cattle and game interests . . . The stock associations are concerned at almost every meeting with the menace of the lion on their ranges."

Dozens of lions were killed and their stomach contents analyzed. Hibben's report was buried when he found that cattle accounted for less than two percent of lion diets, and horses, sheep, and goats were completely absent.

It was not until the 1960s that treed lions were tagged and released rather than killed. The first study of this kind took place in the long slicing valleys and stinging winter cold of the Central Idaho Wilderness. When tagged lions were treed again and again over months and years and the locations of these events were plotted on a map, the puzzle of lion movements could be slowly pieced together. In the 1970s, researchers began to mount small radio transistors on collars. Signals from a collared lion could be followed from a distance by waving antennae from four-wheel-drives or small airplanes. The onerous burden of constant pursuit was eased while accurate data came ticking in as often as researchers—usually staff of state game departments and academics with student assistants—could afford to get out in the field or rent a plane. Every western state and several western Canadian provinces mounted cougar studies. By the time Kerry finished his master's in the early 1980s, it was the established practice to hire houndsmen to pursue and tree lions, which were then anesthetized, examined, and collared. For six months, or a couple of years, or however long their funding lasted, researchers plotted the signals. Lions were now easy to locate whenever a collar needed new batteries or the researcher wanted to look at a particular animal. Some researchers surgically removed one toe from each lion to make the animals easy to identify from tracks.

Kerry didn't cut off any lion toes, but he followed established procedures in other respects for the first five years of his Yellowstone study. Grants to support his work came from an array of sources: the U.S. Fish & Wildlife Service, Yellowstone National Park, the National Geographic Society, M. J. Murdock Charitable Trust, Montana Department of Fish, Wildlife and Parks, the National Fish & Wildlife Foundation, the Mellon Foundation, and former Department of the Interior official Nathaniel P. Reed. The U.S. Forest Service helped with logistics.

As a cat's legs began to wobble from a dartful of immobilizing drug, Kerry and his assistants climbed the trees and used rope to make the catch. Nearly two hundred times on nearly one hundred individual lions, Kerry and team fitted radio collars, tattooed both ears, weighed the animals, noted the sex, and estimated the age and overall health by examining teeth and other bodily parts. Almost every day he or someone on his team tracked lions, usually on foot, and noted where the lions were and what they were doing.

Kerry had been through several dogs in the course of the project. The current one, and the best of them all, was a skeletal redbone named Bo, after an African group famed for its trackers. "Bo Bos!" Kerry would frequently boom to the animal, in the manner of people long accustomed to giving and taking emotional energy from their dogs. Bo would gaze at her master with deep brown eyes and wag her skinny tail. At home, Bo was encouraged to curl up on the living room couch, against the gray, short-haired skin of the caribou Kerry had shot in Alaska, and rest up from the rigors of fieldwork, maybe gain a little weight. The bed was the only place Bo wasn't welcome, and Kerry grumbled good-naturedly over even this small restriction imposed by his wife. Kerry had learned about the African trackers when he honeymooned in Kenya, a rare sojourn away from Yellowstone. It was impossible not to know that he and Sue married on September 1, 1990; the names and date were stitched in pretty needlework on quilts, pillows, and framed samplers. Curly haired, self-possessed, and decisive, Sue worked in the natural resources department of the park and had met Kerry at one of the endless administrative meetings. They courted on lion trails. To the marriage Sue brought her high-ceilinged apartment, built in 1890 as bachelor quarters for the Army outpost at Mammoth Hot Springs, and a three-legged cat. Kitty had an established place on the dining room table in a basket carefully situated within reach of the lazy-susan, where there was a pot of lawn grass for her nibbling pleasure. "I've learned a bit about lion behavior from watching her," Kerry said, "like the way she bites her claws to sharpen them. And the way cougars move through the woods, their postures, are much like housecats."

In this sixth and last year of the project, Kerry was working mostly alone in the field, keeping Bo on a leash and relying on her nose and her behavior to help him pinpoint a lion or a lion kill. His goal was not to disturb or influence the lions in any way while he carried out a kind of study called a predation sequence. This was designed to yield information about the dietary habits of cougars—not just what they ate, but also how often they killed, how long they spent eating, how well it agreed with their digestion, and how far they traveled between meals. Lions to be analyzed in this way were chosen at random from each of the five social classes that make up lion society: adult males, adult females with and without kittens, and subadults of both sexes, defined as independent of their mothers but less than two years old. For a week I tagged along as Kerry shadowed a subadult male who was traveling with his brother. They were still within the wide bounds of the ridges and valleys that their mother habitually hunted but had met up with her only once or twice in the three months since they started hunting on their own. A third littermate had struck off on a solitary trail. "Even as kittens, when we treed them for collaring," Kerry said, "these two stuck together and climbed the same tree, and the other kitten went up a different tree."

To make sure that he found every elk, deer, porcupine, or other morsel that his lion consumed during a predation sequence, Kerry snooped after him like a private eye, day in and day out, mapping his every move, riffling through his every laying-up place. He kept at it until the lion had killed three ungulates, which took about a month. Every morning well before the sun cleared the looming horizon of mountains, Kerry motioned Bo into a wooden cage on the back of a battered old pickup truck and threw our packs into an adjoining compartment, from which arose a remarkably foul odor. Fortunately it did not penetrate the cab. The windshield was cracked and the suspension was shot. We would jounce out of the park and head west of Gardiner, bypassing the entrance arch for which Roosevelt had laid the cornerstone, following along the rushing blue and white Gardiner River for a while and then turning onto a series of gravel roads. Large, fancy log cabins and matching barns sat coyly half-hidden at the ends of long driveways; branded signs hung from log-linteled entrance gates. These were private ranches. Park borders meant nothing to lions, whose geography was contoured by line of sight and curve of sound and scent on the wind.

Along the road, when he could get a clear look at the spot where the cats had been yesterday, Kerry would stop the truck, unbuckle his receiver and antennae from their leather cases, screw the H antennae together, and begin casting his electronic net for signals. Holding the receiver close to his ear, he aimed the antennae this way and that, flicking his wrist with an expert motion that I never quite mastered. Whenever the crunch of tires on gravel announced an approaching vehicle, Kerry quickly lowered the antennae and moved behind the truck. He did not like to have passersby notice him. During lion hunting season he made it a policy not to radiotrack from the road, because the direction in which the antennae pointed gave away the hiding place of a lion. A few years ago, at some dog trials, Kerry overheard local houndsmen joking about having an especially good time running lions. From this Kerry surmised that they knew his radio frequency. He called the radio manufacturer and posed as a houndsman who wanted the same frequency for his dog collars that his friends had, and after he named the houndsmen, the manufacturer gave him their frequency. It was the same as his own. To Kerry's relief no one had yet used it to track down his research lions, but he became cautious about pointing his antennae.

Wind slid along the pickup body making noises like novice flute players at frantic practice, but through it I could still hear the strong, rhythmic beep of the cat's collar, pulsing like a heartbeat. We prepared to hike toward wherever the signals seemed strongest. Kerry had long ago obtained permission from most landowners, but first he was careful to pay courtesy calls on whomever was home. Often it was caretakers, since many of the owners ranched in absentia. Some were gracious and curious, inviting us in for coffee at the end of the day, asking for Kerry's tales and telling their own about the mysterious lives of wild animals in the mountains. Others were truculent and suspicious. It was well documented and widely acknowledged that lions rarely attacked livestock anywhere in the region, Kerry said, so in general ranchers had a reasonably tolerant attitude toward the cats. Attitudes toward the Park Service and government in general were often less accepting.

One of the multithousand-acre ranches bordering the park that Kerry's lions routinely trekked across was owned by the Church Universal and Triumphant. The roughly six hundred highly educated and affluent permanent residents called themselves "a self-sufficient spiritual community in the making." The community was notorious for several things: attempts to tap the geothermal flow that, farther upslope, created Mammoth Hot Springs; an oil spill from huge underground tanks meant to carry the group through bleakest anarchy; and the stockpiling of arms in an era when apocalyptic immolations were associated with many cults. The church was led by a woman whose unlikely but honest married name was Elizabeth

Clare Prophet. Locally, she was called Elizabeth Clear Profit. Relations with the surrounding communities were, at best, strained. A church member once reported to police that one of Kerry's assistants had fired a gun at her from a pull-off along the road. Sue overheard the message being relayed to park headquarters and notified Kerry, who, mystified at first, finally figured out that his assistant was doing telemetry work and that the antennae had been mistaken for a firearm. Church members had previously been shot at from the cliffs at that same pull-off.

In addition to a vegetable truck farm, thirty-five hundred acres of irrigated grains, and various livestock operations, the church ran a roadside restaurant with a dinner theater troupe and a deserved reputation for good food, a campground, a university, and numerous spiritual seminars. Thousands of people traveled to the ranch each summer for courses in the blend of Eastern and Western religious ideas that the church defined as New Age. Kerry had permission to enter church lands any time, although church managers worried that people attending conferences might get scared if they knew how close mountain lions really were.

Attacks from cougars are extremely rare but do occur. Kerry had been threatened by three cougars, all of them females with cubs. "Kenny Logan was studying denning," Kerry said, referring to a fellow lion researcher in the Southwest. "He said that females weren't very aggressive and ran away to come back later, so I thought I should do some denning work, too. But females here behave differently. Maybe it's because our environment has a lot of aggressive predators, and Kenny's area has less. Anyway, I ended up having to use my bear mace on one lion and my assistants have used it twice on lions." As a matter of course Kerry had given me a canister of grizzly bear mace—a hot pepper spray—to fasten to my belt. He had never used it on a grizzly, although the day before I arrived he had climbed a tree twice to avoid a grizzly mother with cubs.

One Sunday morning as he was about to leave for church, Kerry had received a call from a park ranger. A vehicle used by one of Kerry's assistants, a handsome and affable graduate student named Greg Felzien, was parked in the same place it had been yesterday, with snow on it to prove it hadn't been moved. Greg was not scheduled to stay out overnight. None of his roommates or friends knew where he was. Kerry called a pilot and flew over and over the area where Greg was supposed to be but saw only the tracks of his snowshoes following the tracks of a cougar. Rangers followed that set of tracks on the ground to the entrance of a small avalanche chute. The cat had made it safely across but Greg had not. They found him dead and half-buried at the bottom.

There had been a few other accidents with less serious consequences. Occasionally, there were false alarms. Walking down a park trail to investigate a ranger's report that a lion had killed another lion, Kerry surprised twenty men dressed in camouflage with blackened faces. Propped up nearby were twenty M16s. For an instant Kerry thought he had stumbled onto a camp of illegal elk-antler hunters and was done for. Then he recognized one of the men as a ranger he knew. They were a ranger SWAT team on maneuvers—what Sue referred to as the Secret Squirrel Squad.

All things considered, on a day-to-day basis Kerry feared lions, bears, snakes, storms, and poachers less than the simple force of gravity. Falling down, especially on ice, could be deadly. During a lion capture for his thesis work, Kerry fell out of a tree and broke his back. The injury took a year to heal and left him with a little numbness in his right foot and enough distaste for heights that he hired good tree climbers whenever he could. "You trip while being pulled downslope by eager hounds on a leash," he said, "or lose your footing climbing up someplace steep with a heavy pack pulling you backward, and you're in trouble."

These words echoed in my mind as I scrabbled on hands and knees up a nearly vertical slope, grabbing at grass tufts to keep my pack from toppling me the wrong way. I had to keep lurching over and creeping under fallen trees, and picking through brittle fences of dead conifer limbs as fast as I could. My heart was a bird frantically beating her wings against the cage of my ribs. When we reached the top of the slope, Kerry took a reading and then surveyed the dips and swells still in our path.

"What we don't want to do is lose any unnecessary altitude," he said.

"Exactly!" I agreed, so ardently that Kerry hooted with laughter. He was incredibly strong, able to go all day up and down without seeming to tire. I never even heard him pant. The signals would beep loudest from some forested mountain face cleft by a hidden ravine, or from a dome-shaped meadow beyond bare-knuckled ridges. Mountains ringed us, and behind them rose more mountains, some smooth, some wrinkled in convolutions of age. The days were spent clambering through this country, sagebrush tripping our ankles, wild roses raking our shoulders, trying to find or keep up with the two adolescent lions that were traveling together. Using the intersection of compass lines from radio readings taken in two different places, Kerry would point to the middle level of three ledges covered with trees, or a forested dimple along a ravine, and say, "There." Exactly there, hidden in the deep green forest, grooming, dozing, taking a breather or striding along, invisible but right there, were the two cats. Except for the occasional rasp of a hawk and the drift of our voices, the world was quiet. Once, Kerry put his fingers to his lips and pointed to magpies clustered against the silhouette of a hilltop; he was sure we'd find a kill. Magpies often scavenge cougar kills. Raven behavior could be telling, too, but subtler— a silent circling over a lion's resting place. But this time the handsome white and black magpies were only picking at cowpies, looking for maggots.

It was late July, and summer grasses tossed their heavy heads. Wind in Douglas firs was insistent about some weather coming in. On a predation sequence, weather was immaterial to the routine. There was a day when a thick gray sky dispensed its rainy blessing on us, sometimes gently, sometimes rudely. My boots were soaked within fifteen minutes. It turned out to be a long day, and rather miserable. In a diaphanous veil of cold mist the mountains became dreams of themselves, vague, dark, shape-shifting masses of mystery. Kerry suffered from a poor sense of direction and had learned early in the project to rely on the compass, so zero visibility didn't faze him.

The two brother lions were moving more than expected through their high, creek-crazed bowl of watersheds. Their movements didn't conform to any pattern Kerry knew. "Kenny's lions don't move around much during the day," he said, "but mine do, unless they've made a kill and stay put to eat it." Signals bounced confusingly off cliffs and rocky hillsides. Once he lost the cats altogether and quickly arranged a private plane flight to widen his search the next morning. After I left, he found an elk calf that the lions had killed on the last day I hiked with him.

"The first instant you see a kill, it's so startling. For those first few seconds, until you get back to yourself and start to think about business, you're in their world, seeing it as they see it." Kerry said this during a lunch spent leaning back against some boulders in a pleasant little bluff and imagining a video camera affixed to a mountain lion's collar. The virtual reality of a cougar hunt, a cougar kill. The kill distills two million years of evolution to a single sequence of attack, defense, death. Hidden behind a rock or tree or shrub, cougars watch and listen. Their round pupils are adapted to both daytime and nighttime hunting and set close together for binocular vision with superb depth perception, most sensitive in a range of fifty to eighty feet. Small, rounded ears move together or independently to pick up sounds, including ultrasonic frequencies. Smell is less acute than in dogs and seems to be less important for hunting than for interpreting scrapes and other social signals from neighboring lions.

With prey in sight, cougars crouch like housecats, creep, wait with twitching tail, creep again until they are within fifty feet of the rear or side of the victim. Then they sprint, mobilizing a body of tensing muscle and flexing sinew hung on a light skeleton. Hind legs are longer than the front, facilitating forty-five-foot-long bounds and fifteen-foot-high leaps. The tail, long and heavy, balances the split-second pivots. Cougars have brought down pronghorn antelope, the fastest animal in North America. The majority of the carcasses Kerry found in northern Yellowstone were elk calves. Across North America, deer seem to have been the favorite food, but cougars also eat a wide variety of small prey, including squirrels, snowshoe hares, marmots, beaver, birds, mice, raccoons, and porcupines. Small prey are especially important to cougars in tropical latitudes where jaguars compete with them for deer.

Large prey are generally killed by bites to the neck or throat. Before biting, cougars embrace their prey around the neck and shoulders, claws extended and raking. Whiskers help to feel where canines should pierce to sunder the vertebrae and break the spinal cord. When everything goes well, death comes in an instant. Sometimes, especially with large prey or inexperienced cougars, the cougar is forced around to the throat. Asphyxiation takes longer and allows flailing hoofs to injure and some-times kill the cougar.

If the hunt is successful, the immediate reaction of the cougar is to rest from the enormous exertion. If the prey is larger than a porcupine or rabbit, the next step is usually to hide the carcass. "Cats aren't very commonsensical about where they drag their kills," Kerry said. "Some-times, with the same effort, they could have moved it to a good secluded spot but instead end up in someplace pretty exposed." Wherever they decide to drop the carcass, cougars usually try to scratch over it whatever is available—dirt, forest duff, sand, twigs—to protect it from scavengers and, perhaps, from too rapid spoilage in the heat of the sun. Often, cougars stay near the kill for days, bedding down nearby. "They seem to have a hard time getting comfortable," Kerry said. "I see signs of a lot of settling and resettling." Able to eat five to fifteen pounds at a sitting, starting with the heart, lungs, and liver, proceeding to the muscles, and ending with the marrow inside cracked bones, a cougar may consume the carcass almost entirely. Stomach, intestines, head, hide, and a few large bones may be all that's left. Surprisingly little blood is spilled; cougars probably lap it up carefully for the moisture as well as the nutrients. The smell that just about knocked me over whenever I lifted the wooden lid on the back of the pickup was cougar scats in Ziploc bags. Kerry collected them to analyze exactly what animals were eaten (in case he had missed any small kills) and how much nutrient the lions derived from them. The freezer in the basement was overflowing with five hundred bags awaiting analysis, and Sue wouldn't let him bring them anywhere near the living area. Kerry figured that the disintegration in the daily warmth on the back of the pickup wouldn't unduly hurt the accuracy.

Sometimes lions feed only once or twice, then abandon the remaining meat. Spoilage of the meat may be one reason, although in cold climates like Yellowstone this is fairly insignificant. It appears more likely that they are preempted from their meals. Lion kills attract many kinds of life. Cougars seem to play the role of provider, not at all an advantageous one for the cougar. Relationships among predators is one of the frontiers of wildlife science, and as yet little is known in quantified ways about interactions among cougars, wolves, bears, bobcats, and coyotes. There is, however, a growing body of field observations. "Many times I've seen a lion leave a kill abruptly after only a day," Kerry said, "and I've found black bear tracks at the kill. I'm sure the bear has driven the lion away. I haven't noticed grizzlies doing that, but that's probably only because there's so few grizzlies around, and even fewer wolves." In Glacier National Park, where wolves have filtered down from Canada, a colleague of Kerry's had just started a new study. Already, there was clear evidence that both wolves and bears were following cougar tracks. Wolves were treeing collared lions there and had even killed three of them. In Yellowstone, Kerry once found a young cougar treed by coyotes, and an assistant had seen coyotes harass a lion off a kill. Another of Kerry's helpers watched a mother cougar confront a startled black bear that was coming too close to her den. There was snarling, growling, and throwing of punches;

both animals danced around the bushes, separated, and came together again. In the end, the bear ran away wailing, with the cougar close behind.

There is also cooperation, at least within cougar families. The two brothers we followed were hunting; Kerry didn't know for sure but suspected they hunted together. He was sure that mother and young had occasional joint hunts. He saw, as had been noted by other lion scientists, that daughters often lived close to mothers, though sons almost never did. He also observed that mothers and daughters occasionally met, even hunted together, long after the daughters had become independent. The oldest lion Kerry knew was a female that a friend of his treed eleven years after Kerry had collared her as a young adult. Other field researchers have noted similar longevity, and lions have lived more than eighteen years in captivity. The idea of long-lived animal matrons sharing knowledge and passing it on to young—in short, a bioculture—has already been suggested by radical thinkers for the last grizzlies of the San Juan Mountains of Colorado. Somehow those bears have learned to hide almost every vestige of their massive, lumbering selves from prying human eyes. Bioculture is still beyond the frontier of wildlife science.

"Have you seen emotions in cats?" I asked Kerry. We had pulled into a rest stop beside the river and were eating lunch on the mown part of the bank, beneath a big old cottonwood. Human voices almost drowned in the relentless hum of the fast water.

"No, not really," he said. "They're wild animals and they behave like wild animals. I keep reminding myself of that. What's impressed me most is their individuality. Each of them has a life that's as real to them as ours is to us." Reality just then was very pleasant in the dappling shade of the cottonwood, and we felt languid after a long, sweaty hike. Conversation was desultory, but inevitably turned to hunting.

"I don't name my lions," Kerry said. "Kenny has the luxury of not having a sport harvest, but I see lions grow up and move, then die from a bullet. That's why I don't name them. I try not to get attached to them because I don't want to lose objectivity. It could influence my behavior if I ever was in a position to make recommendations on a season, maybe make me want to interfere with a sport harvest directly or indirectly. Making value judgments is not my role."

Kerry held to an idealized vision of lion hunting. "Say someone grew up with hounds, trains his own hounds to track lions, goes to a wilderness area and really roughs it, spends days and days on the trail, does it the hardest way possible. Hasn't he earned the privilege of shooting a lion?"

I took this as a rhetorical question and didn't answer. The sun was slanting down the long valley, glaring from slick rock shoulders of mountains, sharpening the green of the pastures. In the shade of bankside trees the river was diffused into soft, sliding grays. "Anyway," Kerry said, "it's a fundamental Christian value to dominate animals. And it's not sport hunting that threatens lions, not seriously, even though there are places where lions are badly overhunted. I do think state agencies base regulations on guesses and assumptions, since biological data are so sparse and local. And nobody knows what other states are doing, even though they're linked in one continental system, whether they want to admit it or not. But the real threat is that we're losing too much good lion land to senseless sprawl. We need large parcels of high-quality habitat, and most of all we need to get corridors connecting those islands of habitat."

This notion of habitat corridors—wide strips of natural vegetation, perhaps following watercourses or ridges, between parcels of wildland otherwise surrounded by logged or mined or subdivided landscapes— emerged in the 1980s. Practitioners of a new discipline called conservation biology began to apply abstract knowledge about genetics and population dynamics to the real world of diminishing wildland and declining species. The results were startling. It quickly became clear that, from a genetic point of view, small populations faced alarming risks from inbreeding and catastrophes such as epidemics. Even 2.2-million-acre Yellowstone National Park probably couldn't harbor all the cougars needed for long-term survival of a single population. There had to be immigration and emigration routes to other groups of cougars.

A pickup camper pulled into the parking lot, and a little boy jumped out and ran down to the river as fast as he could, yelling loud enough to drown the water noise. Kerry smiled. In a few weeks he would wrap up his project and move temporarily to a residence hall at the University of Idaho in Moscow, to get his Ph.D. That would take two years; he wasn't sure what he would do afterward, except have children. He had put most of his adult life on hold to study cougars, although he hadn't given up quite as much of the American mainstream life as his compatriot in the Southwest, Kenny Logan—but then, Kenny had his wife working with him.

Because lions move across borders, Kenny Logan and Linda Sweanor's subjects weren't as safe from hunting as Kerry thought, but their entire study area had been closed to sport hunting when their ten-year project began. The New Mexico Department of Game and Fish had inaugurated the study and the U.S. Army agreed to host it, opening 750 square miles of the restricted White Sands Missile Range. This encompassed all of the San Andres mountain range in southern New Mexico. Protected within the boundaries of the missile range since 1945, the San Andres had not suffered livestock grazing for half a century, and as a result constituted the largest single remnant of true Chihuahuan Desert remaining in the Southwest. "The difference is tremendous," Kenny said. "In there, the grasses are—" and he held out his arm at waist height.

Because of bureaucratic hassles over security, it wasn't possible to go out in the field with Kenny and Linda. Instead, they came down from the mountains and met me at their house for dinner. They owned an attractive adobe three-bedroom house in a new development on the outskirts of Las Cruces. It was a neat house, tastefully decorated, and except for a few traces of romping by their two cats, had a pronounced unlived-in look. We drank beer and ate pizza at their dining table, where I faced a window that framed their study area. Kenny pointed out the boundaries, from the pass nearby—a great dip in the silhouette of mountain—all the way north as far as the eye could see. The San Andres appeared as a single broad slash of mountain with a wildly erratic edge that plunged to the pass, then ascended to run serrated for a while. The whole long massif had one angle of slant, as if the rim of the world had been thrust upward in warning, evoking visions of primordial forces, vast and incomprehensible.

Desert ecology of cougars had not been thoroughly documented, and Kenny and Linda figured that their findings could be applied from west Texas to southeastern Arizona south into Mexico. The White Sands project was divided into two phases. The first five years were spent doing much the same kind of work Kerry did, documenting the number of cats and their daily activities. The second phase was designed to mimic sport hunting by translocating cats from the study area to other parts of New Mexico. In carrying out the goals of their project, Kenny and Linda were perhaps the first mountain lion scientists to work routinely without houndsmen or hounds. Dogs and cougars would both die of heat exhaustion at White Sands, where daytime temperatures reached 115 degrees Fahrenheit. Besides, trees were rare, and on the ground there was too much risk of dogs killing cats and vice versa. So Kenny and Linda and their several assistants—half of whom were women—set spring activated, leg-hold cable snares along routes likely to be traveled by lions. Snares had long been discounted as a poor way to catch cougars because they had to be set just where cougars would walk, might injure the cougar, and would certainly catch too many other animals. It took nearly a month of trying before Kenny and Linda snared their first lion, and snares continued to require considerably more time than captures by dogs, but eventually they mastered the technique of placing snares where lions were likely to tread.

Of 151 snare captures, they had lost two lions to fatal injuries. A third with a broken leg was rehabilitated and returned to the wild. The few other animals heavy enough to trigger the snares—coyotes and deer—had been set free unharmed. This was one of the safest capture records of any cougar study. The worst seems to have been a very strange 1976 master's thesis on cougar translocation by Texas houndsman Roy McBride. McBride darted more than seventy cats but accounted for only eight translocations, and wrote that "chases in summer months often lead to overheating and death of lions."

Kenny grimaced at the mention of McBride's study; he was himself from Texas, and one of the reasons he left was because he felt there must be other ways to think about predators than the Texas way. He had a dense thatch of black hair with the slightest hint of gray here and there, a sunburned face, and a nervous habit of blinking. Linda was a mere wisp of a woman, lithe, freckled, and tawny, with hair a dark blonde and amber eyes just a shade darker than a lion's. They had met at the University of Wyoming, where Kenny was a graduate student working on a thesis about cougars, and Linda, a recent biology graduate, was working for the university on a bighorn sheep study.

"That was a breakthrough," she said, "for a woman to study big game. In undergraduate school, all the women seemed to end up in nongame research, but that's changing now." She had always wanted to study predators because of their intelligence and importance to an ecosystem. Mountain lions in particular fascinated her because they were the last large carnivores still numerous and widespread enough to exert evolutionary influence on their prey. When Kenny was offered the job of lead researcher at White Sands and asked her to marry him, Linda decided to base her master's thesis on the work. It was entitled "Mountain Lion Social Organization in a Desert Environment." In it she elaborated, refined, and—because cougars show great variation in adapting to different environments—occasionally refuted the findings of researchers in more northern climates. To call cougars solitary is misleading; they are highly social in the sense that their behavior and whereabouts depend on the behavior and whereabouts of neighboring lions. But neighbors keep their distance. Even in much wetter habitats than the Chihuahuan Desert, with much more numerous deer and other prey, lions spread themselves across the landscape in lower numbers than the amount of food would support. In the San Andres, three to five adult cougars lived in one hundred square miles; if young ones still with their mothers were included in the count, the number went up to six to nine cougars per hundred square miles.

"Just for comparison," Linda said, "New Mexico has twelve hundred people per hundred square miles."

To maintain enough elbow room, lions behave according to a code of land tenure as deliberate and complicated as in human societies. Because of it, Linda wrote in her thesis, "Lion populations appear to be self-regulating." Other researchers had advanced this idea, but few showed the mechanisms of self-regulation in operation as clearly as Linda did. Every lion seeks an area of adequate cover and food, called a home range. In Linda's thesis, home ranges were plotted into attenuated geometric shapes, calculated according to several standard methodologies. They are a useful but deceptive visual aid. Straight lines run blindly through steep ravines and across sheer cliffs that no one in his right mind would cross. And the heavy black lines give a false impression of immutability. More like oil drops on slowly moving water, home ranges are fluid as well as fixed, sliding around and over each other as seasons and circumstances change. Males usually claim an area that overlaps the territories of several females and spend their time hunting and traveling, always on the lookout for females in heat. They readily shift the boundaries of their ranges in response to the presence of new lions or the death of old ones.

Females, on the other hand, prefer to remain in familiar areas, where they know cover and prey are available for raising kittens. Motherhood requires enormous amounts of energy. Most females don't give birth until they are about two years old and, on average at White Sands, have a litter every seventeen months. Cougars breed year-round, but some regions have a surge in births at particular times of year. At White Sands, it occurs during late summer and fall, when mule deer also give birth and lion food in the form of fawns is abundant. Equal numbers of males and females are born, although, as with humans, adult lion populations tend to have slightly more females.

It's not uncommon for females to share parts of their range with other females, and even male ranges have been known to overlap in a few locales, but rarely do cats meet face to face. They communicate their presence in several ways. Males usually scrape little heaps of dirt, topped with urine or feces. These are the signs that hunters search for. Lions like to leave these scent signals in particular places along their travels, under especially big trees, or in the saddle of a ridge, and sometimes the same places are used by several males. When sniffing these signals, lions make a lip-curling grimace called a flehman, which is thought to engage a special olfactory organ in the roof of the mouth. Little is known about other body signals. Communicating by voice—that centerpiece of cougar lore—is extremely varied. There is no question that cougars whistle, chirp, meow, growl, and purr. Screams have been heard from caged cougars, and Kenny and Linda believe they've heard screams from lions in heat at White Sands, but many other people question whether cougars really scream in the wild. The latest theory, proposed by a long-time lion researcher in Utah named Frederick Lindzey, is that porcupines scream in a way that might be mistaken for lions.

Social intolerance, expressed through territoriality and maintained through various forms of lion communication, is one complicated way that cougars regulate themselves. Dispersal of young is another. Kenny and Linda figured that 32 to 64 cougars lived throughout 750 square miles, and about half were adults with established home ranges. Most of the remaining lions were kittens still with their mothers. Kittens that survived their first year and a half of life (the time of greatest death) began, gradually, to drift away. This group of drifters constituted about 10 percent of the population. Of 70 kittens that survived to dispersal age, only 17—mostly females—remained within the White Sands study area. The others traveled, especially the males, one of whom finally settled down 124 miles away. Travels of twice that distance have been documented. The "transient" lions mentioned frequently by other researchers were probably, Linda concluded, dispersing youngsters looking for a place to live. Very little is known about dispersing lions except that they are a terribly vulnerable segment of the lion population. Not only does traveling expose them to a constant barrage of threats, but they are also inexperienced and, like adolescents of other species, sometimes reckless. These are the lions most in need of undeveloped corridors from one block of wildland to another.

The most dramatic way that lions regulate their own numbers is by killing each other. Slightly more than half of known cougar deaths at White Sands resulted from attacks by other cougars. All males that Kenny and Linda examined carried scars from fighting. Males killed other males and even females that trespassed on their home ranges, although males didn't kill females they had mated with, nor their own kittens, as long as the mother was present. Unattended kittens were killed. Kenny got up from the table and rummaged in a back room to bring out three skulls from lions found dead during the study. All had puckered places where bone had healed over puncture wounds, inflicted, Kenny was sure, by other lions. All three had survived those particular encounters. Others weren't so lucky. In every case it was males who were aggressive. Three females were bitten in the head and died, and a fourth was chased off a cliff and fell to her death. One female and her kittens were cannibalized; another died of unknown causes and was eaten by her three eight-month-old kittens. One young tom was chased by a much bigger tom up a power pole. He climbed to the top, grounded a hot wire, and died. A few months later, another young but larger and meaner male arrived in the same territory. The older cat made room for the younger for two years by shifting to the north. During that time the younger one killed two females and mated with a third, siring a litter of kittens. Then he tried to expand, but this pushed the older male against the ranges of other cats farther north. Eventually the elder killed the younger lion. This kind of thing was known to happen in other cougar societies, but more rarely, and in some ecosystems hardly at all. Kenny and Linda theorized that the more intense the competition for food—and in the sparse desert landscape it was very intense—the greater the hostility between lions.

The routine by which Kenny and Linda lived and studied lions was to spend ten days in the mountains, broken in half by one trip for supplies and to check on their housecats, then four days off. Once a week Linda flew; she had done eighty percent of the radio locations from the air. In the mountains they and their teammates lived in separate camps, composed of tents or shacks built from discarded missile crates. The camps were accessible by four-wheel-drive, but days were spent hiking. Every morning without fail, everyone checked their snare lines for lions. Afternoons, they followed signals and searched for lion sign. "Dust storms are the worst," Linda said, "when there's nothing remotely resembling a shower within reach." They had no social life. The house, bought as an investment six years into their ten-year stint, constituted their main claim to middle-class life. "It's not like we miss friends in town, because we've never had them," Linda said. "We have no roots here but in the mountains. The lions are like our family."

This was dangerous ground. Linda pulled out a picture album. Just as in Charley Leeder's book, grinning people held limp, sprawling cats, but these cats were alive, if somewhat glassy eyed, and there was no blood anywhere. "This is Mr. Onions," she said, pointing. "We found him as a cub near a wild onion patch." It took some time to get through the album because she had other names to explain, whole family histories to recount.

"Yes," Linda said. She was unequivocal and unafraid. "We do have emotions for individual lions. When they die, it's hard, but if the causes are part of their own world, well, that's their life, you can accept it, although you miss them, you're always thinking, gee, what if he could have made it? But the human-caused deaths are difficult. A female that we had marked as a four-week-old kitten died from foot injuries from a trapper's steel leg hold trap. That shouldn't have happened. A male was killed by a hunter. To the hunter—well, who knows what goes through a hunter's mind? But to us—I mean, that hunter didn't know anything about that cat, and yet he has him hanging on the wall. We knew that cat's parents and grandparents. We learn their life histories, all the trials and rigors of their lives, and then *bammo,* somebody shoots the sucker."

"We try to be objective, " Kenny said. "My mental approach is to think of lions as nothing more, but nothing less, than another earthling. We're outsiders observing, but yet in the process we get to know those lions better than anyone else does, and certainly better than we know our own neighbors here. And we find that there are correlations between human behavior and other animals—territoriality, aggression, and so on. This brings up a red flag of anthropomorphism. You realize that you are observing qualities similar to those of human beings; we just express those qualities in more sophisticated ways. Our emotions are sophisticated manifestations of survival instincts and techniques. Memories and communication are others. It's not anthropomorphic to recognize that, but some people are afraid to admit it."

Their voices raced with passion, and often both of them jumped to speak at the same time. More often than not, Linda deferred to Kenny. As they spoke, I glanced often out the window to watch a delicate, deep pink sunset slowly turn the mountains an inky blue.

"I wouldn't be surprised," Kenny said, "if a mother that finds her kittens eaten feels loss. I've heard a lion mother purr from twenty yards away while she called her kittens to her. How deeply she feels the loss and how long are impossible to measure. I believe also that these animals think to a certain degree and make decisions based on experience and learning. I used to be an avid hunter. I wanted to kill one of everything in North America." He grinned. "But then I grew up. What most influenced me was seeing just how tough it is for animals to survive in their world. Trophy hunting lost all its importance. It just seems frivolous now."

Lion hunting is anything but frivolous for the lions themselves: hunting is by far the largest single cause of lion death. "And this degree of killing by humans is new to their evolution," Kenny said. "It changes the direction of natural selection." Yet in all the decades of mountain lion science, Kenny and Linda's was the first study ever designed specifically to assess the impacts of hunting on a lion population, although Fred Lindzey in Utah had recently adapted his long-term radio monitoring of cougars to do something similar. Lindzey simulated a hunting season by moving to another area cougars of a gender and age matching those typically shot. The cougar population did not recover by the next season to the original level. Enough cougars died from natural causes that Lindzey questioned the long-held theory of compensatory mortality, which asserts that loss of animals through hunting is offset by the survival of more of the remaining animals, because more space and food are available to them. Kenny and Linda had also moved a group of cougars but felt it was too early yet to comment, although Linda speculated that hunting increased fighting among lions by increasing the opportunities for competition over empty territories. They still had three years to go to finish the final phase of their study.

"What will you do," I asked, "when the project is over?"

Linda groaned. "I hate it when people ask that. The thought of not going back into the mountains is terrible."

"We need to manage for lion hunting," Kenny said. "So much of the funding for wildlife research comes from hunting licenses." They envisioned themselves giving workshops on how to age and sex lions and gather other kinds of data, and attending commission meetings to change any hunting regulations that needed to be changed. They planned to advocate for corridors and land-use planning. They did not want their ten years of work to end up hidden away in a file, so, a few months after I left, they signed a contract with the New Mexico Department of Game and Fish to develop a statewide cougar management plan after their fieldwork was completed. "Cougars are our last chance," Linda said, "to get it right before we have to go back and try to restore what we've destroyed."

"The world has given us so much," Kenny said. "We're always reaping it in, a sunrise, a bird song. Most people are so bombarded with other people they can't begin to conceive of what other earthlings are like. But life is so precious. Look up at the stars and consider how many have solar systems, how few have life, and here we so often squander it. So we feel an obligation to conserve lions, and cultivate an appreciation for them. Even if we need to change our lives. Somehow we need to learn how to become the new Natives, how to accommodate other earthlings."

"Our values need to change," Linda said. "I look around the house and think, I'd like to have this or that. Then I go to camp and hear a whip-poorwill and I ask myself, why do I need anything more than a shack and a propane lantern?"

"Why," Kenny asked, "is a gram of gold worth more than a butterfly that weighs a gram?" There was, of course, no answer. Beyond the dining room window, the evening had progressed to a velvety black night, pricked with stars.

It was understood that when the project ended, Kenny, like Kerry Murphy, would get his doctorate at the University of Idaho. Their connection there is a faculty member named Maurice Hornocker. They, Linda, and many of their helpers are his students. Hornocker was the first to tag lions in Idaho in the 1960s, when he pioneered many of the techniques in use today. He has also conducted ground-breaking research on other predators, from wolverines to otters to Siberian tigers. A dapper speech giver and a brilliant grant writer, he founded his own research institute and continues to design cutting-edge mountain lion studies. He is respected, but not beloved.

The grand old man of the cougar coterie, the first researcher willing to probe beyond lion science and the one whom others refer to as the lion philosopher, is Harley Shaw, a retired staffer of the Arizona Fish and Game Department. Harley's parents were Oakies who moved to Arizona in the Depression. Harley grew up in the country, where his young brother died from a scorpion sting. Harley has a round, ruddy face framed in pure white—hair and beard both. The beard is neatly trimmed and reveals a tenderness around the mouth. Eyes are deeply set and brown, but with something green and gold and reflective in them. Most of Harley's sentences end with a chuckle. He wears wool shirts and fancy vests with geometric designs native to the Southwest. One morning when I was visiting him, I came downstairs to find him oiling his Redwing boots. "They're good even for hiking," he said. "I wore tennis shoes through my childhood. Spent hours picking cholla out of them, so as soon as I could afford a pair of leather boots that's what I got and I've worn them ever since."

Harley began working for Arizona Fish and Game as a student in the 1950s and never left. It was not a happy union, and he took the earliest possible retirement, which he called "divorce with alimony." One of his first projects had been studying fall hunting impacts on turkeys, and turkeys remained an abiding interest. "I didn't used to think fall hunting was bad," he said, "but now I wonder if maybe by killing off the older hens while poults are still young, we lose some flock memory—like where to go for unusual kinds of food when the usual foods fail." When he retired, Harley began a book about turkeys, his second book. His first was entitled *Soul among Lions*. It was an odd book for a biologist, with intimations of morality, even mysticism. "In sustaining our image of objectivity, we as biologists pretend that we study wild animals," he wrote in the preface. "In reality, we inevitably study an interface between ourselves and other species . . . we modify not only our knowledge of the species being studied [but also] our feelings for it . . . Research thus becomes a process of personal change."

Harley's office was spread through the house that he and his wife, Patty, leased from the city of Prescott. The house was at the site of several springs used for Prescott's early water supply and had been built for the pump mechanic just after the turn of the century. The original bricks patterned the inside walls. It was heated by a wood stove in the living room. Books were everywhere, slouching on tall shelves, spilling over the coffee table, stacked in corners. Outside, a few hundred yards away, half a dozen big cottonwoods hosted a great blue heron rookery. It was too early in the spring for nesting but there were always a few flying by, legs trailing. Patty was a devoted birder whenever she could get a few minutes off from work. She had short gray hair, clear green eyes, and a pert, friendly manner. She ran her own printing business, which consisted largely of a real estate advertising magazine for booming Prescott. It was a mortification to both Patty and Harley that she was making money on development that they both abhorred.

Though Harley kept his preretirement habit of rising early—his coffeemaker was set for four 4 A.M.—he hated anything that bound him to a rigid schedule. For that reason he taught only sporadically at several local colleges, but nevertheless he had managed to attract an informal following of young people. He took me along one day with his group to his old lion study area, the Spider Ranch, where he had started tracking lions nearly a quarter of a century before. The ranch was privately run but had an allotment on Forest Service land. I slid out of the truck and nearly stepped on a lion track. This I took to be a sign that I was in the right place at the right time. It was a perfect late winter day, blue sky and green mountains, everything fresh and clean. A chaparral of manzanita, turpinella oak, sumac, mountain mahogany, and scattered junipers covered small hills. Some of the hills were studded with boulders, and stands of Gambel oaks stood in cool spots. For five years Harley rode on horseback through this land, following lions down roads and trails and striking out cross country. It had not been a good time in his life. The ranch owner and the ranch hands were supportive but his own agency often was not, imposing mindless bureaucratic obstacles that amounted to irrational harassment. First one marriage fell apart, and then a second broke up as he left the Spider Ranch to study lions on the Kaibab Plateau. Through it all, several of his most beloved lion dogs died under painful circumstances. "Cougars," said Harley, "are associated for me with a lot of sadness."

Harley's students were soft spoken and keen eyed. Several were students, several were teachers, and one was a librarian at a high school. There were two babies in the group; they passed from arm to arm before being settled in their parents' backpacks. The women tended to be thin and lanky, almost bony. One was named Caroline, blonde and beautiful, quiet and retiring, but avidly studying lion tracks, leaning over them, sloshing through streams, with a one-year-old on her back. It made my back ache to watch her. We walked along a dirt road and people fanned out along the sides, especially at washes, to look for tracks. When they found a well-defined one, they held a glass plate over it and traced it with a magic marker, then traced it again from the glass onto paper, which they could then reproduce. That particular day, they were out to sharpen their skills in habitat analysis. Harley was training them to make quick and dirty assessments of the value of a particular spot for wildlife, a strategy useful for evaluating and mitigating the potential effects of logging, ranching, or development. We all tried estimating the amount of forest canopy by raising our arms, quartering the sky, and estimating the percentage of trees in each quarter. Later, the students would average it all and compare it with measurements from the $90 standard measuring tool, a densimeter, that one of the teachers had borrowed from a lab.

"Without institutional support you can only do low-tech things," Harley said.

We found a good run of lion prints in the hardened mud of the road. People measured the stride and assigned legs—front right, left rear. Harley pointed out an unusual overstep of hind foot over front. He was hoping to interest his group in running track counts along one of these roads on Spider Ranch. If they counted tracks every day for a couple of weeks in a row and repeated the count annually, they could get an idea of how many lions were around.

"We have hardly scratched the surface of learning what drives animal population declines and rises," Harley said. "There may not even be a strong cause and effect. I'm coming around to chaos theory, where one tiny difference makes a huge impact in the very long run. Our hope of predictive models is slim if that's the case. We've oversold the notion of wildlife management. It works only because natural systems work, and because the worst of the poaching is controlled. That's why I'm a great advocate of monitoring populations, so at least you can see what's really happening." The problem with lion research as Harley saw it was that ten years was much too short, but few projects went even that long. "A five-year study can't ever get past the descriptive phase. But it's easy to get in and 'do research'—these techniques become a fad. How many more lions need to get their rear ends darted? Until these agencies are willing to fund twenty-year projects and get onto an experimental phase, like the project at White Sands, they are doomed to repetition."

But it was not in the nature of bureaucracy, Harley believed, to foster long-term studies. Nor did he think biologists generally wanted to spend a lifetime on one project; they wanted to move on in their careers. For their part, administrators didn't believe things were that complicated, and wanted conclusive results in, say, three years. Harley visited them in their steel and glass towers, utterly removed from the mud that mired him in the Kaibab, and he came to feel that people in charge of game agencies didn't really want populations monitored. It might show up their poor decisions, and the last thing a career type wanted was failure. As long as they didn't know, they could raise a smokescreen. "Government administrators are not always honorable," Harley said. "They make the rules so they can break them or change them anytime without accountability. If I had to choose between businessmen and agency administrators, I'd say the businessmen would be more trustworthy, because they're accountable for their decisions and depend on their reputations."

The bitterness was tempered by the evenness of his voice and by his appreciation of the cold beer waiting in coolers at the end of our hike. And by the acknowledgment that the same system he criticized had given him a living and supported him in at least some of his endeavors. During his tenure with the state, Harley hosted the third mountain lion workshop at Prescott. "Biologists often reflect the species they're studying," he had said once, "and lion researchers tend to be silent, solitary, and distributed at low densities over large territories." Despite any innate reclusiveness, lion biologists from the twelve western states and several Canadian provinces with lion populations managed to congregate four times over several decades. The first workshop, held in 1976, focused on describing where and in what condition the lions were. The second, held eight years later, did the same, with some emphasis on research and on comparative hunting regulations. The fourth, called rather hurriedly in the early 1990s as lion attacks on humans escalated, was entirely devoted to mountain lion-human interactions.

Harley's role as chairman of the steering committee for the third workshop gave him the opportunity to schedule an entire session on population monitoring. At the end of the conference, participants agreed that the greatest need in lion science was the development of a nonintrusive field method for accurately counting lion populations—some statistically reliable way to count tracks or scats or scrapes on a continuing basis. Of course, this would mean a long-term commitment of agency personnel to do the counting. No such method has yet been developed.

Harley's own work, driven by agency politics, focused on lion predation. The Spider Ranch, in conjunction with the adjoining Cross U Ranch, ran nine hundred cows, many with calves, on about 175 square miles. Harley found that about a third of what the local lions ate was calves, representing a possible loss to the two ranches of $25,000 a year. More than a hundred other ranches in central and southern Arizona reported similar losses. Virtually all of the lions that Harley tracked ate a calf at some time or other, so it wasn't a question of one or two confirmed stock killers. This situation was confined mostly to Arizona, where a relatively mild climate allowed year-round cattle operations in good lion country. It was sheep that lions took in other places across the West, but sheep losses were usually very localized and often the work of a single lion. After sifting through much contradictory and confusing data, Harley finally concluded that a change in cattle management— bringing the herd down from the mountains and out of lion habitat during calving season, which just happened to be the time of year when deer numbers were at their lowest ebb—might be far more effective than killing lions. Undisturbed, lions did not simply multiply indefinitely but reached a point of social saturation and stability. Once lion society was disrupted by control—the euphemism for killing—empty territories would attract dispersing lions from other regions, who might just eat even more cattle. Lion control, which was a considerable operating expense, would have to be continuous until all lions were eliminated, or else it might well be counterproductive.

On the Kaibab, Harley tried to understand the impact of lions on deer. Mule deer were by far the largest part of the lion diet there, and mule deer had been declining for years. To human deer hunters, it was obvious that lions were reducing the deer population and should be hunted more heavily. Harley found he couldn't really confirm or deny their assertion. He watched the Kaibab deer herd as it began to recover immediately after the lion population crashed from unknown causes, although sport hunting played a part. But those years were exceptionally wet, a factor thought to stimulate deer births throughout the arid West. Taken as a whole, the work of other researchers was just as inconclusive: some found that prey herds multiplied despite unhindered lion predation; others found that, in circumstances where prey numbers were low to start with, lions could keep those numbers from rising. All Harley could conclude was that at current levels of hunting and habitat, sport hunting did not seem to threaten the population.

Lion hunting was troublesome for Harley. "My whole generation has a Leopoldian view of wildlife management: game is a crop, and managing means to hunt under controlled conditions," he said. "It's hard for me to be antihunting. My roots are too deeply into it. I shot a deer about three years ago, but then asked myself why. If there's no fire in the belly, what's the point? I could not bring myself to shoot a lion because I wouldn't know why I was doing it. But I can see someone wanting to shoot a lion. It turns me off, but to males in a certain stage of life it has a value. I do think there is a biological basis to the hunting urge. What I can't understand is how some houndsmen can go out every year and shoot a lion again and again. The chase I fully understand, the skill I value. Perhaps there could even be some vague advantage, in the interests of human diversity, to maintaining a group of people who hunt." He paused. "On the other hand," he said, and paused again. We were eating a stew of lamb that Patty had raised. She was listening intently and nodding agreement. The indoor dog and the cat waited politely at a little distance. "I don't think the world would end if we stopped hunting some of these species," Harley continued. "Lions do fine just left alone."

They seemed caught in a transition, both of them—too keenly aware of the bad in the old ways to trust tradition, too uneasy to be comfortable in the new age.

Just before dinner, in the late afternoon, Patty had gone to feed her horses at a pasture down the road. Harley and I sat on the stone patio, drinking a beer, watching chickens scratch and shadows slant, and shooting the breeze. This was Harley's forte. Capitalism, democracy, peasantry, environmentalism, human progress on material, technological, and spiritual levels—all were grist for his mill.

"It's not as simple as just how do you look at lions," Harley said. "It has to do with how we look at each other, the poor serving the rich, accepting the idea of exploitable human beings." When I wondered aloud whether a society that was taught to value animal life more would of necessity value human life more, he laughed and said which came first, the chicken or the egg? Those damned rhetorical questions.

It's too early for a full conclusion, although time is getting short. Much is now known about lions, but that knowledge must mobilize social change if lions are to survive. Whether lion scientists will help lead the necessary cultural changes remains to be seen. Even from this small sample, it is clear that science can work in various guises, as can myth.

Texas Varmints and
California Dreamers

TWO THIRDS OF THE WAY DOWN THE RIO GRANDE'S LONG RUN FROM THE Colorado Rockies to the Gulf of Mexico, it bends back on itself to outline a huge pocket. Looking down from an exceptionally good vantage point, the Great Spirit decided to dump all the rocks left over from making the world into the toe of that pocket. More prosaic theories rely on inland seas, volcanoes, eons of deposition, uplift, and erosion to explain the chaos of the Chisos Mountains. From the Chihuahuan Desert floor, they jut straight up to nearly eight thousand feet. Other mountains stand in silhouette against the far blue distance of West Texas, some long and smooth, some crumpled as if by a giant fist. Bounded by the Pecos and the Rio Grande rivers, West Texas is a world unto itself. Nine thousand years ago, before a long desiccation began, it was a moister, lusher world, with a metropolitan nucleus at the juncture of the two rivers. There, the hunter-gatherer Pecos people lived in sheltered ravines in a limestone plateau and painted what have been called the most outstanding pictographs on the North American continent. The most prominent figures in these paintings include elongated, colorful gods; puny, pale humans; and large, sometimes beweaponed mountain lions. Lions seem to straddle a middle distance, more divine than humans, but more profane than gods. Perhaps, in a world that worked differently than ours, lions were able to channel power from gods to humans, and convey messages from humans to gods. Traces of hallucinogenic mescal beans have been found in painted caves. Reality has always been pliant in West Texas.

In the glare of desert sun, reality was as sharp as the shadows cast by contours in a pawprint. Tracks riffled the dry sand of Cottonwood Creek. This is a favorite lion travel route in and out of the Chisos, and thus in and out of Big Bend National Park, which contains the Chisos Mountains in their entirety. "A lioness and two kittens," said the blonde young woman, as she crouched over the tracks to measure them. She was documenting lion use of the park and depended on strong sun to show up the tracks. Without shadows, tracks disappear into the subtle textures and random patterns of sand. Through much of the 1980s, biologists in Big Bend and in Guadalupe Mountains National Park, along the New Mexico border at the northern extremity of West Texas, tried to study lion ecology. Their research was hampered by the fact that radio-collared lions that wandered beyond park boundaries tended to have very short lives.

Long after every other western state enacted regulations to govern the killing of mountain lions, Texas—it would be fairer to say West Texas—continues to hold out for the frontier. The essence of frontier is lack of law. No laws govern the killing of Texas lions. They can be dispatched by anyone with a valid hunting license, anytime, by any means. There are no bag limits, no closed seasons, no obligation to report any kills. Certainly no obligation to fill out any forms. Unlike other states that permit lion hunting, Texas has no problem with poaching, because there are no laws to break. With jaguars, wolves, and grizzly bears killed off long ago and black bears reduced to a pittance, the mountain lion takes center stage as the biggest little varmint in Texas.

The Lone Star Chapter of the Sierra Club tried unsuccessfully in the 1970s to persuade the Texas legislature to change the lion's legal status from unprotected nongame to game animal. Game status would enable legal protections like seasons and bag limits. They tried again in the early 1990s. Texas was, after all, by then an urbanizing state, and attitudes were changing. Even the sports editor of the *Houston Chronicle* endorsed game status for lions. As in the 1970s, ranchers from West Texas flew to Austin for the committee hearing. They came dressed in a finery of flannel shirts, polished boots, flashing belt buckles. Environmentalists wore sandals and T-shirts emblazoned with images of mountain lions. The ranchers did not restrain themselves from voicing their opinions. "I can see," said the committee vice-chairman, "that for some people it would be a cold day in hell before they let any bill close to this pass." It was not a cold day. The bill died.

Texas knows very little about its lions. Three mountain lion workshops were held in the 1970s and 1980s; in the published proceedings, tables and bar graphs show Texas as blank fields and wide open spaces. The position responsible for mountain lions in the Texas Parks and Wildlife Department seems to be something of a hot seat, and occupants came and went rapidly during the first half of the 1990s. Whatever their personal opinions—some gave subtle signs of professional embarrassment about the lack of lion data—all dutifully echoed the agency line, which is that the cats are increasing in number and expanding in range. There was, therefore, no need to change the legal status of the lion. To buttress this position, a Parks and Wildlife staff report quoted the supporting opinions of three people closely acquainted with lions in Texas. One of them worked in livestock protection and another in wildlife research; both were supported in part by state funds.

The third was, in the finest Texas sense of the word, an independent citizen named Roy McBride. Lion hunter extraordinaire for ranchers and researchers alike, McBride was in his early fifties and already a legend. Conservationists, biologists, and ranchers all deferred to his field expertise, gleaned from more than thirty years of tracking lions in Texas and Mexico, wolves in Mexico, jaguars in South America, and leopards in Africa. McBride began his career at age twenty with a job as predator-control agent for the government. After more than a decade he quit to hire himself out directly to ranchers. He believed that ranchers ought to pay for solutions to their own problems. "Why should our tax dollars subsidize agriculture?" he said, when I was lucky enough to catch him by phone. "Why don't we have government weeders for our gardens, or government plumbers?"

It was McBride's great good fortune that just when lions were almost exterminated, endangering his job as lion killer, the environmental movement came along to place new value on living lions. Lion researchers began to seek out his services so that they could collar the lions he treed. Every year he flew with his hounds to Florida to track panthers. It didn't matter much to McBride whether the lion he was tracking was going to be shot or studied. It was the chase he was addicted to. He was interested enough in lions to earn a master's degree in wildlife science from Sul Ross

University in the small town of Alpine, in Big Bend country, where he lives. His thesis was entitled, *"The Status and Ecology of the Mountain Lion of the Texas-Mexico Border."* Rambling and vague, it hinted at the death from overheating of dozens of lions who were caught and darted; the lions then disappeared from the text. McBride noted the lengthy journeys undertaken by West Texas lions—sometimes more than a hundred miles— and felt that such movements were as much a nervous trait as an ecological safeguard against overhunting. Lion lives seemed to him nomadic and lonesome. His own life wasn't much different, although now he sometimes works with his sons Rocky and Rowdy. McBride greatly admired the hunting ability of lions and believed them quite capable of selecting the biggest, strongest buck, even when weaker deer were present. With people, he said, they were pussycats. Many times he crawled into caves harboring lions, which reacted only with growls.

His experience in Texas inspired McBride to formulate a theory on the fall and rise of the state's cats. "By the early 1960s, persistent lion control, mainly by sheepmen, had reduced the lion population through- out the entire state of Texas to less than two dozen animals, and those were mostly in West Texas," he said. "Without the influx of cats from Mexico, we'd have won the battle to eliminate the lion."

In his spare time McBride ran a few head of cattle. He did not care for sheep. "You can still see the scars that sheep grazing left on the land," he said. Nonetheless he invented and sold internationally a sheep collar containing a toxin, Compound 1080, to kill any predator unlucky enough to bite it. Sheep ranchers have historically been the lion's most virulent enemy and the most frequent users of government predator control. There are horror stories, true ones, in which a rancher in good lion country loses thirty sheep in a single night to a lion. Something in the domesticated stupidity of sheep causes them to mill around instead of fleeing when one of them is attacked. This is the antithesis of customary prey response and seems to charge up a lion's hunting instinct. In the overall picture, ranchers so hard hit are few in number. It's a matter of record that domestic dogs, feral hogs, and coyotes kill far more livestock in Texas than do lions. And despite the legal right to shoot lions at will, Texas sheep ranchers declined steadily after their peak production year of 1943. At that time, more than ten million sheep ruinously overgrazed much of Texas, particularly West Texas. Range depletion, tighter immigration controls that drove up labor costs, falling wool prices, and competition from New Zealand and Australia combined to bring the number below two million by 1990. This repeated an earlier pattern of high sheep numbers in the late 1800s, falling to around two million by 1920. "If wool growing comes back strong again," McBride said, "lions will be in trouble again. But for now lions have rebounded as far as they can. They're at carrying capacity in parts of their range. There's two dozen lions just in Big Bend National Park. There's no need to mess with lion status."

The belief that lion numbers were up, maybe higher than at any other time in the twentieth century, pervaded the West in the 1980s. It just made common sense that with bounties gone and sport killing regulated in most places, lions would repopulate old haunts. Some biologists simply had a gut feeling that lions were increasing. State wildlife agencies have traditionally assumed that the number of lions killed by hunters and livestock owners represents a stable proportion of the lion population. When the number of lions killed goes up, as it did in the 1980s in several western states, wildlife managers conclude there must be more lions out there to kill. Snowy winters that make lions more vulnerable to tracking, droughts that push deer and the lions that follow them into unfamiliar and therefore dangerous territory, new roads that open up previously inaccessible lion habitat to hunters, electronic aids that make hunters more efficient—all these influences are entirely omitted from the formula.

Nor is there much field evidence to confirm gut feeling. No state undertakes the periodic track and sign counts that Arizona researcher Harley Shaw advocates, and without monitoring lion populations, managers don't really have a clue about what's happening in the field. In Texas, Parks and Wildlife points to rising numbers of sightings, and sightings in areas where lions haven't been seen in decades. An official report plots on a map of Texas a recent decade's worth of sightings by county as an indication of lion range, but most lion researchers dismiss lion sightings as worthless. Harley Shaw once said of them, "After years of chasing UFOs—unidentified furry objects—I now discount out of hand any sightings of lions, even from professional biologists. The human mind is a strange and wonderful thing, and it's totally unreliable."

Body counts are more concrete. Another official Texas map plots the same decade's worth of lions killed in Texas by county, which causes lion range to shrink considerably from the sightings map. But the body count is suspect, too. The only reliable numbers come from the Animal Damage Control program, heir of Roosevelt's Bureau of Biological Survey. Texas has the largest ADC program in the country. Its trappers respond to landowner complaints of losses to lions by bagging several dozen cats annually. Other kills—by landowners acting on their own, hunters, and motorists—are reported sporadically, voluntarily, and in no statistically reliable way. And even dead cats can deceive. Three lions were shot in separate incidents in 1991 in the Pineywoods ecological region of East Texas, where wild lions hadn't been documented since the turn of the century. "This supports the consensus of staff that lion range is slowly expanding in the northern and eastern areas of Texas," a Parks and Wildlife report stated. "However," the report continued, "staff recognizes that these lions were possibly released from captivity." A declawed lion had been killed in the Pineywoods two years earlier. The market for pet wild felids is a booming and—not surprisingly—a largely unregulated business in Texas. Inevitably, some owners of lions grown beyond the cute kitten stage can't cope with them and release them somewhere out of sight.

One such cat mauled an eight-year-old boy in Big Bend National Park in 1984, the first recorded mountain lion attack on a person in a national park (another occurred in Glacier National Park in 1990). The child required several episodes of plastic surgery to smooth his scratched face. The cat was immediately tracked and shot. Soft, uncallused foot pads and unusually white teeth testified to the former captive status of the young male. He was scrawny, driven by hunger but betrayed by lack of hunting experience. Park management began to distribute information to park visitors warning of danger from lions. A sign along the scenic road to the main visitor's center portrayed a lion in silhouette and advised hikers to check with rangers. It quickly became the most photographed feature of the park. In 1986 a couple and their small child were walking in the Chisos Mountains when the husband saw a lion approaching. He followed park advice by picking up his child and standing his ground. His wife panicked and did the one thing she had been advised by park literature not to do: she ran, triggering the cat's instinctive spring. Her wounds were superficial. This lion was killed, too. He was a member of the most dangerous category of lions—wild, adolescent males, rash and brash in many species.

Park managers felt the need for data and offered to subsidize field work for a master's thesis by the young woman who would analyze those brightly lit tracks in Cottonwood Creek. It was a tightly focused study, designed to identify lions that were likely to attack people. The majority of attacks and other lion encounters had occurred in the Chisos Basin. Almost half of all the people that visit the park come to the basin, which offers a campground, lodge and gift shop, restaurant, web of trails, and nearby at Panther Junction, the visitor's center and park headquarters. Most of the other visitors concentrate on the Rio Grande. For nearly two hundred miles it is a designated Wild and Scenic River, cutting through elegant red and white canyons that are occasionally closed to visitors to allow endangered peregrine falcons to rear young in peace. Some people come for the extraordinary birding: 407 documented species, more than any other national park in the country.

The Chisos Basin comprises about sixty-thousand acres, less than one tenth of the park's total. Year-round water is available at Oak Spring. Basin soils have an underlying clay layer that holds water far longer than desert soils, yielding lush green grasses when drought parches other areas. Several inches more rain fall in the Chisos than the average thirteen inches at lower elevations. Sewage lagoons contribute a permanent standing pool. In short, some of the most intense human use of the park occurs in the most ecologically rich area of the Chisos Mountains, which are themselves an island of lush habitat in the surrounding desert. It came as no surprise to find that deer liked the basin, especially during dry seasons. Del Carmen white-tailed deer are common in the Chisos, roaming the pine-oak-juniper forests above forty-five hundred feet. At their lowest range they mingle with tough and hardy mule deer that inhabit the desert. Javelina also use the basin heavily, as do skunks. All those species are important lion food. Because prey is so plentiful and the hunting so good, with thick plant cover providing plenty of ambush sites, lion ranges are smaller in the Chisos and seem to overlap more than in the desert.

During the two years of the study, the basin was occupied primarily by one female lion and her litter. They used the basin most during dry seasons, and again when the kittens were ready to become independent. Another female with a neighboring home range also shifted into the basin when her kittens were ready to disperse. The study concluded that the plentiful prey probably made the basin a prime dispersal site. During the study there were several lion incidents, including a lunge on a pet dog leashed in a basin campground. A hiker spent the night in a tree while a mother lion and two large kittens prowled around beneath him. One lion climbed up the tree, to be met with a kick, but none of the lions so much as took a swipe at the hiker, who described them as "polite but curious." For the most part, the researcher exonerated adult lions. It was a very small proportion of the young ones, and mostly the dispersing males, perhaps desperate with hunger, that were likely to overcome their fear of humans.

The study concluded with management options to deal with the potential of lion attacks. Park employees could be discouraged or prohibited from owning pets, whose food and water attract skunks and javelina, and from watering lawns, which entice deer by the dozen into the midst of the residential area. Children could be discouraged from walking alone at night or playing in drainages and rock piles. Perhaps there should even be a curfew for children, because their small size and irrepressible motion make them the most vulnerable targets for lion attacks. Garbage should be more carefully contained, not because lions raid it but because it attracts lion prey. Like employees, visitors could be discouraged or prohibited from bringing pets into the park. The student conducting the research observed dogs illegally off their leashes on several back-country trails; one was chasing a small herd of javelina. As part of an overall visitor-education program, parents could be advised not to let children roam unattended. Hikers could be warned about traveling solo and during dawn, dusk, or at night, when lions were most active. Some trails might be restricted to adults or altogether closed when high-risk lions were present. Except for the emphasis on children, measures such as these were common in many parks where bears, buffalo, elk, or other large wildlife posed occasional threats to people.

Funds were tight, black bear incidents began to upstage lion attacks, and lion research in the park ceased. In the meantime, the state was doing some lion work of its own. Black Gap State Wildlife Management Area, which lies east of the Park, in the 1970s hosted an attempt to restore native bighorn sheep. Lions killed so many that the project was moved. A subsequent project at Black Gap consisted of killing lions and coyotes and measuring the response of mule deer. Mule deer had declined in much of the West through a series of droughts in the 1970s until the mid-1980s, when they seemed to stabilize. The Black Gap study was a dismal failure. After years of surveys there was disagreement within Parks and Wildlife about the numbers of mule deer, much less the impact of lion predation. New waterholes had been dug, muddying the data by adding a highly influential factor for deer survival.

West of the park, Parks and Wildlife staff at Big Bend Ranch State Natural Area began in the early 1990s to collar and track lions. The Sierra Club protested that the study's goals and methods were too vague to produce usable data and sent copies of the study proposal to other wildlife researchers, who agreed. Eventually Parks and Wildlife asked Kenny Logan in New Mexico and Harley Shaw in Arizona for advice on handling lions in the desert. (Parks and Wildlife also inaugurated a lion study in the brushlands of South Texas, one that the Sierra Club applauded.) During all this controversy over how to study the lions at Big Bend Ranch, a decision on whether simply to eliminate them was pending. There was political pressure to make deer hunting a featured attraction at the ranch.

Deer are dear in West Texas. Sometimes they bring more per head than cattle, when a hunter pays a thousand dollars or more to ride around a fifty-thousand-acre ranch for a few days. Parks and Wildlife has a landowner assistance program that includes advice on wildlife management. Losing deer to lions is a concern voiced to Parks and Wildlife staff. If the landowner has already improved deer habitat as much as possible, staff might advise lion control. The landowner has to pay for it, has to hire a hunter like Roy McBride, but if that's what they want, they can get it. Private landowners own ninety-six percent of Texas, and what they want drives the use of the land. It is conventional wisdom that landowner attitudes will govern the future of wildlife in Texas.

When the formation of Big Bend National Park in 1944 inaugurated the unusual complex of public land in West Texas, the small towns in the region welcomed it: tourism promised to boost a depressed economy. But ranchers there cursed their bad luck. To them the park was a permanent breeding sanctuary, out of which lions would forever wander.

There's something about the Chihuahuan desert that makes you want to wander. Maybe it's the challenge of maneuvering the small, empty spaces that form convoluted paths through plants that stab or slice any reachable body part. Maybe it's the slowly unfolding deception of the place. Flat, seemingly desolate expanses turn out to be riven with canyons small enough to clamber into but wide enough for easy traveling along the wash. Following washes, lions have been known to travel the thirty miles from the Chisos to the Christmas Mountains in a single night. The Christmas Mountains rise just beyond the northwestern park border. Looking south from them, the Chisos loom charcoal gray with red tones so deep you could drown in them, as a lion did years ago in one of the natural stone bowls of rainwater called tinajas.

Slopes of green cactus and scrappy piles of red rimrock give the Christmas Mountains a festive look. Somewhat drier than the Chisos, they nonetheless offer an oasis in the surrounding desert. Until the early 1990s, when they were purchased by a mysterious entity—to be annexed, rumor had it, to the park when the political climate was right—the Christmas Mountains were part of Terlingua Ranch Resort. The name refers to three languages—Spanish, Comanche, and English. A ghost town of the same name not far away bears silent witness to the quicksilver mining that yielded a hundred thousand flasks of mercury between 1900 and 1941. Every cottonwood tree for miles around was felled for mine timbers; every deer glimpsed was shot for miners' food.

Selling off the Christmas Mountains left Terlingua Ranch with just over two-hundred-thousand acres, bought by a corporation from ranchers in the 1960s. Much of the land was subdivided into lots and sections, average size forty acres. About thirty-thousand acres were held out for hunting preserves. Only a few hundred of the five thousand or so owners actually live on their properties. Many come just for hunting season; some, interested only in investment, have never set foot on the place. It is not an easy place to get to. The nearest supermarket is seventy-five miles away. At the turnoff to the resort, near a slum of mailboxes, a sign pleads: "Lodge 10 miles. Persevere." Abandoned shacks along the road, their tin coverings no longer pegged down, flap like broken-winged birds in the wind. Resort headquarters consists of a few stone houses and a handful of trailers, a motel, and a restaurant. In the dusty parking lot, a large wire enclosure holds aluminum cans for recycling. The office was hazy with cigarette smoke when I dropped in. Reba, the receptionist, wore a huge platinum mound of sticky hair. Her eyelids exploded like firecrackers, all color and glitter. The general manager at the time was a large man from Baltimore named Bill Palmisano, whose fancy Stetson had fledged so many feathers it looked ready to fly. But it was handyman George Ellington, known as Geep, who really ran the place. Geep had been with Terlingua through many general managers and eventually took the position himself. His eyes were the sharp merciless blue of a desert morning. He sat down in an overstuffed chair upholstered in Naugahyde, pulled a big Buck knife from a sheath at his belt and began to clean his fingernails.

"I guess I killed a couple dozen lions in the eighties," he said. "I go after them when I think there's too many. They go right along with the deer herd. One of the signs is porcupines. When owners start complaining about porcupines, I know there aren't many lions around, because lions will eat them up. But we haven't seen porcupines around here in three or four years. Lions must be moving out of the park again." He neatly flicked away a paring. "I wouldn't be against making lions a game animal. Just so long as ranchers can control them on their own land."

One of the best-known ranchers in West Texas lived a short distance east of Terlingua Ranch across a narrow part of Big Bend National Park. I heard about Mrs. Stillwell as soon as I started talking to people in West Texas about mountain lions. She lived in a trailer next to the Stillwell Store. Her daughter ran the store, which encompassed an RV park, gas station, laundromat, tent campground, and guiding services for fishing in the Rio Grande, as well as scenic horseback and jeep tours. It also held some whitewashed shelves of canned goods. When I met her, Mrs. Stillwell was two years older than the twentieth century, then entering its nineties. She had been born in eastern Texas, but her father, whom she revered as a "natural-born pioneer," moved west in stages until he finally settled in Alpine, because there were schools for his children. He disapproved of her fiancé, who was twenty years older than she, and who occasionally drank and gambled. Hallie eloped anyway, in 1918. In her autobiography, she writes of her relief when her family accepted her husband and "never treated him any worse than any other member of my family."

Once married, Hallie left off schoolteaching to saddle up every morning and ride herd like one of the cowboys on her husband's cattle ranch. They couldn't leave her alone in the one-room ranch house because of the deadly marauding of Pancho Villa. It was a year or two before Hallie could get a bedroom added on to the ranch house. She made curtains for it out of flour sacks. She longed for a porch but was afraid to make such an extravagant request and settled for an arbor. It was her pride to keep the dirt floor under the arbor swept clean and moistened with water for coolness.

Hallie admired her husband and his men and wanted their approval. She slept on the trail when necessary and learned to throw, rope, and tie cattle. When the mother cows bawled piteously as their calves were taken away, she told herself, "That is the way it must be, I must not let it hurt, I must steel myself like the men do, cast those feelings aside, mount my steed and ride away." Her husband was so taciturn, even by the standards of West Texas, that she had to learn to read him like sign—the looseness of his posture on a horse, maybe the tilt of his hat. One of the times she could tell she pleased him the most was when she shot a mountain lion. The lion had killed a deer and her husband found the covered carcass.

"Would you like to kill a mountain lion?" he asked her.

"Yes, I sure would!" She rode out the next dawn. Her knees shook but she held her 30-30 steady enough to hit the lion between the eyes, and made a rug out of him.

Mrs. Stillwell was slow-spoken, gracious, and dignified. She wore a blouse with a big agate brooch at the throat, a sweatsuit jacket, skirt, nylons, and sneakers. She had on lipstick and rhinestone earrings. Her hands were as gnarled as the desert. She believed that she had come to love the harsh, arid land. "You've really got to work for what you have in this hard country," she said. "You've got to love it. We love the birds. I've almost gone broke buying birdseed for the quail, and now we're getting wild turkey."

After her husband was crushed by an overturning hay wagon, she managed the ranch with the help of her two sons. During the drought of the 1950s, she earned a much-needed salary as a reporter for various newspapers. Her comments on ranching brought her regional fame as a defender of traditional views.

"Don't get me on my soapbox about predators. You're a tourist, you don't have to make a livelihood on this country," she said softly, courteously. "My living depends on how many calves I send to market."

"How many calves have you lost to lions in your years of ranching?" I asked.

"None," she said. "That I know of. We've had lions to kill some saddle horses. Lion prefer deer to beef but would rather have horsemeat than anything. What are they good for? Coyotes eat some of the small rodents and help keep them down, that's the only thing I could see them do, but I don't see where the lion is important at all. They'd be just fine in a zoo. What right do they have to kill the beautiful deer and antelope I love to see? It's a shame for predators to kill all the good animals."

We were sitting on the porch of the store. A few vehicles passed. The landscape rolled away from us in a dusty blaze of noon, toward a horizon of rough, broken rocks brooding beneath their own shadows. Mrs. Stillwell stared out at them. "I'd just as soon not have a single lion in all this country," she said.

For the loss of a single lion from her Big Sur landscape, Margaret Owings ignited a revolution in California. She lit the fuse with a phone call in 1962. The explosion finally came in 1990, when California voters passed America's first citizen's initiative to ban trophy hunting of a traditional game animal. That animal was the mountain lion.

Margaret Wentworth was born in Berkeley in 1913 into a family that venerated trees. Her father was treasurer of the Save the Redwoods League. She married an architect, Nathaniel Owings, of national renown. He enjoyed talking to her so much in the evenings that instead of isolating herself in her studio, she set up her work in the living room. She was an artist in many media. Together they designed a house at Big Sur, on a point of land named after Captain Grimes, who in the nineteenth century had assiduously sought out and killed most of the few remaining sea otters for their commercially valuable pelts. The Owings's house was called Wild Bird. It perched six hundred feet above the ocean. A deck faced the sea and was cooled by breezes. Beneath the craggy cliffs, off the beaches of colored pebbles that shone like a rainbow with every wave, sea lions lived. A state proposal to reduce the sea lion population by 75 percent turned Mrs. Owings into an activist. The defense committee she put together included a Roosevelt and a Rockefeller, and her circle encompassed Rachel Carson, George Schaller, Henry Moore, and Georgia O'Keefe.

Writer Wallace Stegner described her as "tall and beautiful . . . a bearing that should make her seem reserved and unapproachable, but that only makes her regal . . . a woman acutely sensitive to natural beauty and friendly to wild things . . . And she is scared of nobody." The forces she set in motion defeated the proposal to kill sea lions. Sea otters entranced her, too, and she spent decades defending them against abalone fishermen and oil interests.

When she turned inland, Mrs. Owings faced the splendid rucked hills of the Coast Range. It was good land for lions. In the early 1960s she began to hear whistling noises in the canyon below the house, the sort of sounds, she learned, that a mother lion uses in conversation with her kittens. Once she heard them while walking her Pekinese, Muffet. The dog's hair stood straight up. The dust of the driveway was impressed with large-lobed, rounded, clawless prints. Mrs. Owings felt uneasy in the presence of a wildness that justifiably terrorized her little dog, but she also felt pleased. The idea of balance—in nature, in herself—was fundamental to her. She thought of mountain lions as glorious, magnificent animals. The lion disappeared and the local paper ran a story about the young man who had shot her. He was awarded a $60 bounty and acclaimed as a hero. "I was just sick to hear it, and I knew then it was going to make a change in the pattern of my life," Mrs. Owings told an interviewer from the University of California's regional oral history office in 1987, "because I was going to do something about it." She called her state senator, Fred Farr. Would he be willing to introduce a bill to remove the bounty on mountain lions?

Lions bounties in California originated with sixteenth-century Spanish Jesuits in the southern part of the state. To wean their Indians away from worship of a creature that ate the livestock the missions were trying to raise, Jesuits offered a bull for every puma killed. It was many years before Natives could be persuaded to kill the revered predators on whose success, signaled by buzzards, they had themselves subsisted. As in Texas, some Natives, particularly the Chumash and Yukats—whose drug of choice was jimsonweed—portrayed lions in their pictographs. California is a place of convergent realities: a student researching cougar history remarked on the striking similarity in style between those pictographs and high Californian street art of the late 1960s.

The state inaugurated a lion bounty in 1907 of $20 per puma, a handsome sum in those times. In 1917 the reward for a female lion was raised to $30; later, bounties for both sexes were raised again. A man could make a living killing pumas, and some did. Most notable among them was Jay Bruce. At the age of twelve he crippled his hand while playing with a bomb on the Fourth of July and ceased going to school. Instead, he went fishing. The hand that couldn't hold a pencil was fluent with a rod, and Bruce supplied as many trout as he could catch to whoever would buy until, alarmed by declining fisheries, the state passed a law prohibiting the practice. Bruce blamed great blue herons as the true destroyers of trout. He had begun hunting predators at age ten by shooting a bobcat and, with an older brother, in short order killed half a dozen foxes and bobcats. He figured that the squirrels he and his brother killed for their own table were merely one sixth of the three hundred squirrels those predators would have taken had they been allowed to live. This obsession with the economics of predation ruled him all his life. He called the mountain lion "the only predatory animal in California which is apparently of no economic benefit to the human race . . . but is simply a liability which probably costs the state a thousand dollars a year in deer meat alone to support each member of its lion population, or at the rate of $15,000 to maintain each lion during its natural existence." By this standard, applied to his own tally as bounty hunter and salaried state cougar hunter from 1910 to 1947, Bruce saved California something on the order of $10 million.

Margaret Owings's father heard about Jay Bruce while on a camping trip with his family and took his daughter to meet him. The lurid tales Bruce told of lions made the young girl glance fearfully at the boulders around her tent, but even so she felt sorry for the lions Bruce shot. "I was just born with this feeling," she told me, "of wanting to guard everything, the birds from the BB shots of boys, the wildflowers from being picked." When she decided to fight the lion bounty, she again put together a committee. Olaus Murie joined her, and her old friend Ansel Adams, and Joseph Wood Krutch, and David Brower. The Roosevelt she knew was Nicholas, who had been hunting in the Grand Canyon with his uncle Teddy when Teddy decided there were too many lions there. Nicholas Roosevelt had seen deer herds explode and starve after the predators were extirpated; he joined her committee. Mrs. Owings also invited Rachel Carson to join and asked her to write to one of the members of the state Fish and Game committee who supported the lion bounty for the love of beautiful deer. A note from Carson changed that member's vote. The bounty was rescinded. From 1907 to 1963, California had paid $389,345 for 12,461 lions.

Removal of the bounty was a victory, but Margaret Owings soon realized it was only a partial one. Pumas were classified as unprotected mammals and could still be hunted virtually without restriction. In 1969 California reclassified lions as game animals. The first regulated lion hunting season was held during the winter of 1970-71. Eighty-three lions were killed. A second season the next year resulted in the killing of thirty-five lions. These numbers fell considerably below the predictions of the California Department of Fish and Game, which had contended that lion populations were stable and could withstand hunting. To the conservationists assembled by Margaret Owings, it seemed clear that lion numbers were very low and getting lower. In 1971 they succeeded in gathering enough allies in the legislature to vote for a four-year moratorium on lion hunting, except for those lions that killed livestock. Fish and Game, which strongly opposed this threat to its management prerogatives, was directed to assess the state's population of lions.

In an echo of Jay Bruce's obsession with figures, the number of lions living in California became a topic of heated debate. Bruce, in fact, laid the foundation for the argument by calculating a total of 475 California lions in 1924, although his figure of 600 for a few years earlier is the one commonly remembered. With characteristic precision, Bruce divided the number of lions throughout the 21,600 acres that he considered prime puma habitat, which lay between 3,000 and 5,000 feet in elevation in the northern Sierra Nevada and Coast Ranges, and up to 7,500 feet in the southern mountains. "Some of these assumptions," a later Fish and Game report stated, "were obviously in error." The agency estimated 2,400 lions in 74,000 square miles of lion habitat in 1972, based on more than eight hundred interviews with former state-paid lion hunters, sport lion hunters, ranchers, sheep herders, houndsmen, game wardens, and others believed to be knowledgeable about pumas. Many of these people had an obvious interest in the continuation of hunting. Field investigations to verify the estimates consisted of observations of five sets of lion tracks. A person present during the fieldwork in Santa Barbara County said the investigator "never got out of the car the whole time he was here." A second Fish and Game study in 1974–76, conducted in 175 square miles of Coast Range in Monterey County, relied on individual houndsmen to capture lions during weekends, holidays, and whenever else they had time off from their jobs. Seventeen lions were collared over two and a half years; there were never more than eight animals being tracked at any one time. When the signals from some lions disappeared, the investigators assumed equipment failure instead of considering the possibility that the lions were transients rather than residents. This study concluded that the previous official estimate of lion numbers was, if anything, conservative.

There were some good data in the Fish and Game studies, but Margaret Owings was not much impressed. She secured funds from Defenders of Wildlife and the National Audubon Society to hire Carl Koford, a University of California wildlife researcher. For three years Koford analyzed lion bounty records, interviewed people, inspected habitats, and tracked cats in six types of habitat by car and foot along dusty roads, trails, passes, and ridges. His overall conclusion was that the total range where pumas were actually bearing young had shrunk below the 21,600 square miles estimated by Bruce in 1924. Koford believed there were fewer than a thousand lions in the state, though some of his colleagues felt he analyzed the data with a bias toward the lowest possible number.

With Koford's report as ammunition, Mrs. Owings worked to extend the moratorium on lion hunting. Often leaving home in the middle of the night, she logged an enormous number of miles driving back and forth to Sacramento for legislative hearings. When time ran short, or she needed to gather up scientists or sympathetic ranchers or other witnesses for a hearing, she would charter a small plane. Once she was caught with a novice pilot in a terrible storm near the Santa Cruz mountains. The plane dropped to twenty feet above the ocean. They flew along the coast, then turned into San Francisco Bay. Through dark, swirling tendrils of fog, Mrs. Owings saw the great lacework of the Bay Bridge above her. "Are you sure you are allowed to go under the Bay Bridge?" she asked the pilot. "Oh," he replied. "I didn't see it." Sometimes, after picking up four or six people in a single-prop plane and arriving in good time for the scheduled hearing, she would be told it had been postponed until the following week or canceled altogether. This was a favorite ploy to discourage those who traveled from afar.

It didn't work with Mrs. Owings. The legislature passed a series of moratoriums on lion hunting through the 1970s and into the 1980s. Mrs. Owings asked Robert Redford to write to the Chairman of the Fish and Game Commission—the only conservationist's letter that commissioner was ever known to answer. Her work so influenced Jimmy and Gloria Stewart that they persuaded Governor Ronald Reagan to sign a moratorium that he had planned to veto. In 1985, Governor Deukmejian did veto it. Fish and Game announced that cougars had increased to fifty-one hundred, give or take a thousand, and prepared to open a sport-hunting season. By this time the constituency for lions had grown large, organized, sophisticated, and determined. Environmental groups sued, citing the lack of data, and the season was postponed. Then they began to seek something more permanent than a moratorium. A lawyer and environmentalist named Bill Yeates, who had earlier drawn together a coalition of groups to work for lions, founded the Mountain Lion Preservation Foundation, with Margaret Owings as first chairman of the board.

When I visited it some years later, the foundation was located in a blue clapboard Victorian house in Sacramento. Beside the house stood an enormous, defoliated elm, with beetle holes in the trunk. The four-person office was on the second floor, above a mental health clinic where dazed people sat on wooden steps. The director, Mark Palmer, was a native Californian, a burly, bearded blond fellow in rumpled clothes who would have looked right in a pickup truck with a rifle rack. He was not ideologically antihunting; he had tried hunting ducks once, but it didn't appeal to him. Neither was the foundation ideologically opposed to all sport hunting—only to that of predators, on the grounds that it was biologically unnecessary and undesirable. When the lion moratoriums ended, Palmer, who was then on the foundation's board, helped direct efforts toward a ballot initiative to ban forever the sport hunting of mountain lions. The campaign was long and emotional. In brochures, fact sheets, advertisements, and videos, the foundation melded the mythic power of the lion as the last remaining symbol of California wilderness with scientific data that debunked old myths of lions as wanton killers. The foundation's mailing list totaled almost forty-thousand people. In June of 1990, 52 percent of voters passed the California Wildlife Protection Act. Known as Proposition 117, it prohibited sport hunting of lions and also required the state to dedicate at least $30 million annually, from already existing revenues, for the next thirty years on purchases of wildlife habitat for all species. Within a few years, as California's budget hemorrhaged, legislators began to look for ways to snatch away that $30 million, but revoking Proposition 117 altogether would require the consent of four fifths of the legislature or a whole new ballot initiative. For the moment, even Fish and Game conceded.

The Department of Fish and Game occupied a highrise a few blocks from the foundation, past a little park that I had been advised not to stroll through even in the daytime. The official most closely concerned with lions was a tall, pencil-thin, very handsome and elegant man named Terry Mansfield. In his pin-striped suit and red-checked tie, with a gold pen clipped to his pocket, Mansfield would have looked right as a lawyer for some affluent environmental organization. He had been born and raised in the Central Valley and joined Fish and Game during the first lion moratorium. He felt that Proposition 117 had been sold through emotional extremes. He was frustrated at having his hands tied in dealing with lions. Worst of all, Mansfield said, as lion populations grew unchecked, threats to human property and safety could only increase.

Requests to kill lions that killed livestock soared from a dozen per year in the early 1970s to a couple of hundred per year in the late 1980s, when they leveled off. Most incidents involved goats and sheep, but pets were also fair game. A woman looked out her back sliding door and saw a mountain lion jumping over the fence with the family dog in his mouth. Another homeowner looked out to see a lion eating a Doberman next to the Jacuzzi. Dogs let out at night never returned, and lion tracks were seen on dusty road shoulders. A few nights before I spoke with Mrs. Owings, she had let in her Pekinese and miniature Yorkie just as something crashed through the garden gate, ripping it from its hinges. She felt sure a lion had been stalking the dogs through the yard. "A lion would love to eat them," she said. "That's not a criticism."

In Calimesa, a puma put muddy pawprints on a picture window, looking for a way in after the housecat that had been sunning there. Finally he tore through a window screen and chased the cat around the living room. Vases and furniture were upended and the walls were soiled. The lion escaped but the report neglected to mention whether the housecat did. California has a huge number of feral housecats, and Mansfield thought it possible that lions could pick up new diseases from eating them. But since lions didn't meet the criteria for endangered or threatened programs or generate money through hunting licenses, he couldn't justify spending money to research such matters.

More sensational than attacks on pets are attacks on people. In 1986 lions attacked two children in separate incidents in Caspers Regional Wilderness Park, a seventy-six-hundred-acre enclave in the Santa Ana foothills owned by Orange County. A five-year-old girl was watching tadpoles in a creek when a cougar dragged her into the bushes. A cougar suspect was tracked and shot and proved to be a young male in good health, but there was no proof that he was the culprit. The child was blinded in one eye and partially paralyzed. About six months later a lion seized a six-year-old boy who had lagged behind his group of play-mates to crouch down and tie his shoe. That lion was never caught. The boy suffered multiple lacerations on his head, chest, and back. Officials closed the park for several months. When it opened again, they barred minors from most trails and required adults to sign waivers of liability before entering. The parents of the little girl sued the county for know-ingly harboring a dangerous animal without giving adequate warning. A jury ruled in their favor, awarding damages of $2 million. The park launched an appeal, which succeeded in reducing the settlement slightly. At least one politician called for the elimination of all lions from the park, but many voices rose in defense of lions and the rightful role of risk in wild places.

The controversy caught the attention of wildlife scientist Paul Beier, then at the University of California at Berkeley. Beier compiled and analyzed a list of all documented cougar attacks on humans in the United States and Canada from 1890 to 1990. In the course of that century, ten people had been killed in unprovoked attacks by mountain lions, and forty-eight were injured. For perspective, Beier reported that two dozen people are killed *every year* by dogs, two-hundred-thousand are injured badly enough in canine attacks to require stitches, a dozen people are killed by rattlesnakes, three or four dozen by bee stings, and nearly a hundred by lightning. Most lion victims were children who were either alone or with other children; all fatalities (except for one adult who died from rabies carried by the lion rather than from the wound itself) were children unaccompanied by adults. Most adult victims were alone. A few of the attacking lions had dramatically invaded human space, one crashing through the window of a cabin, another loping into a garage. Many of the cougars were promptly shot, and the few facts recorded about some of them suggested that they were less than two years old and perhaps underweight. In ten cases, no cat was caught, and within two years three more attacks had occurred within fifty miles of the earlier incidents. Beier interpreted this as weak evidence that a cougar that attacked a human once might do so again.

Hikers in Yellowstone and Glacier national parks who encounter grizzly bears are advised to stay quiet, avoid eye contact, fold up into a fetal position, and play dead. The opposite is true for mountain lions. Beier found that victims who fought back, yelling and beating the cougar away with sticks or rocks or anything close to hand, or even just with hands, were usually able to drive the cougar away. Those that played dead, went limp from shock, or ran away fared much worse. Stance seems to be important. Children, because of their small size, and adults who bend over or sit down, making themselves smaller and placing their necks within easy reach, probably appear more like prey than those who stand upright. Another important factor seems to be eye contact. Cougars and other wild cats, which attack from the side or rear, can be stalled by a direct stare. Staring a lion down might sound like folklore, but a number of people who have skirmished with cougars reported that the cats moved quickly toward them when they broke eye contact. In India, where tigers kill about sixty people every year, woods workers wear face masks on the backs of their heads to confuse the great cats.

There were more attacks by lions from 1970 to 1990 than in the eighty previous years. Cougars need to be hunted, for bounties or for trophies, to keep them afraid of humans! So went the clamor in hunting magazines. The catch in this argument is that more than half of all the lions that attacked humans did so in British Columbia, where hunters kill hundreds of lions every year. By far the greatest concentration of attacks has been on Vancouver Island. Some of Beier's colleagues speculated that the island's lack of small prey, like porcupines and rabbits, makes young cougars, who rely heavily on such creatures while learning to hunt bigger prey, more desperate for food. Others wondered whether the very intensity of cougar hunting on Vancouver Island—which has the largest number of women cougar hunters I've ever run across—had winnowed out the more passive lions, leaving cougars that were willing to kill dogs and rake humans to escape being hunted. Maybe different regional lion populations have different learned behaviors, or maybe there is some kind of genetic difference. Maybe the loss of wolves and grizzly bears from most of their habitat is making cougars cocky. The only certainty is that more and more people are pushing into the wild places where cougars live. Incidents occur most often on the fringes of suburbia, along what is termed the urban-wildland interface. Confusion and concern prompted the fourth workshop on pumas in fifteen years, a symposium on mountain lion-human interactions, held in Colorado in 1991. A few months before it convened, a lone male jogger was killed by a lion on a trail less than a mile from his high school in Idaho Springs, Colorado. There was speculation that he had stopped and bent down to tie his shoe. A few of the conference participants called for more trophy hunting to keep cougars in line, but most felt differently. Most wanted to educate the public on coexisting with cougars, through commonsense control of pets and children.

In 1909 two people in California died from rabies inflicted by cougar bites. There were no other cougar-related deaths in that state until 1994, but in that year there were two. One was a marathon runner, a 120-pound woman, killed while running along a trail in a state recreational area just west of Sacramento. There were signs of a brief scuffle. The woman had been partially eaten and buried under leaves. A week later an 82-pound nursing female cougar was shot very close to the spot. Tissues with the runner's DNA were found in the cougar's anus. One six-week old kitten was discovered. No one could read from the signs whether the woman had stopped to tie her shoe, or whether the cougar mother had perceived some sort of threat to her young. A friend of the deceased runner started a trust fund for the two young children left motherless, which in a couple of weeks accumulated about $9,000 in donations. At the same time, the nearby Folsom City Zoo pledged $15,000 from an existing account to house the orphaned cougar cub, received a promise from a single anonymous donor for an additional $5,000, and collected about $2,000 from individual contributors.

Newspapers across the country reported that the cougar's account was more than double the children's fund. Nationally syndicated radio talk-show host Rush Limbaugh jumped at the opportunity to excoriate animal-rights wackos for their repugnant priorities. Listeners from every state and from Canada and New Zealand responded with outrage and cash; the bank refused to release exact figures but acknowledged that the children's trust fund had risen to six figures. Limbaugh did not respond to letters and phone calls from the Folsom zookeeper explaining the situation, including the fact that no animal-rights people were involved. With much less fanfare, Safari Club International, National Rifle Association, and livestock groups used the woman's death to lobby for two bills challenging Proposition 117. The bills didn't make much headway, but it became clear to those who had worked for Proposition 117 that what had seemed like a final victory over trophy hunting was in fact far from irrevocable. And cougar attacks kept happening: one headline, in a variation of the man-bites-dog story, read "Woman Knifes Mountain Lion." The article described the third case in American history of a rabid cougar attacking a human. Another story reported the death from bites to the head of a fifty-eight-year-old woman watching birds in Cayamaca Ranch State Park. The adult male cougar killed in retribution had ingested human hair. In yet another incident, echoing the old stories of attacks on horseback riders, a mountain biker in 1995 fended off a lion in Angeles National Forest; the presumed attacker was tracked and shot.

Paul Beier had been hired by Orange County and the state of California after the two 1986 maulings of children in Orange County to do a detailed study of cougar ecology in the Santa Ana Mountains. I sat in the audience at Northern Arizona University in Flagstaff, to which Beier had recently moved, when he gave a seminar on his work. Dressed in a purple Hawaiian print shirt, bald on top with flyaway hair, he was, I thought, too conspicuous to be a cougar man. The cougar men I knew liked protective cover. And in fact Beier was finished with cougars. He found it too difficult to get funding to continue studying them. In the five years that he followed them, though, lions vouchsafed to him some startling secrets. Beier radio-collared a total of thirty-two lions in eight-hundred square miles of chaparral, oak woodlands, coastal sage scrub, conifer forest, grasslands, and orange and avocado orchards west of Interstate 15 between Route 76 and Route 60. The study area abutted seventeen incorporated cities. Beier showed slides of endless housing tracts, with a single green ravine or tiny remnant creek bottom threading through them. He would point to a spot in the ravine or along the creek and say, "There's a cougar."

These were dispersing yearlings; one of Beier's goals was to examine their travels. He followed eight young males and a female. They hunted in terrain avoided by adult cougars. With adults established in the more secluded and preferred interior portions of the habitat, dispersers wandered almost inevitably toward the edges of suburbia. All came within three hundred feet of urban areas and heavily used parklands. One spent several hours trying to get around a noisy and well-lighted silica factory. A young male daybedded in an oak grove between exits on I15, where tens of thousands of motorists clogged the freeway within six hundred feet of him on Christmas Eve. Not one person reported seeing him. Another male hunted for several nights and bedded during the days in some small canyons below a busy construction site, without incident. The young female followed a finger of remnant vegetation to within earshot of hammering carpenters framing new houses. Dozens of people and machines surrounded her all day long; she had to wait until dark to unobtrusively extricate herself. A male was hit by a car and survived for six months with one front and one rear leg broken and a dislocated hip. He moved hardly at all and killed 'possums and raccoons in a small area of intense human use. During that time he was briefly glimpsed only twice, and never showed aggression toward people or pets. This was typical cougar behavior. Beier concluded that Santa Ana lions were remarkably adept at avoiding humans and could hardly be more reclusive.

The presence of roads posed enormous risks to cougars. Four of the nine young dispersers died on roads before they could find a place to settle down; a third of all cougar deaths during the study were caused by cars and trucks. There are thirty-two million people in California. Only in Florida, where a similar tidal wave of people is surging into formerly undeveloped places, are roads such a menace to pumas. Half of California is publicly owned land, so there are many good core refuges that can each support a few cougars, but those cores must remain connected for necessary emigration and immigration to take place. Roads are severing these vital connections. Cougars either die trying to cross or are altogether prevented from crossing by the incessant traffic and human sprawl associated with roads. When small core areas become isolated from other cores, cougars die out. That's what happened to the San Joaquin Hills. The hills offer relatively pristine woods and plenty of prey. Cougars lived there from time immemorial until the 1980s, when a ribbon of urban growth thickened into a three-mile belt between them and other refuges. Beier searched intensively for cougars there but found no trace. He believes that they might have been saved by fenced, unlighted undercrossings lined with native vegetation and situated along known animal travel routes.

At the northern end of the Santa Ana Range, Beier tracked cougars moving back and forth to the Chino Hills through box culverts and a vehicle underpass under Route 91 at the mouth of Coal Canyon. It was the last remaining wildlife corridor between the two ranges. The city of Anaheim approved a combined residential and commercial development on 663 acres in Coal Canyon, with the stipulation that more lanes be added to Route 91. There were no stipulations for a viable wildlife corridor. The Mountain Lion Foundation had by then dropped "Preservation" from its name and broadened its mission to habitat protection in general. It joined with other environmental groups and even the Department of Fish and Game in a lawsuit over Coal Canyon. Not just pumas but a dozen rare plant and animal species were jeopardized by loss of the connection. This was one of the first lawsuits over a wildlife corridor, and it was lost. The foundation resigned itself to more long-term battles: an appeal of the court's decision and a petition to the U.S. Fish & Wildlife Service to list the Santa Ana lions as an endangered population under the Endangered Species Act.

There was one very unexpected dimension of Beier's study. Female Santa Ana lions behaved differently from those in other studies. A lion mother found the body of her son where researchers had left it. (The young male had been treed by domestic dogs, fell out of the tree when darted, hit his head on a planter box, and died a week later; Beier could find no skull or neck injuries to explain his death.) The lion's mother tore a strip of muscle away but did not eat it. She covered the body with grass and leaves in the typical cougar fashion but did not return to feed on it. For the next three days she bedded within 750 feet. She died two weeks later not far away; Beier suspected a disease caught from the son's body, but could identify no pathogen to prove it. Another female was blue eyed, had an unusually large home range, and was never seen with cubs or even consorting with a male. Four out of twelve adult females failed to reproduce. This sort of thing had never been previously reported. Beier duly noted that it made the extinction risk higher.

Strangest of all, adult female cougars met regularly, and on many occasions pairs of them remained close together for several days. Sometimes they traveled together. These visits occurred in twenty- to twenty-two-day cycles, perhaps reflecting synchronous estrus among neighboring females. Bears are known to sometimes synchronize their cycles, as are women who work or live together. The lions vocalized a lot, by screaming, yowling, and calling hoarsely when they were near each other. Over the decades of cougar observation, there have been a few reports of females socializing, but nothing like this. When it comes to social experiments, Californians set the trends.

THE FLORIDA
PANTHER PEOPLE

TWO SQUEALS AND A GRUNT. THIS WAS UNMISTAKABLE PIG TALK, NOT IN barnyard dialect but in accents of the wild, the subtropical wilds of South Florida. I heard them, though not a blade of grass stirred in the red-brown prairie sweeping before me, not a leaf shivered on the shrubs that made a green island in the middle. Wild pigs are wily creatures. One of the few living things to escape the clutches of Spanish conquistadors, European pigs fled into the flat, watery savannas that defeated the Spanish, French, English, and until almost the mid-twentieth century, even the Americans. Tasty and remarkably fertile, feral pigs in an almost inaccessible landscape maintained panthers in South Florida for more than a century after they were believed exterminated in eastern North America.

The eastern races of the cougar had mostly disappeared by the 1890s, when hunter-naturalist Charles Cory wrote about his subtropical chases. He described the small feet and more rufous coloring that later helped establish the Florida panther as the cougar subspecies *Felis concolor coryi.* He wrote then that the animal was "not uncommon in the unsettled portions of the state." By 1946, when Stanley Young and Edward Goldman published their classic compilation, *The Puma, Mysterious American Cat,* the Florida panther's former range from eastern Texas to South Carolina had been reduced to isolated parts of South Florida. But by then, the shift in attitudes that had started in earlier decades and was so eloquently expressed by Aldo Leopold had taken hold in Florida. In the 1950s, it became one of the first states to enact legal protection for mountain lions. Federal protection came in 1973 with the Endangered Species Act, which listed the Florida panther as an endangered subspecies. In that same year, the World Wildlife Fund brought Texan Roy McBride and his hounds to Florida. They treed one cat, proving that panthers still existed, a fact which had been doubted by many. In 1976 the Florida Audubon Society sponsored a conference to pull together the little information that existed on Florida panthers. Shortly afterward, the U.S. Fish and Wildlife Service inaugurated a cooperative state and federal recovery program.

This was the start of a decades-long epic of institutional ambivalence. Personnel and philosophies of four agencies meet in excruciatingly slow and politically choreographed motion. The U.S. Fish and Wildlife Service has jurisdiction over federal endangered species programs; the National Park Service manages a large chunk of panther habitat in South Florida; the Florida Game and Fresh Water Fish Commission is responsible for wildlife management throughout the state; and the Florida Department of Environmental Protection identifies and acquires habitat for sensitive species. Committees, subcommittees, task forces, and working groups meet endlessly to formulate and implement a recovery plan. All this costs more than a quarter of a million dollars annually in federal money and roughly as much in state money. The goal: to save the last few disease-ridden, parasitized, incestuous Florida panthers squeezed between the relentless westward reach of Miami and the eager eastward grasp of Naples.

From three-thousand feet in the air, the land east of Naples looked like a geometric jigsaw puzzle. Rectangles, squares, and trapezoids were outlined by drainage canals and roads. Clots of buildings suddenly dissipated to a few houses in every block, as if the city had flung itself beyond its own reach and was regrouping for another thrust. Then hard-edged shapes softened into the circles formed by cypress domes, and straight lines began to wander between islands of trees and expanses of prairies. Forest canopy thickened to the east; when the plane tilted, a sheen of water revealed it to be the type of wooded swamp called a strand. A state biologist in the front seat, who was listening intently to earphones, made a hand signal. The pilot tipped onto a wing, cut the motor, and—in a nasty ambush on my stomach—fell, spiraling, to five-hundred feet, then started the motor and began to circle. Directly below, hidden beneath maple leaves in the Fakahatchee Strand, dozed one of the twenty-one panthers that were radio-collared at the time. Every winter, Roy McBride and his hounds look for any panthers not yet collared, and all collared panthers are monitored by plane several times a week, year-round. The biologist plotted a point on the map, the plane rose, and the searching and spiraling continued.

Few animals anywhere in the world have been as intimately studied, at least on a biological if not on a behavioral level, as the thirty to fifty Florida panthers remaining in the wild. The early years were spent gathering basic information, such as how many panthers there were and their age and sex. Then the health and genetic condition of the cats emerged as crucial. Field workups on every panther tranquilized came to include nasal, rectal, vaginal, oral, aural, and skin samples for tests, electroejaculation of males for the frozen sperm bank, and various vaccinations. Differences from western cougars began to show up. Female Florida panthers reach sexual maturity at an average age of eighteen months—quite a bit earlier than other cougars. Adult male Florida panthers claim some of the largest territories yet documented for any mountain lions—up to four hundred square miles in the wettest and, for panthers, poorest habitats of the Everglades. Even in that vast space, the few remaining males fight and sometimes kill each other. It was clear from radio locations that family members were mating in the absence of other partners. Blood and tissue analyses revealed that mercury poisoning in the Everglades had killed at least one panther and was probably debilitating others.

It was even known that when biologists were sweating through a 103-degree-Fahrenheit day, the panther they were after was likely to be hidden beneath head-high saw palmetto at a cool 77 degrees.

"Where is the panther while you're measuring the air temperature in the place he's just been?" I asked Dave Maehr in his Naples office, where he worked as director of panther field research for the Florida Game and Fresh Water Fish Commission. His job, with its authority to design studies and its intimate exposure to panthers, is the heart of the panther recovery project.

"He's out scouting for another daybed," Maehr said. Maehr's very blue eyes and sandy brown hair could have belonged to a surfer, but he was hardly a frivolous person. He had taken the job for the Florida panther project five years out of graduate school. Since then he had raised a family on a piney, pretty five-acre lot outside Naples that he left mostly to its own tangled self. He had radio-tracked a panther through his backyard. Once he had to have rabies shots against infection from a panther that died of the disease, only the second such death documented in North America at that time. From shelves on each side of him peered the animal skulls requisite in any self-respecting wildlife biologist's office. Closeup photos of Florida panthers in trees hung on every wall.

"I would estimate the disturbance of our work on panthers as nil, absolutely nil," Maehr continued, anticipating my question. "They might get walked in on once a month on the average, and the knowledge we gain from that is critical." Something in his tone suggested that he would be a difficult man to argue with. By his own definition, he was "an opinionated asshole." It was hard not to like someone who perceived himself so unabashedly, but he had critics who felt that his research amounted to harassment of panthers. There had been two acknowledged panther deaths caused by official fieldwork: one in the earliest days, when a panther was fatally overdosed with immobilizing drug, and another much later, when a fifty-pound youngster died from a bacterial infection that apparently resulted from handling during capture. Rumors constantly circulated about other, secret deaths. The criticism didn't bother Maehr, and he laughed out loud at the rumors. He knew that human disturbance was a tremendous factor in the lives of many panthers, but he also knew he wasn't causing it. The cause was the months-long disturbance called hunting season. When hunters and their dogs entered the woods, panthers went traveling.

The hunting of hogs and white-tailed deer has a long, strong tradition in South Florida. In the early 1940s it reached a point of frenzy, when hunters were paid to exterminate deer because deer hosted a life stage of a particular species of tick. The tick caused cattle fever. Cattle ranching, too, has a strong tradition in Florida. Deer were reduced to such low levels that the tick life cycle was broken. Panther numbers probably reached a corresponding low point when the deer nearly disappeared, and it was surely wild hogs that saved the cats from quietly starving to extinction. Hog populations seemed to remain relatively stable; deer were restocked. How many of those deer were available to feed panthers became an issue in the 1980s. As data accumulated, it became clear that panthers who fed mostly on deer and hogs were larger, healthier, and more successful at reproducing than panthers who lived on smaller prey, such as raccoons and armadillos.

Staff in several of the agencies, as well as members of the public who were following the project, questioned whether human hunters were killing so many deer that not enough were left for panthers. This was a discomfiting possibility for the State Game and Fresh Water Fish Commission, whose raison d'etre had always been to provide opportunities for human hunters. Managing deer for panthers turned the agency's mission on its head. One of the people who questioned hunting was an employee of the Commission; his career was shunted onto a side track, and he was eventually transferred away from field duties in South Florida. The Commission then accused the National Park Service, which administered Everglades National Park and Big Cypress National Preserve, of avoiding responsibility for improving those habitats for deer. The argument was that by removing the several kinds of exotic plants that crowded out natural deer food, seeding deer forage in appropriate spots, and burning more regularly to stimulate native grasses, deer would multiply because they would have more to eat. This strategy was firmly rejected by the National Park Service because it targeted specific species for manipulation and violated the holistic ideology of ecosystem management that was policy. The tug-of-war went on for years.

For most of the late 1980s, Dave Maehr and his team studied the deer herds in Big Cypress National Preserve. Massive mismanagement of water has devastated wildlife throughout South Florida and brought the Everglades ecosystem to the verge of collapse, but Big Cypress National Preserve, on the northwestern edge of Everglades National Park, is somewhat less vulnerable to destruction because it's higher and drier than the Glades. It is nonetheless stunningly flat. To say that the landscape of South Florida is not spectacular is to be kind. Imperceptible changes in elevation cause dramatic changes in vegetation, but to an uneducated eye it all looks like soggy fields and scraggly forests. Epiphytes sprout from trees in seemingly inappropriate places, like ear tufts or nose hairs. An educated eye recognizes many of them as rare orchids and perceives nearly a dozen different plant communities, including wet and dry prairies, pine flatwoods, groves of hardwoods (called hammocks), strands of jungly thickets, and cypress forests knee-deep in water. The best deer habitat in most of the region lies in the uplands of the preserve, in an area called Bear Island. Some of the last black bears in South Florida still hide out there. For a number of years a panther female raised her young there, giving birth in May and moving them away by fall, but on the whole there were fewer panthers than there should have been in that good habitat.

My husband and I camped at Bear Island several times, tucked away among cabbage palms and tent-stabbing saw palmettos. We walked through prairies where strands of a million spider webs floated like a gossamer carpet across the grasses, and through forests where the breeze rustled like small animals scurrying. Once, beside a puddle that reflected lingering twilight, we thought we saw a panther's footprint. Our hearts rose in our throats as we traced three lobes in the heel pad. Dusk was gathering in the bushy, contorted crowns of pines strung sparsely along the horizon, and guttural cries of birds filled the air. The hairs on the back of my neck prickled. "Our bodies pull the wilderness in," Enid Shomer wrote in her poem *Stalking the Florida Panther,* in her book of the same title.

Another visit was very different. To induce private landowners to sell to the preserve, the National Park Service agreed to allow the continuation of off-road vehicle travel. ORVs included homemade swamp buggies— a blend of tank and battleship—that could smash through the thickest clumps of saw palmettos and slog through foot-deep swampy mires. Mining and oil drilling were permitted, as were trapping and hunting. These last two activities were regulated by the state Game and Fresh Water Fish Commission. Combined seasons for all game ran from early fall through spring. The gun season for deer and hogs, which were by far the most popular game, ran from about mid-November through early January. Bear Island was the preserve's major game-checking station. A bulletin board there listed dozens of trophies: deer were small, averaging under a hundred pounds, but many hogs weighed over two hundred. A blood trail spattered the gravel road, dripped from a deer trundled on an ORV. Bear Island was, we realized as gunshots reverberated while we put up the tent, a traditional hunting camp. On top of that, it happened to be New Year's Eve. Stunned by our own stupidity, we considered driving the thirty miles of back roads to Everglades City for a motel, but realized we would arrive at the height of party time. No: we had made our beds, and now we pressed into them, figuring that a ground-level prone position was safest. ORVs prowled and growled all around us. Shrieks and whistles sounded like some raucous flock of Florida cracker birds roosting nearby. They were not the sounds of sobriety. Gunshots of many calibers punctuated the night. An artillery barrage announced the arrival of midnight, then slowly, very, very slowly, sputtered into silence.

No wonder the panthers moved out.

A few other researchers, mostly from Florida universities, continued to contend that deer were overhunted in Big Cypress, but Maehr concluded that hunters were not depleting the herds and that deer numbers were probably about as great as the landscape could support (unless, of course, managers burned more and planted food crops). The problem was not the deer; it was too many hunters spread over too much of the area for too long. Reluctantly, and in the face of clamorous opposition from hunters, the Game and Fresh Water Fish Commission over a period of years outlawed the use of dogs and reduced the number of combined hunting season days from 270 to 170. General gun season days went from 58 to 49. The National Park Service inaugurated ORV permits and a system of designated trails to consolidate traffic and avoid the best denning and laying-up places. After these changes had been in place for a few years, Maehr's team detected a female panther denned up only fifty yards from a designated trail. She gave birth at the start of hunting season.

"She didn't move away despite caravans of ORVs and people on horseback and even a prescribed fire that the Park Service set by mistake and that just missed turning three panther kittens into crispy critters," Maehr said. "Apparently she became acclimatized to noise that stayed predictably in the same place, the way herons and egrets hunting in roadside canals will ignore traffic. Maybe a balance has been reached." But no sooner had he said that when the argument erupted again over proposals to provide new access into the preserve from Interstate 75, only three air miles from the Bear Island campground.

With so many hunters and guns in the woods, panther advocates at first feared that poaching might be occurring on a large scale. Poaching later proved to be a problem for cougars reintroduced in northern Florida, but Maehr documented only two poached panthers in South Florida in more than a decade—exactly as many panthers as had died because of research efforts.

One of the poaching incidents occurred on the Big Cypress Seminole Indian Reservation. Indians had moved into Big Cypress Swamp in the late 1700s. They were Creek peoples from throughout the southeastern United States—the original range of the Florida panther—fleeing white settlers in the last remaining wildernesses. They built palm-thatched houses called chickees in hardwood hammocks. Like panthers, the Creeks, who became known as Seminoles and Miccosukees, were isolated in remote areas as whites pressed inexorably south. The Seminole Wars of 1817-1845 and the Indian Removal Act of 1830 reduced but did not eliminate the Indian presence in South Florida. The Big Cypress Reservation was created for the Seminoles in 1911, by executive order of President Taft; the Miccosukees weren't officially granted land until the 1960s. Small groups of traditionals from both tribes reject those compromises with whites and continue to live by the old ways outside the reservations. Distrust and dislike of whites continues strong. The Seminoles are periodically invited to participate in panther recovery project deliberations but rarely respond.

Southeastern Natives have traditionally placed a high value on panthers. One of the most arresting pieces of all Native American art is a wooden figurine from Marco Island off the Gulf Coast, dated to the fifteenth century. The features are unmistakably those of a panther, yet the animal sits on his haunches like a human, invoking the commonality of panthers and people. The carving came from the Calusa culture, which had died out from Spanish diseases before the Creeks entered Florida, but Creeks also had ideas about panther power. A story I heard on the Big Cypress Reservation, while sitting around a chickee campfire in a new, tribally owned tourist facility called Billie Swamp Safari, told how a panther caused illness in a village after noisy children had heedlessly scared the deer away.

During a nighttime hunting expedition with friends in 1983, Seminole chairman James Billie saw green eyeshine in a tree, and shot at it. He dressed the hide and draped it over a cypress tree, where a wildlife officer, who was apparently tipped off, found it the next day. Court proceedings were set in motion and resulted in a trial in 1987. James Billie's cousin and spokesman Sonny Billie called the panther "a most powerful medicine" whose hide, tail, and claws would be used in tribal ritual, but Billie himself testified that he had not shot the cat for religious purposes—that he had not, in fact, even thought about what he would do with the panther. The court reviewed the intricate legal history of Native sovereignty over hunting and fishing on reservation lands, and affirmed the protected status of panthers under the Endangered Species Act. But James Billie was acquitted when, after complicated courtroom discussions of subspecies definitions, the hide could not be shown to belong to a Florida panther rather than some other subspecies.

The purity of Florida panther genes was a touchy subject. At the beginning of the recovery project the official definition of the Florida panther included the white flecks around the head noted by Young and Goldman, plus a cowlick and a kinked tail. The white flecks were then found to be caused by tick bites, and cats began to turn up without the cowlick or the kinked tail.

"There's simply no such thing as a Florida panther," Frank Weed said, as we walked down a sandy path between cages of big cats. Weed made a living on large cats; he bred and sold them and made them perform for photographers. Many of the leopard, black leopard, and cougar pictures in glossy magazines were snapped through a hole in a protected wire enclosure in a large, naturalized cat run on Weed's property near Bear Island. Weed teased the cats across the ground with a feather on a string, or prodded them with a stick. He said he had supplied the three mixed-breed cougar skulls and skins that Billie's prosecutors could not distinguish from those of Florida panthers. He lived in a trailer on a tiny slope above the cages, with his wife and a shy bobcat. Photos, books, and videos about cats covered every flat surface. Housecats of all colors lay about everywhere, inside and out.

Weed was in his seventies and his face was worn and lined. He had been a vocal critic of the recovery effort for years. He spoke in a weary lecture tone, as if he had said it all many times before.

"There's reports of cats from all over the state. I think there's a good two hundred of them out there, not the thirty to fifty the state claims. People don't bother them now. They used to shoot them because they thought the cats ate too many deer, but I think that's stopped. People know panthers aren't hurting deer." He unlocked a gate and stepped into a cage. "Cougars are the most affectionate of the big cats," he said, petting a large, light-colored male named Morris behind the ears. Morris's response was an unmistakable meow.

Weed said he had never released new blood into the native panther population, but he knew people who had. At a place called Everglades

Wonder Gardens in Bonita Springs, a family named Piper raised more than half a dozen young panthers orphaned or found by hunters in the 1940s and 1950s. Some of these were bred to other cougars in the Piper collection, and seven of the offspring—referred to as the Piper stock— were released with approval into Everglades National Park in the 1950s and 1960s. And, with an estimated one thousand to two thousand captive pet cougars in Florida, it was a safe bet that some of their owners got tired of caring for demanding large cats and opened a cage door in some unobserved spot.

"Can I put my hand in?" I asked as we stood beside the cage of a female cougar.

"No, she's actually very bad," Weed said. "She's not one that I raised. Some of them will let you touch them but generally you don't trust any of them. Some I won't breed. I take a specimen I like and breed it to another one I like. I want to breed a light color and a small shape. I always have a waiting list of customers, although the state of Florida wants me to go out of business and keeps making it harder." To tame his cougars Weed put the days-old kittens in his bathtub under a heat-lamp. He handed me a tiny, spotted, mewing bundle that scrabbled blindly around my shoulder with still unopened eyes.

The eyes of a grown cougar are pale gray and shimmering yellow, and so translucent that the color lies as if at the bottom of a well. The eyes of Tracker, who years earlier had been a kitten in Weed's bathtub, were fixed on Jim McMullen as he entered her cage. McMullen had raised her and was about to give her a frozen whole chicken. He was the author of *Cry of the Panther,* a strange book about obsession and symbol in the Florida swamps. A Vietnam veteran haunted by memories and unable to make meaning of his life, McMullen read a story in a newspaper about the extinction of the Florida panther. Something clicked. Finding a living panther became McMullen's cause, his meaning. He moved from Illinois to the Everglades, whose swamps conjured and then vanquished the terrors of Vietnam. He trained his senses, his body, and his mind toward one purpose: to track panthers. McMullen wanted to *be* a panther, and said he had tried everything, from soaking himself in cougar urine to eating panther kills to crying in imitation of the cat until his throat was raw, to find "affinity." After many months of tracking he found it by gazing into the eyes of a panther he named Shakespeare, because the cat's movement reminded him of the poet's fluid verse. Afterward he lived for weeks at a time in the swamps, tracking Shakespeare and, he said, dozens of other cats, although biologists like Dave Maehr said McMullen was recounting the same cat's tracks.

McMullen made his living as a naturalist and sometimes taught survival school. Even on a relaxed Saturday afternoon he wore a large knife on each hip. A panther claw necklace rattled around his neck. Tracker was the draw for presentations McMullen gave, for a fee, about the Florida panther. She chirped at him while he leaned against her cage. "OK, OK," he answered, testing with a knife the chicken's state of thaw, then prying out the plastic-wrapped organs from the cavity. Tracker rolled on her back and batted her paws in the air.

McMullen detested the intrusive aspects of panther recovery. He was a leading opponent of the plan, proposed in the early 1990s by the U.S. Fish and Wildlife Service, to remove cats from the wild for breeding in captivity. He feared that many of the cats would die in the process. Dave Maehr scoffed at that but worried about social disruption among cats remaining in the wild. Of the more than three hundred public responses to the plan, most agreed with one or another of those assessments. There was a large contingent of the public in favor of benign neglect.

Melody Roelke, who became Florida's panther veterinarian after the first research-related death of a panther, and who thought to aim her career at working with free, wild animals, turned out—perhaps inevitably—to be the leading proponent for captive breeding. She was a strong, stocky woman with deep-set eyes and a taste for coffee and melancholy folk music. Pinned among a clutter of notes and cartoons on her office bulletin board was a photo of a long, lean, utterly relaxed cheetah lounging in her arms. Roelke had begun her career by tending cheetahs in zoos and had contributed to the pioneering genetic work on cheetahs featured in *Scientific American* and *Science*. The framed covers of those issues, with their somber cheetah faces, hung on her wall, along with one of the "Panther Crossing" signs that have sprouted along South Florida's highways ("Less than 30 remaining. Please drive carefully."). Cheetahs had been found to be so genetically similar that they could exchange skin grafts as if they were identical twins. This was thought to result from inbreeding after a population crash perhaps ten thousand years ago. Cheetahs' low fecundity, high rate of kitten death, and extreme vulnerability to diseases were considered textbook examples of the threats associated with lack of genetic diversity. The forces of natural selection operate most profoundly at the genetic level; the ability to evolve such adaptive traits as disease resistance depends upon genes sufficiently varied that at least a few genes are capable of responding to changing conditions.

Roelke's comparative analysis of mountain lion genes revealed a dangerous lack of diversity in the cats isolated for many generations in southern Florida. By some measures Florida panthers had even less genetic diversity than cheetahs. The consequences seemed to bloom even as Roelke studied them: increasing numbers of males appeared with an undescended testicle, which had never before been reported in a wild cat population. Their sperm was malformed. Heart murmurs and other cardiac defects, again unknown in wild cats, killed more and more kittens and debilitated adults. Infectious pathogens associated with disarmed immune systems killed kittens and adults alike. Occasionally the jargon of science includes a term so elegantly succinct and expressive that no lay phrase can substitute. *Extinction vortex* is one, conveying an image of panthers sucked helplessly into a silent hurricane of genetic destruction. Statistical models, after tumbling all the data ever compiled about panthers into various configurations, predicted extinction within twenty-five to sixty-three years if panthers were benignly neglected. Thirty to fifty panthers, even a hundred or two, were simply too few to maintain enough genetic diversity for long-term survival. Conservation biologists estimate that something along the order of five hundred free-roaming animals are the necessary minimum for a single population, and that at least several such populations should exist within reach of each other for exchange of genes.

Because captive breeding was what she knew best, Roelke advocated it not merely to enlarge the panther population, but also to preserve whatever unique Florida panther genes might remain in the wild. "How many other cats are out there swimming and dealing with mosquitoes that can bleed a cow to death?" she asked. "Those are the kinds of adaptations we can't quantify. And because we want to maintain the integrity of this particular animal, it's forcing us to push forward our understanding of feline reproduction, how to manipulate it, how to augment it, and we can use that knowledge on other highly endangered animals like the snow leopard and tiger." Not long before, Roelke had been the anesthesiologist on an all-woman surgical team that collected 141 eggs from eight cougars for the first in-vitro fertilization of a large cat. Ten resulting embryos were implanted in two of the females. No litters matured—the procedure was hardly fail-safe—but knowledge of cougar reproduction took a great leap forward. At the same time, embryos from an African bongo antelope were successfully implanted in elands, Chinese Monal pheasants hatched from eggs laid by an artificially inseminated hen, and the world's first test-tube tiger was born. Control over animal reproduction—even the splicing of genes from one species into another to engineer desirable qualities—came within human grasp.

The captive breeding plan relied on such sophisticated reproductive technology. Its goal was to achieve a studbook-managed zoo population of several hundred panthers and another couple of hundred in the wild. Unlike captive breeding projects for three other endangered species—red wolves, black-footed ferrets, and California condors—which removed the entire known population from the wild, only individual, unrelated panthers would be identified for capture. Eight adults and eighteen kittens were to be taken over three years. Several zoos had agreed to host some of the panthers, but space and resources there were severely limited. Most panthers would go to White Oak Plantation, a private facility that appeared, like a fairy godmother, in the nick of time to donate a portion of the necessary facilities and expertise to the recovery project. The corporate retreat of the Gilman Paper Company, White Oak's fifteen square miles of pines and live oaks near the Florida-Georgia border had a golf course, tennis courts, and good quail habitat for hunters. It also catered to Howard Gilman's interest in endangered species of the world. Rhinoceroses, tigers, zebras, cheetahs, giraffes, and dozens of other species were bred there, in a much less disruptive setting than a zoo, to contribute to the worldwide gene pool. In a generous gesture, Gilman offered a potential home to a small number of Florida panthers.

Roelke's further work, undertaken with researchers at the National Cancer Institute, showed that the few panthers living in the Everglades were genetically different from panthers in Big Cypress. This helped precipitate a revolution in biological thought. The classic categorization of species and subspecies is based on easily visible physical characteristics. With subtle but real biological racism, taxonomists have traditionally viewed miscegenation as an unnatural contamination that produced hybrids. Glimpses into the molecular world through laboratory methods, unknown when the Endangered Species Act was written, are now turning traditional concepts of taxonomy upside down. The method Roelke used involved an analysis of mitochondrial DNA (mtDNA). Mitochondria are self-replicating structures that regulate energy transfer within cells. They contain their own DNA, but in contrast to the DNA found in cell nuclei, to which both parents contribute and which influences physical and behavioral traits, mtDNA is inherited only from the mother and has no apparent effect on how an animal looks or behaves. A single mating between animals of two separate species or subspecies can inject the mother's mtDNA into generations of descendants, without any other detectable evidence of her other characteristics.

Researchers at the University of California examined the mtDNA of two other endangered species undergoing controversial recoveries, red and gray wolves, and found evidence of coyote genes. The Farm Bureaus of several western states promptly petitioned for the removal of the gray wolf from the endangered list because "the gray wolf may not be genetically pure because of hybridization between wolves and coyotes." The American Sheep Industry Association petitioned for delisting of the red wolf because it was "clearly a hybrid." When Roelke found that the Everglades panther population had at least one maternal ancestor from Central or South America—probably from the Piper stock—the question that came up immediately was whether at least some panthers were not legally entitled to protection under the Endangered Species Act. And if Big Cypress panthers mate with Everglades panthers, their offspring, too, will be hybrids.

In a rare instance of bureaucratic alacrity, the Department of the Interior denied both petitions to delist wolves and declared that all wild panthers in Florida were protected under the Endangered Species Act. It then plunged into a complicated internal debate over the formulation of a new policy to account for genetic hybrids. While this debate dragged on, young male panthers began to turn up with both testicles undescended, which made them sterile. In an abrupt change of policy from captive breeding, project leaders proposed outbreeding. By this they meant bringing in half a dozen alluring young Texas cougar females to the South Florida wilds. Florida panthers had once met Texas cougars at the western extreme of their range; outbreeding therefore would "restore historic gene flow." Outbreeding would by its very design eliminate whatever purity might remain in Florida panther genes, but there was a solid biological argument for recreating as closely as possible the natural mixing of panther populations. Besides, captive breeding—even with the Gilman contribution—was enormously more expensive than outbreeding, requiring space, money, and time. Outbreeding was finally approved in 1994—with the stipulation that the desired progeny be genetically and morphologically profiled so that the term *Florida panther* could be defined.

By the time outbreeding became the preferred option Roelke had resigned to take a job in Africa, but before she left she brought the captive breeding plan to the brink of implementation. Capture of the first panthers for breeding was set to begin when the Fund for Animals, an animal-rights group, put it on hold by filing a lawsuit against it. The group's main complaint was that the captive breeding plan took animals out of the wild without any provisions to ensure that there would be a "wild" to put them back into when captive breeding had created a sufficiently large population.

The issue of habitat was the single nerve that ran through all the divisive clashes of perspectives, personalities, and gender and unified the recovery project people and their critics. Some forms of habitat preservation and improvement were well under way. The federal government had spent large sums to expand public lands in South Florida, and the state of Florida had legislated one of the most aggressive public land acquisition programs in the country, with spending slated at $300 million a year for ten years. Construction projects that received federal money had to be critiqued by the U.S. Fish and Wildlife Service for threats to endangered species; as a result, the state road known as Alligator Alley was made safer for panthers during its reconstruction to an interstate. Being hit by cars was the leading cause of panther deaths, claiming fifteen panthers in a dozen years and severly injuring four more. Tunnels were built at known wildlife crossings and at regular intervals, and highway edges were fenced down into them. Almost immediately, bears, raccoons, alligators, deer, and panthers began using the underpasses. The National Park Service finally began a program to eradicate the pretty but prolific hollylike exotic known as Brazilian pepper and restore native vegetation to parts of the Everglades. Unlike the National Park Service, the U.S. Fish and Wildlife Service had no qualms about single-species management, and began experimenting with food crops and feeders for deer as soon as it acquired the nearly thirty thousand acres west of Big Cypress that became the Florida Panther National Wildlife Refuge.

In short, most of what could be done with public lands was being done. It was habitat on private land that was disappearing. Florida's human population nearly doubled between 1970 and 1990, and thousands of people were still moving into the state every week. Nearly half of Florida's native vegetation was already converted to urban and agricultural uses. Smoke from land-clearing fires smudged the horizon. Trucks laden with rolls of sod for new yards were always blocking the road. The citrus industry was pushing south after years of frosts in north-central Florida; square miles of orange trees in rows with mowed grass between them promised nothing for panthers. Recovery project people and their critics alike all watched as condominiums and resorts and airports and subdivisions chewed up the land where panthers lived.

Dennis Jordan fussed with stacks of papers in his office on the campus of the University of Florida in Gainesville. "We've done maps that show that fifty-three percent of the range occupied by panthers in South Florida is private land," he said. Jordan had been the Florida panther recovery project coordinator, a U.S. Fish and Wildlife Service position, since 1987. For two decades before that he worked for the service throughout the Southeast; a southern accent lent his bureaucratic euphemisms a certain charm. In one sense he was the ultimate administrator of the recovery project, because legally his agency had final authority over all actions concerning Florida panthers. But in reality he was boxed in by bureaucracy, because neither he nor his agency had enough political clout to take the lead. Decisions depended on a group of the top administrators from each of the four agencies involved, called the Florida Panther Interagency Committee, which itself was only one (although the most powerful) of several interagency panther groups.

A former member of one of these groups named Ken Alvarez, who worked in the state park system, had recently published a scathing book on the administration of the recovery project. Alvarez got so tired of endless bureaucratic befuddlement that he resigned from the recovery team to write *Twilight of the Panther,* in which he stated that "to the long list of threats, a new one can be added: bureaucratic extinction—brought on by bureaucratic ineptitude." The only player given good marks for professional conduct was the U.S. Fish and Wildlife Service, but with no power base it was "the sick man" in interagency negotiations. Alvarez described the four institutions as tribal, pinpointing their culture of loyalty and self-interest. It was these, he argued, and not the biological needs of panthers, that guided agency policy. Managers proved adept at going through the motions of doing what was necessary to save panthers without actually doing so, whenever what was necessary contradicted long-held ideologies or threatened customary prerogatives. The bureaucratic mode was, in essence, a way of not-knowing. Eventually it caused Dave Maehr to resign from his job as leader of panther research. Jordan chuckled without much mirth when I mentioned Alvarez's book; he was, then as almost always, frustrated with waiting for one or another of the agencies to make a decision.

Everyone's office had panther range maps, panther photos, and plaster casts of panther tracks, but Jordan's was further distinguished by a panther planter. This was a small, reposing ceramic figure with a few anemic plants growing from a flank. "Wal Mart, K Mart, one of those places," Jordan replied when I asked where it came from. Though it was mass produced, the creator of the original mold, like the Calusa Indian that carved the wooden figurine centuries ago, saw in the panther certain ideals of grace and beauty. The planter sat on top of a bookshelf, to which Jordan turned and, after some rummaging, found the report he was looking for. Maps showed the toe of the Florida peninsula surrounded by blue and blotched with red, dark green, light green, and yellow. "Private lands tend to be the drier uplands, with the hardwood hammocks and pine flatwoods that panthers prefer, and the panthers there are the biggest and healthiest of all," he said. "Hunting is restricted, so that kind of disturbance is much less. Public lands in South Florida seem to be capable of supporting no more than about twenty-two panthers. It's very clear that private lands are essential to survival of the Florida panther."

Restricted to public lands for living space, without room for the number of animals necessary to sustain genetic viability, the Florida panther could survive only as an intensely managed object. The eventual scenario would be an engineered approximation of nature, with human tinkering replacing evolution and freedom in the wild. Small enclaves of panthers, hauled in by radio collar if they set foot over the line, would be mixed and matched with zoo animals to maintain a genetically healthy metapopulation. Females would be implanted with embryos created in zoos, released to bear the young in the wild, then recaptured for repeat duty as surrogates. Their progeny would be brought in whenever managers felt the need to manipulate them for whatever purpose. Without systematic efforts to preserve habitat outside of public lands, this would become the inevitable fate of the Florida panther, and what happened in Florida would presage the future of large wild mammals throughout America. County land-use plans, theoretically capable of maintaining open space, were proving ineffective. There seemed to be nothing stopping Naples and Miami from meeting in the middle of South Florida. Private lands were fragmented and disturbed but still intact enough to provide wildlife travel corridors to the protected core of public lands. What was needed was a plan to keep the current proportion of developed to undeveloped land.

For years, recovery project people had grumbled in low voices about the need to target private landowners for habitat preservation. Action began when the Fund for Animals agreed to settle out of court and allow captive breeding in return for a habitat preservation plan. Under pressure from the lawsuit, government bureaucracies finally confronted what in American capitalist democracy constitutes their dreaded Other: the Private Landowner, who in South Florida was rendered even more menacing by Business Interests.

What is spectacular about the Florida landscape is not looking at it but being in it, especially in one of those islands of subtropical forest called a hammock. The word derives from a Native word for shady place. Hardwood hammocks grow where slight increases in elevation offer roots some protection from waterlogging. Gumbo-limbo trees grow there, and strangler figs, and live oaks draped with Spanish moss like ladies in dishabille. Hammocks are another world, an ancient world, and arousing in an indefinable way. In dry season the smell is rich and dense, and there is no fetid crush of crowded green. On the contrary, there was a shadowed spaciousness beneath the canopy, on a warm winter day in a nameless hammock on the grounds of Collier Enterprises. Brown leaves made a sound in the breeze like monkeys chattering. The air was moister and cooler than outside. David Land, the company's president for natural resources, knew just where the wild citrus trees grew. He cut open an orange for me to try. For hours my lips stung and puckered. The wild grapefruits were much better, fibrous but sweet.

Land was tall and lanky, beginning to bald, but it only made him look scholarly. There were shadows beneath his eyes. He had been eager to get out of the office, sitting ready to bolt on the edge of his chair at his desk. A map behind him showed a checkerboard in red and green. Each square was a township, six miles on a side. The green belonged to Collier Enterprises, the red to the Barron Collier Company. Barron Collier came to South Florida from Tennessee by way of New York City in the early 1900s, with millions of dollars from selling advertising on the sides of streetcars. In Florida he saw paradise and purchased about a million acres of land, most of it in the county named after him. Much of the public land in South Florida—portions of Everglades National Park, Big Cypress National Preserve, Collier-Seminole State Park, and the Florida Panther National Wildlife Refuge—was donated by or purchased from cooperative members of the Collier family. Even though the Colliers had kept the mineral rights to the land, donations were a good public-relations move and a way to get profitably rid of a lot of swampland that would have been hard to develop. What remained was roughly three hundred thousand acres, which Collier's descendants split into two companies. Collier Enterprises grew cattle, oranges, bell peppers, watermelons, potatoes, cucumbers, squash, but most of all tomatoes. In the spring of a good year Collier provided seven percent of the nation's supply. David Land had joined Collier Enterprises and returned to his native Florida after working internationally as an agricultural consultant. On his office wall were hand tools he had collected in Asia and the Middle East, lovingly mounted on a burlapped board. He explained that this oddly shaped one was a hoe, and that long curved blade a type of machete. Ever so slightly, he sneered at the computer on my lap and made a joke about my having to take notes by hand, as I did while riding in his four-wheel-drive through Collier territory.

"I hope I don't get us lost," Land said, negotiating a maze of gleaming white shell roads through the Gopher Ridge orange grove as oranges popped and squished beneath the tires. The grove was fifty-four hundred acres, but of that about thirty-four hundred acres was actually covered with short, bushy trees, lined up between grassy strips, and the rest was ponds, reservoirs, and marshes. Florida's water management districts had the authority to require permits for land drainage—citrus trees as well as vegetable roots needed well-drained soil or they would rot—and permits usually stipulated that the first inch of a rainfall be retained on site and that the net flow of water off the property not exceed the volume before development. To meet those requirements, drainage ditches funneled water into small wetlands, either preexisting or manmade, called retention areas. The result was a mosaic of naturalistic swamps interspersed through intensively managed agricultural fields. On some of these islands of habitat stood large trees in various stages of death and decay. They had been upland hammocks or patches of pinewoods before being designated as retention areas, and when water was channeled into them, the trees died. There was no permitting system to protect the uplands that panthers preferred.

"The Florida Audubon Society criticized citrus groves as being no different than a parking lot," Land said, "but they were thinking of wall-to-wall citrus, like the monoculture in northern Florida. This is quite different." He turned into a pasture and drove cross-country a short way, the truck bucking like a horse. "And people thought it was all pristine land before we started planting, but actually for the most part it was vegetable fields. We just drove over old plow furrows. No more than twenty percent of our agricultural land was unaltered native vegetation."

We continued driving through what was known as unimproved pasture, consisting of varied wild vegetation. The heavy sweet smell of molasses emanated from a cattle feeder at which six wild pigs feasted, hardly twitching a tail as we passed. On the other side of the road was improved pasture, where much of the vegetation had been burned or bulldozed and replaced with cattle forage of grasses and legumes. Even the government's panther habitat preservation plan conceded that such pastures were also nutritious for deer. Land believed that the plan, drafted by recovery project officials and distributed to landowners in the previous few months, overlooked the value of the mix of agricultural and natural lands to deer and thus to panthers. "Telemetry data show that panthers will reside and raise kittens in the midst of heavily farmed vegetable and citrus areas provided there is an adequate prey base within a reasonable distance and adequate corridors to reach that prey base," he wrote in a rebuttal of the plan.

Although landowners were not yet speaking with one voice—a situation Dave Maehr hoped to rectify in his new job with an environmental consulting firm—Land spoke for many agribusiness owners of the nearly one million acres identified by the plan as needing to be preserved. The most fundamental point of agreement was that if panthers were doing so well on private land, then private management must be doing something right and ought to be left alone to keep doing it.

"Our lands are valuable to panthers because development everywhere else has squeezed them onto us," Land said. "Why should those who have chosen not to develop but to manage in an environmentally friendly way be penalized?" The plan proposed a variety of strategies for preserving privately owned habitat: outright purchase, different kinds of conservation easements, leases, tax incentives, tax reform, and land-use regulation. It was this last idea that agitated landowners the most. "The government probably won't have enough funds to purchase all this land, especially if they calculate full compensation," Land said. "We're an integrated operation—we have greenhouses to grow our seedlings, packing houses to process our harvests—so there's a multiplier effect, an added value from all the equipment related to our use of the land that elevates the land value far above the basic market price. So then they'll turn to regulation. The plan even covers land where panthers have never been radio-tracked but where they could be reintroduced. It's one thing when an eagle lands in one of your trees and builds a nest. But it's another thing when an endangered species is put on private lands and then use of those lands is restricted."

I saw no eagles on Collier property, but I did see wood storks, an endangered species, feeding in drainage canals with herons and ducks, and there were deer tracks in some hardened mud. On a tour of Pacific Land Company's 15,000 acres along bird-rich Camp Keais Strand, I saw great egrets, cattle egrets, kingfishers, moorhens, and anhingas working the drainage ditches, while killdeer wailed their plaintive cry. Raccoons, wild turkeys, and bears lived on or near the property. Some of the orange tree saplings had been rubbed to death by deer with itchy antlers. In another part of South Florida, Alico, Inc. had installed automatic feeders for deer and wild turkeys on its 150,000 acres of timber and pasture, which also hosted a population of sandhill cranes. Both businesses owned prime habitat for many wildlife species, and their managers had cooperated with assorted government agencies for wildlife protection. Both now felt that existing land-use regulations were sufficient to protect panther habitat.

"All they have to do is enforce existing laws," echoed Bobby McDaniel, sitting at an elegant glass and bamboo dining table. He and two of his four sons were on lunch break from planting watermelons on the McDaniel township, which had been in the family since the 1930s. Mrs. McDaniel and a smiling Hispanic maid served platters of food from the kitchen; they themselves never sat down. McDaniel had raised mostly cattle in the past, but when his sons grew old enough to want to make a living, he diversified and intensified. Tall and bullet shaped, his face reddened from outdoors work, McDaniel was one of the handful of landowners who refused the recovery team permission to enter his lands to find panthers. "They're just harassing those animals," he said. He believed there were more cats than officials admitted, and that no habitat preservation plan was necessary. He had seen panthers; his wife saw a black one from the kitchen window. "Look out that window," he said, gesturing toward the backyard view of a large pond and dock with chaise lounge and pots of flowers. Beyond the pond were pasture and pinewoods. "That's as cleared as it will ever be." Two grandchildren sat at the kitchen island, giggling, eating, and growing up.

Even if McDaniel descendants want to keep the land in its present state, they might be forced to sell large chunks of it to developers to pay inheritance taxes. Joe Hilliard knew about inheritance taxes. "The number-one incentive to keep family land in agriculture would be to do away with inheritance taxes," he said in the Hilliard Brothers office on the northern fringe of known panther habitat. To the east lay that desolate plain called the Everglades Agricultural Area, ditched and rolled to frighteningly blank flatness, where even the canals were bereft of birds. Hilliard Brothers raised rice, corn, sugarcane, nursery plants, citrus, and timber on sixty-thousand acres and would have been growing them on seventeen thousand more acres if the government hadn't required millions in taxes after an uncle died some years ago. Action was under way in Congress to amend the estate tax code to favor certain kinds of conservation easements. In general, conservation easements were legal agreements, written for specific tracts of land and attached to the deed, to maintain the existing natural character of the land. Subdivisions and conversion of forests to other uses were usually prohibited. Conservation easements had been successfully employed for years throughout the nation, but Florida landowners had mixed opinions about them. Some, like Joe Hilliard, were cautiously willing to consider them, if full compensation was provided. To others, easements meant locking up land in perpetuity, an unacceptable loss of business flexibility.

Another issue on which landowners were divided was the need for purity in Florida panthers. Although some resented the recovery project's plan to bring in Texas cougars—which would almost surely ensure the perpetuation of cougars in South Florida and their need for habitat— Hilliard was an outspoken advocate of outbreeding. "We need to bring more cats in so they're not so worshipped, so precious," he said. He was a large man but tight, firm, and decisive. He was, at the time, on the board of the Game and Fresh Water Fish Commission, having been appointed by the governor, and he considered himself Dave Maehr's boss. "I get these biologists in a closed room and they all agree there's not a thing wrong with bringing cougars in," he said. "The thing is, the panthers are dying out by themselves."

The urgency of saving panthers wasn't what animated the jeering and heckling audience at a meeting in Fort Myers, sponsored by the Florida Farm Bureau, about cats and their habitat in South Florida. It was the height of the wise-use movement, a grass-roots backlash to environmental regulations. Fueled by money from extractive industries, its adherents touted private property rights as the most American of all principles and proclaimed their private interests as first priority. Recovery project officials sat woodenly on the stage. Trained for the most part in biotechnical sciences, they could hardly be blamed for shrinking from their role in stoking a sociological revolution. At the moment, the revolution was meeting with a bit more success in northern Florida.

It was hard to distinguish between the monotonous rows of pines on Gilman paper company lands and the same piney monotony on the Osceola National Forest, near the Florida-Georgia border. Trees stood like soldiers in plantations burned frequently enough to keep the saw palmettos below knee height. Clasping the top railing of a fire tower and taking in a 360-degree view of flat land flashing with sunlit pines, I felt like I was in the center of a fish-eye lens. On the ground, the sand was perfect for tracks: raccoon, bobcat, armadillo, maybe a fox, definitely a dog, a cow and calf. Inexplicably, mosquitoes were worse than anywhere else in Florida. Despite the large areas of pine monoculture, seven cougars brought from western Texas and released here in the late 1980s managed to find enough cover and sufficient deer to make themselves at home for a short while. As an experiment to determine whether panther habitat still existed outside South Florida, the first reintroduction of cougars began auspiciously. Sterilized to keep their genes to themselves, the cougars established overlapping territories, killed deer and wild hogs regularly, and began to develop a social structure. Then hunting season drew near. One cougar was already dead, probably from poison; two more were shot. The remaining cougars left their new ranges and began to wander erratically. One climbed a tree in a Jacksonville backyard; two others threatened livestock. All were recaptured earlier than planned.

The untimely end of that first reintroduction experiment left Chris Belden at one of several low points in his career. Belden held one of the longest tenures of any Florida panther bureaucrat. After completing hog studies in the Great Smoky Mountains in Tennessee, he moved to Florida to work on mammals for the Game and Fresh Water Fish Commission. Shortly thereafter Belden was named the first leader of the panther recovery team. It was Belden who was transferred out of South Florida after raising the early questions about disturbance from hunters in Big Cypress. When years later he was assigned the job of using Texas cougars to test the feasibility of reintroducing Florida panthers to northern Florida, Belden once again had to deal with hunters. To woo sportsmen afraid that panthers would commandeer the woods, the commission promised not to restrict hunting in any way on behalf of the panther. After the first batch of cougars succumbed to disturbance,

Belden recommended that a much larger number, perhaps thirty to forty, be brought in to form a widespread social web that would bind them within their territories despite the invasion of hunters. He was ignored for years. A second reintroduction project was inaugurated in 1993, not with the dozens of cats Belden wanted, but with at least a few more than the first attempt. Ten cougars were released in the same area as the first batch. Four were lost in short order: one cat was killed on a highway, and three were shot by hunters, although one was only wounded and was eventually rehabilitated.

"Our biggest problem is still with hunters," Belden said in a soft Appalachian drawl. He was bearded, and his black hair nearly matched the color of the wild boar's head mounted behind him in his Gainesville office. "Some are supportive—one hunting club adopted a cougar as part of a program that a new group, the Florida Panther Society, is starting. But we invited fifty-eight clubs to a meeting and only two clubs showed up." Of the three poachers, two lived in Georgia and were found and prosecuted; the Florida poacher was never arrested. "That's about par for us," Belden said.

To compensate for these losses—and for later ones, such as the time a kitten died from complications from a dart and an adult cat died in a snare—other females with young were released. The new arrivals prospered. When a female began to consort with a male, her youngsters dispersed in the normal pattern. Another female gave birth—quite an unexpected event, since the males had all been sterilized, although this time the females had not. Rumors flew that there were wild cats in the area, but Belden figured that she became impregnated by one of the transplanted Texas males in the few weeks between the vasectomy and the disappearance of his sperm. There were a few incidents with livestock—in one, a cougar killed a pig in a pen and got the carcass hung up in a fence, where he ate it—but owners were satisfied with recompense, which was provided as a civic contribution by Barnett Bank of Florida. All of the nine cats that were being monitored established home ranges. And every one of them was on private land.

That wasn't too surprising. The Osceola National Forest was relatively small, and the Okefenokee National Wildlife Refuge, like the corridor of Pinhook Swamp that connected the two, was very wet. The dry countryside surrounding those public lands was owned largely by a handful of wealthy individuals, mostly absentee landowners, and a dozen or so timber companies in addition to Gilman, including ITT Rayonier, Champion Pulp and Paper, Champion International, Union Camp, Nekoosa Packing, and Continental Forest Investments. Belden and his colleagues modeled their landowner contacts on the successful red wolf reintroduction program in North Carolina, which relied on key contacts rather than attempting to reach the entire public at large. "There's only been one problem landowner," Belden said, "a man who owns a hundred-thousand-acre hunting camp and demanded we remove a cougar that settled there. He's a very selfish man who thinks all the deer belong to him alone. But most people like the idea of the cats' being around."

Once landowners had been contacted and permission for tracking panthers on their lands secured, they were left alone; no agency assigned personnel to work with them. Belden hoped that the new, grass-roots Florida Panther Society might eventually act as a liaison with private landowners. In the timidly rolling countryside, where woods, orchards, and pastures alternated with such occasional surprises as a Hare Krishna day lily farm, there was much less pressure to urbanize or intensify land use than in South Florida. There was some clear-cutting, but that didn't seem to bother the cats, while it increased the amount of browse for deer. After the first year of the second reintroduction, Belden was on one of the few highs of his career with panthers. He speculated that if things kept going well, males from the South Florida stock would be brought up to mate with the Texas females. The recovery plan calls for "three viable, self-sustaining populations within the historic range of the animal." Belden saw that viability and self-sufficiency were still a long way off, but at least two of the three populations were in process, and two dozen possible sites had already been identified for a third. (Belden's old stomping grounds, the Great Smoky Mountains, ranked first). If Florida panthers were reintroduced, there might be some attempt to write a local habitat preservation plan, as in South Florida, but at the moment that was no more than an amorphous shape in the bureaucratic distance.

"Right now there's a tremendous level of public support," Belden said. "I'm a little surprised how great it is. That's the most important thing. It's how the public feels that will determine the success or failure of reintroduction." A local survey Belden had done before beginning the first reintroduction had been so overwhelmingly positive that it was clear some kind of transformation was taking place in public consciousness. Consider poet Enid Shomer, who was born in that most institutional of cities, Washington, D.C., but spent her adult life in Florida. Raised in a household prejudiced against cats, feeling no particular attachment toward any other wild felines, Shomer nevertheless came to view the Florida panther as "an emblem of all that I prize when I speak of 'the wilderness,' which for me encompasses the natural landscape as well as the bodily sensibility which we all possess, the wilderness within." In an unpublished essay about Florida panthers, she wrote that the cat aroused in her "not the cuddly, fuzzy feeling people exude for domestic kittens, but a heightened awareness of the link between knowledge and the physical self . . . as we increasingly lose our relationship with the land and our animal roots."

Maybe some archeologist in the unfathomable future will dig up Dennis Jordan's panther planter from a landfill, carefully wash off the detritus, and puzzle over its symbolic meaning to the society that created it. By then they would know whether that society had been content with the symbol and had let the reality die. When I traveled through Florida, I looked in vain for a reproduction of the Marco Island panther in Native shops. I finally saw one in a New Age store in northern Florida. It was made in New Jersey.

THE SPIRITUAL
CHALLENGE OF THE
EASTERN PANTHER

SOMETIMES IT SEEMS AS IF I AM THE ONLY PERSON OF MY ACQUAINTANCE who has *not* seen a cougar in the mountains of western Virginia, where I live. Reports come in from all sides. Lori saw a black one playing at the foot of Little North Mountain not far from here, but she is a poet and a writer of fantasy novels and sees things in the shadows that other people don't. My neighbor Willy was startled the other night by a big, long-tailed cat that ran in front of his car; he is a hunter and said he never saw anything like it in the woods, but it was night and he barely got a glimpse as the animal streaked by. David saw one on the outskirts of the small city down in the valley where he lives, but he is, sadly, too often in his cups. Gil was riding his mountain bike just across the state line in West Virginia and swears he saw one gliding through the green gloom, but he runs a bike touring company, and if tales of eastern panthers spark up his clients' experience, so much the better. Dave is a self-taught woodsman who lives what is called an alternative lifestyle, and he is convinced that the eyeshine and yowling beside his campfire one night was a cougar, though he couldn't find any sign. Larry watched a mother and kitten in his rifle scope for several minutes one brilliant autumn afternoon while he was squirrel hunting. He is a professional biologist, and his story is not easily discounted.

Every year, hundreds of people across the East report that they've seen an animal believed extinct since the early twentieth century. The last wild cougar killed in Virginia was shot in 1882; in New York, 1894; Maine, 1938. The pattern of extirpation is similar in virtually every eastern state. So is the pattern of sightings. Scarce and scattered at first, reports of eastern cougars had swelled by the 1950s to the point that several popular nature writers proclaimed the cats on a comeback trail. Whether through the power of suggestion, or because the rare cats actually were increasing, a great upsurge of sightings began in the 1960s. This helped make the eastern cougar subspecies (then known as *Felis concolor couguar*) popular enough to be listed as a protected animal in the 1973 Endangered Species Act. By the late 1970s cougar reports in the Great Smoky Mountains of North Carolina were coming so thick and fast that a coalition of garden clubs threatened to sue the U.S. Forest Service unless it stopped clear-cutting the Nantahala National Forest.

This sent up a red flag. If cougars really were present on public lands, logging would be only one of several human practices likely to be challenged as disruptive to the recovery of a wide-ranging endangered species that preferred undisturbed wild habitat. Chasing bear, deer, and raccoons with dogs, riding all-terrain vehicles, and other methods of noisily intruding into the forests might be curtailed. The Forest Service joined with the U.S. Fish and Wildlife Service to sponsor a field study. To carry it out, they selected Bob Downing, a wildlife biologist from Texas who had been working for Fish and Wildlife in the Southeast. Downing worked with his diminutive wife, Pat. She worried about his safety alone in the field and had acted as his officially recognized but unpaid assistant for most of his career. Fieldwork won out over having a baby, which would have meant staying home.

When they started the cougar project, the Downings quickly realized that dirt tracking, so revealing on the dusty back roads of the West, was impractical in the much wetter East. Instead, they hit the road every time it snowed in the southern Appalachians. Downing lined up some suitable hounds for use in case he found a fresh track to put them on. Notices in national publications, state conservation magazines, and local newspapers urged readers with recent reports to contact him. In snowless seasons Downing tracked cougars and their prey through recent history. Deer had been hunted almost to extinction throughout the East by the first decade of the twentieth century. Logging laid bare such vast tracts of land and caused such devastating floods that Congress authorized the purchase of millions of acres of national forests in the central and southern Appalachians and in a few other regions in the East. Even with the second-growth browse on these federal lands, deer didn't rebound until state game agencies began to stock and protect them in the 1930s. Native deer endured in a few places, like the rugged and isolated Great Smoky Mountains, where more than a hundred thousand acres of virgin timber remain today, and the huge estate near Asheville, North Carolina, that George Vanderbilt purchased and protected in the 1890s.

Downing became convinced that the prey and seclusion in these few places could have sustained a few cougars through the worst of the deer famine and logging elsewhere. By rummaging in various agency files and talking with local people, he tallied up to a dozen cougars reported killed in the mountains of North Carolina since 1900, and another dozen or so in nearby states. Most of these couldn't be authenticated, but he did locate a 1965 specimen in Louisiana and mounted trophies in Arkansas and Tennessee from the 1970s.

If any cougars had made it, Downing figured they'd be in clover now, because since midcentury, deer have proliferated into a widespread nuisance. Tens of thousands are hit on the roads every year. Lyme disease, carried by deer ticks, has spread widely from the Northeast in just a few years. Some states have inaugurated special hunting programs to reduce the damage deer cause to farm and orchard crops. Browse lines through the woods at the height of a deer's uplifted head signal a habitat diminished by the artificial abundance of this one species. When I see the browse lines in my own forest, I think of Aldo Leopold's heartache in Germany. With the disappearance of large carnivores, small predators have also multiplied—raccoons, opossums, skunks, weasels. They prey on birds, salamanders, and other smaller creatures, with ultimate effects in the life of the soil. There is no end to change.

Maybe the abundance of deer and small mammals for prey accounted for the fact that the Downings found no livestock kills that could be unequivocally attributed to a cougar. They did examine half a dozen deer that were positively killed by a cat: one full-grown deer had been dragged some distance before being covered, and another had been covered by an animal whose reach extended more than a yard. A very large bobcat might have been capable of these feats, and in the absence of any cougar tracks Downing could not reach a definitive conclusion. The only tracks that he judged might be cougar occurred along the Blue Ridge Parkway in North Carolina. New snow blurred them before the Downings could get there, and the contours of the feet weren't discernable, but the prints were widely spaced in a long stride. They traveled along guardrails and logs as cats are wont to do, and jumped almost six feet from one log to another. The Downings returned repeatedly to look for additional sign but found evidence only of bobcats. They never had occasion to call for the dogs Bob had lined up. In many places, they saw scratch hills that might have been cougar scrapes, but so many other animals routinely root around in the leaf litter—the introduced wild hogs in the Smokies among them—that such disturbances simply couldn't be evaluated. A few handfuls of likely-looking scat turned up in North Carolina, Virginia, and West Virginia, but techniques of analysis weren't advanced enough then to be useful.

Downing ranked the elusiveness of cougars high on his list of searching problems. His favorite story tells of a cougar in a 530-acre park within the city of Seattle in 1981. Three hundred people lived within the park, a former military base; five people reported seeing the cougar. Game officers and a hunter with hounds spent twelve hours searching for him, without success. He was seen again twice over the next two days; searches were repeated, then called off, with admonitions about "cougar hysteria." For several more days visitors and residents reported seeing him but were dismissed by officials. Then an unusual track was found, the dogs were set on it, and after ten hours a ninety-five pound male cougar was flushed.

After three years the Downings had flushed no cougars in the southern Appalachians. They wanted to find proof of a comeback, but they disappointed themselves. Bob had to report that he was "unable to confirm self-sustaining populations of cougars." At the same time, the U.S. Fish and Wildlife Service was also funding a study of western cougar tracks. Searches for tracks in snow were successful one hundred percent of the time. Even when snow was lacking, or high winds or precipitation had disturbed the ground, physical evidence of cougars was found at a quarter of all sites searched.

That settled the matter of eastern cougars as far as the wildlife establishment was concerned. Whatever outcry might arise over clearcutting and hunting with dogs, concern for eastern cougars couldn't justifiably be part of it. Downing wrote the recovery plan required by the Endangered Species Act, but—like many other recovery plans—it wasn't implemented, and no recovery team was appointed. The eastern cougar became de facto extinct. Yet sightings continued.

Sightings as evidence of a cougar's presence are held in very low esteem by lion biologists in the West. Researchers like Harley Shaw in Arizona and Paul Beier in California told me story after story about a housecat or a coyote emerging from bushes where someone had absolutely seen a cougar enter. Screams are even more suspect because so many other animals can wail like a woman being murdered, as a cougar is supposed to. As for tracks, few people have the kind of field knowledge necessary to rule out dogs, otters, bears, foxes, bobcats, and lynx. The majority of eastern cougar sightings come from hunters, who have some knowledge of the woods but are subject to conditions of poor visibility—dappling forest canopy, half-light of dusk or dawn, thick undergrowth, misleading or no reference points by which to judge size, the instantaneous nature of sightings, or great distance from the animal. The second largest category of reports comes from motorists, who suffer similar handicaps—vision distorted by headlight glare, distraction of trying to keep the vehicle on the road—and often lack woods knowledge. A deer is the same color as a cougar. A dog may be the same size and color and have a long tail to boot. Housecats can reach large sizes further exaggerated by excitement. Reports of bodies by the side of the road or tied to a hunter's fender come in, but the tangible evidence always seems to evaporate. Delusion persists even in the presence of reality: twice, people reported dead cougars to Bob Downing, but the investigators he sent found dogs.

Yet the people who think they've seen a cougar resist the obvious and logical explanations. "It was a dog," I told Lori, Willy, Gil, and Dave, only to be met with angry stares. They *want* to believe they've seen the rarest and arguably the most dangerous animal possible where they live. Surely these cougars are cultural projections, drawn perhaps from guilt for our collective ravaging of the continent, and from yearning for the exoneration that the survival of cougars would confer. Psychologists say that knowledge of humankind's assault on the natural world is a painful source of modern Angst. Surely, too, there is an element of thrill-seeking in the sightings, in a culture addicted to the fastest, biggest, highest, and fiercest, whether in machines, mountains, or animals. Maybe the image of cat goes deeper than culture. Maybe it has been permanently etched on human consciousness by eons of fear and admiration. Cat sightings may be a primal expression of the human understanding of nature.

Sheer defiance of the system drives some believers. Take Hal Hitchcock, who taught biology for twenty-five years at Middlebury College in Vermont. When officials of the state game agency ridiculed him for reporting tracks in the 1940s, insisting that the panther was extinct in Vermont, his dander was aroused. He set out to prove the agency wrong. "I'm not a particularly belligerent person," he said, "but I felt that the game department was ignoring and denying perfectly good evidence, and that set me off. I've collected and evaluated sightings and track reports for years. Now I'd stake my life on the presence of panthers."

Hitchcock carried on a strong tradition of cougar certainty in Vermont. In March 1934 the Reverend William Ballou took a troop of Boy Scouts on a hike near Chester. He found huge tracks that had, in places, broken through a hard crust of snow. Ballou had grown up in Wyoming where he learned to know cougar tracks, and he didn't hesitate to proclaim these as such. The Boston newspapers took up the story with stinging skepticism, implying that the whole incident was fabricated. A white-haired Congregational minister with a sense of humor, Ballou responded with a chicken pie dinner meeting in Chester open to all those who had seen panthers or their tracks. About a hundred people came. The evening began with a prayer beseeching God to guide those present in veracity as well as protect their reputations, and proceeded through the singing of specially composed panther songs, the telling of many firsthand panther tales, and the unveiling of a mounted panther shot in 1867 by the great-grandfather of several of those present. The Irrepressible and Uncompromising Order of Panthers was founded, with Ballou as Grand Puma, a treasurer designated as Grand Catamount Keeper of the Catnip, and a songmaster called the Grand Caterwauler. Everyone believed that a real panther would soon appear, verifying their claims. As no cats obliged them, after a while everyone's enthusiasm petered out.

Except Ballou's. He began to pursue fresh panther reports whenever he could, even running off from his duties at the altar on the day he was supposed to marry his son. His was apparently the first such effort, followed up a decade later by Hal Hitchcock, but a number of other individuals and small, local groups have devoted themselves to collecting panther reports through the years. There is about them a definite aura of the outcast as well as an unquestioning faith, as if the great challenge of eastern panthers is merely to believe in them. I know a woman in Pennsylvania who saw her first cougar when she was three and now goes into the woods regularly to pray for another glimpse. If any one leader ever emerges to unify them, the eastern panther people might qualify as some sort of harmless cult.

The most comprehensive work on sightings was undertaken by a radio reporter in Baltimore named John Lutz, who was assigned to investigate the killing of livestock by an unknown predator along the Gunpowder River in 1965. Lutz never saw the culprit, but those who did during the seven months that the killings occurred identified it as a puma. A thin, pale, delicate-looking man, Lutz became fascinated by the strength and the mystery of the animal he dubbed the Phantom Cat. For fifteen years he limited his investigations to Maryland, but in the early 1980s he began to expand. A decade later, he had totaled more than two-thousand sightings, tracks, and screams. Pennsylvania has far and away the largest number, followed by Maryland and West Virginia. Around 8 percent of the sightings include kittens. More than a quarter of them specify black cats. Lutz estimates that there are fifteen hundred to two thousand panthers in the East, and he believes he knows their breeding grounds by the clusters of sightings. Like Hal Hitchcock in Vermont, Lutz encountered ridicule and rudeness from wildlife agencies. When he visited the office of a Maryland state biologist with a plaster cast of a verified cougar track from Garrett County, where a confirmed cougar kitten had been killed in 1920, the man snapped, "You could have made that anywhere." Lutz's unorthodox theories—that the many sightings of black cougars indicate a species as yet unknown to science, or that the black cats descended from black leopards brought to the United States through Asian traders who sold them to American slavers—don't help.

Black cougar sightings are hard to figure. Reports of them date to the earliest days of exploration in both Americas. One or two black or dark gray cougars have been documented in South America, but no

North American specimen or photograph has ever come into scientific hands, although a reputable amateur naturalist mentioned seeing a black pelt from Colorado. The simplest explanation for the sightings is the power of suggestion invoked by the eastern name, *panther.* The term is an Old World carryover that in recent centuries has come to refer to the black color phase of the leopard. A panther is by definition black, so when easterners see an animal that they think is a panther, the inclination will be to paint that animal black. Black panthers are not uncommon in the most tropical parts of the leopard's range. Tigers, golden cats, servals, and caracals—all native to tropical or subtropical habitats—also occasionally produce black individuals. In the New World a black jaguar turns up now and then, which could account for some of the sightings in colonial days, when jaguars may have roamed as far north and east as the humid lowlands of South Carolina. A small, steamy region in South Florida has yielded ten black bobcats, six of them since 1970. The recent discovery of a black bobcat in New Brunswick skews the theoretical connection between black cats and tropical habitat but opens other possibilities for confusion with black cougars.

Despite the chaos of cultural images, there is in the mass of sightings that Lutz and others collect a small core that can't be laughed or argued away. These include statements by highly credible people—prominent hunter-naturalists, respected biologists, a superintendent of Shenandoah National Park, even a retired director of the U.S. Fish and Wildlife Service. There are also descriptions by ordinary people that give accurate details of cougar looks and behavior, such as the small size of the head in proportion to the body and the habit of tail twitching. In 1993 electrifying news came from the eastern maritime Canadian province of New Brunswick. An employee of a timber company there had found large, unusual tracks and contacted the provincial wildlife department. Two biologists came out the next day and followed the tracks for more than two miles in excellent snow conditions. The tracks were clawless and wider than they were long, both feline characteristics. The walking and running strides averaged nearly four feet. One leap measured sixteen feet over a clump of three-foot-high saplings whose dome of snow was untouched. Where logs poked up above the snow, the trail led along the top of them. A scat was discovered and sent to the Canadian Museum of Nature in Ottawa. Through elaborate microscopic analysis the scat was found to contain the remains of snowshoe hares and hairs from the foot and leg of a cougar. These were presumed to have been ingested when the animal groomed after eating. "There is, thus, little doubt," stated a letter from the museum to the provincial biologists, "that the scat was produced by a cougar."

Cougars may not even have existed in New Brunswick before the coming of white settlers and the disturbances they induced. Naturalists in the nineteenth and early twentieth centuries gave completely contradictory accounts, one declaring that there was "not a solitary authentic record, or any other authentic evidence, of either the present or former occurrence of the panther," another stating that the cat's presence was "well-authenticated." The first indisputable evidence came in 1932, when a cougar was shot. All that remains is a photo of the triumphant hunter holding up the skin with a long thick tail. Reports of sightings and tracks, which had been circulating at a low level for years, intensified and caught the attention of Bruce Wright, a wildlife biologist for the province and, later, professor at the University of New Brunswick. For decades Wright painstakingly examined and cataloged the details of every panther report brought to him. He theorized that panthers had retreated north as New England forests were cut and deer were almost exterminated. Fascinated by reports of black cats, he traveled to British Columbia to obtain a freshly killed cougar skin, filled it with water, and photographed it from various angles to see whether he could mimic the conditions that would make it appear black in the wild. He could not and concluded that not everyone who saw a black cougar could be mistaken.

Bruce Wright was a pupil and friend of Aldo Leopold's. When in 1947 Wright presented his former teacher with the evidence of panthers in New Brunswick, Leopold believed him. Leopold said, out of fear of well-heeled hunters who would go anywhere to get a rare trophy, "We must not tell anybody." Wright did tell, however, in several books and numerous magazine articles. No sportsmen flew in from distant places, but Leopold's anxiety for the animals' safety was validated by New Brunswick natives themselves. The overwhelming tendency for those who encountered animals that they thought were panthers was to shoot at them or, if they didn't have a gun handy, to throw a rock to make a killing.

Leopold was one of the few professional colleagues whom Wright succeeded in convincing. Wright's cause was later taken up by Ted Reed, who was not a biologist but a manufacturer of heating equipment. In 1974 Reed traveled to Nova Scotia over Memorial Day weekend to pick a vacation campsite on a tract of a few acres along the Bay of Fundy that he had bought the year before. He had grown up in the Berkshires of western Massachusetts and passionately loved the outdoors. While he was looking over his new property it started to snow, so he got in his car and headed back. Shortly after he turned onto the paved road he noticed, out of the corner of his eye, a large brown animal running along the right side of the car. He thought it was a deer and feared it would jump in front of his car, which it did, leaping across the whole width of road. Reed already had the image of deer formed in his mind and it took him a second to register that this animal had a long tail curved at the tip in the direction of the leap.

"Astonished is much too mild a word for what I felt," he said. He was a small, neat man whose gray hair was thinning when I met him exactly two decades later. "I pulled into a turnout and sat and tried to understand. I knew it was a mountain lion—that was the name I had grown up with—and I said to myself out loud half a dozen times, Ted, you've seen a mountain lion."

We were sitting in a hotel lobby, with other small groups around us. Reed's voice was quiet but urgent. "As a wildlife experience, it was a supreme emotional event. There was a sense of wildness, of power far beyond simple size and weight, that was fearsome, that made me gasp. There was power in the shoulder muscles, even in the tail. The combination of size, quickness, and agility—this was not a lumbering animal that you could run away from. It's not just me; I get this kind of response from other people who have really seen a panther in the right sighting conditions. Those are the ones that *have* to tell their story, *have* to share the experience, as if it's necessary to their emotional health." After composing himself by the side of the road that day, Reed drove to the nearest phone and called the provincial wildlife agency. The man that answered was not surprised; several reports had come in during recent months. He referred Reed to Bruce Wright.

At the time, Reed was enmeshed in business and family responsibilities, but he vowed that he would pursue the matter when he retired. In the late 1980s he sold his factory, settled into a retirement home in New Hampshire, and tried to contact Bruce Wright. Wright was long dead, but his widow gave Reed some of his papers. Reed found them absorbing and convincing. He thought about the best ways to look for panthers and realized that few eastern wildlife personnel had any field knowledge about cougars. He contacted Jay Tischendorf, an agile, serious young veterinary student in Colorado who had recently changed careers after studying cougars with Kerry Murphy in Yellowstone. Kerry called him the best tree climber he ever had. Before that, Tischendorf had been in touch with Bob Downing about cougars in the Appalachians. Born and raised in Ohio and excited by the possibility of cougars in the East, Tischendorf agreed to give track identification workshops in the Northeast. He and Reed collaborated in 1994 to put together a conference on the eastern panther. Tischendorf, who as organizer gave the opening remarks at the conference, dedicated it to a friend and former coworker who died in an avalanche in Yellowstone, Greg Felzien. He showed a slide of Greg, and broke up, and couldn't continue for several minutes. He also dedicated the conference to Jammer, and showed a slide of him, a good old lion hound from those days.

While he worked with Tischendorf, Ted Reed also began to compile cougar reports throughout the Northeast, much as John Lutz was doing farther south. The first issue of Reed's newsletter announced a home video of an eastern panther filmed in May 1990 near the village of Waasis in New Brunswick. The video documented a dramatic change in how the people of New Brunswick reacted to cougars. The mere fact that the observer grabbed a camera instead of a gun pointed toward a sea change. The cameraman was looking out the window of his brother's woodworking shop, toward the edge of a field where woods began. He had never used the camera before. The first several of the ten minutes of the action were blank because a control had been misset. The remaining video was rough and chaotic in parts but showed a cat-like animal walking, standing, sitting, and leaping. Jay Tischendorf believed the cat was a young puma, perhaps eight to twelve months old, looking for a home range. The sister-in-law of the cameraman also observed the cat. A few months later she wrote to Ted Reed of her ambivalence with an eloquence that transcends misspellings and poor grammar:

"From the first look I was captivated . . . He had chosen me . . . It bothers me to think that the deer are natural prey, but he is a carnivor . . . As he crossed the road I became apprehensive of where he was going. Not too far back was our fishpond, my husband and two smaller children . . . My smaller children, 8 and 11 no longer play on long, lazy days across the field and in the woods to their forts. Now left silent by the cougars crossing. The long walks in the woods are now not alone. For the disbelievers just let him cross your path but once. Then come and tell me that the eastern Cougar no longer exists . . . When I learned of his rarity I felt privileged that such an animal could find peace on our homeland . . . The cat for a moment looked straight at me, his big bleak brown eyes signaling a warning . . . A closing message for you, my little one (cougar)—walk softly as there are those among us who, out of fear, might kill you . . . Thank you for living at peace with me as I grew. Thank you for the moment of eye contact (through binoculars) in which our souls met and we understood each other."

Given the video and the confirmed cougar scat, New Brunswick could hardly continue to deny the presence of cougars. And since both the scat and the film had been obtained within easy cougar stride of the Maine border, the implications were obvious. In the fall of 1993 Ted Reed interviewed a Maine hunter who had unexpectedly come upon a large cat with a death grip on a bobcat. After about fifteen seconds the cat turned and stared at the hunter, who was transfixed by the piercing, burning eyes of an animal he described as looking like a female African lion. Maine biologists came and collected hairs from the scene for analysis, but the hairs got lost in a bureaucratic shuffle and no report ever came back to Reed. A photo of a Maine cougar published in the May 1994 issue of *Audubon* magazine caused a brief flare of hope until several biologists closely examined the shrubs and trees and pronounced them to be western species. It was known that the photographer went west regularly to hunt cougars. There have been a handful of hoaxes over the years. My husband once pressed a perfect cougar footprint into the mud beside our pond, but it didn't take me long to figure things out.

Lost hairs and hoaxes didn't matter, though, because another Maine hunter saw a cougar with two kittens early in 1994, and the tracks were confirmed by the Maine Department of Inland Fisheries and Wildlife. And later that same year, the National Fish and Wildlife Forensics Laboratory in Oregon confirmed that a scat found in the woods near Craftsbury, Vermont, belonged to a cougar. "Three cats were reported in that case," said Cedric Alexander, district biologist for the Vermont Fish and Wildlife Department. "So they are apparently producing young. Of course, their origins are in question."

This kind of remark made Reed chuckle. "The state agency line is beginning to change. They don't want to be found wrong. After I came back from World War II," he remembered, "people started to see wolflike animals in the woods. At first the agencies said, no, it wasn't possible. Then when people started to shoot coyotes, state biologists said they were coydogs, from a few odd individual coyotes that people brought from the West and released, and that had bred with dogs. Now it's well known that wild coyotes have infiltrated every eastern state. The bureaucracy will follow the same pattern with eastern panthers. Before they acknowledge that native panthers have managed to survive, they'll claim they're all escaped captives."

Circus train or truck accidents used to be a popular source of escaped captives, especially black panthers, but such crashes just don't happen very often. A speaker at the eastern cougar conference named Loren Coleman neatly traced the birth of that folklore to the 1952 movie, *The Greatest Show on Earth,* which featured a circus train wreck that loosed wild animals on the countryside. Coleman, with less credibility, also proposed that the very occasional sightings of maned lions were of surviving Pleistocene American lions, *Leo atrox,* and that the more frequently seen black cats were their off-colored mates. Like other captive cats, African lions do sometimes escape from zoos and roadside shows. A carcass that somebody salvaged from a dumpster in North Carolina and claimed in the late 1970s as a cougar trophy was found to be a female African lion. A ditch in North Carolina also yielded the skeleton of a young African lion in 1982.

More pertinent is the astounding market, legal and illegal, in exotic feline pets. Frank Weed, the Florida cougar breeder, can't keep up with the demand. I've read ads in newspapers and magazines for cougar kittens and out of curiosity wrote for a price list from an animal farm in South

Carolina. Cougar kittens were on sale at the time for $850. Adults were cheaper at $600, and jaguars, leopards, black leopards, Bengal tigers, and something called a "leopard jaguar" were available upon request (and—this was noted in small print—with proper Department of Interior permits) for $1,250 to $2,000. Federal laws are a maze and states have varying or no regulations, so estimates are virtually impossible, but where exotic cats can be reckoned, they number in the thousands. Endearingly cute as kittens, they grow into unpredictable, voracious adults, and some unknown percentage of them are turned loose by fearful or exasperated owners. In 1974 one cougar was killed and another was captured in West Virginia; the kind of parasites they carried and the behavior of the survivor strongly suggested prior life in a cage. A Tennessee cougar killed and mounted in 1971 had no toenails and was probably an escaped or released captive. Tissue from a cougar killed in 1992 in Quebec was analyzed by new techniques and showed Chilean genes. This might have been due to captive breeding or to the travels of a drug-smuggling former owner (wild cats seem to be popular among drug smugglers—and it's not uncommon for pumas to be confiscated when the owners are busted). A small adult female cougar was killed in Pennsylvania in 1967; some odd deformities suggested she was a former captive. With her was a larger companion, who escaped.

At the eastern cougar conference I met a gray-haired, florid-faced woman.

"What is your interest in cougars?" I asked.

"They're killing my sheep!" she boomed with British heartiness. She was from Cornwall, in England. Her small farm was named Ninestones, after a local Stonehenge. Four years ago the sheep she raised as a retirement hobby started dying from mysterious attacks. She had photographs of a woolly carcass with ribs sticking up into the air licked dry as sun-bleached driftwood. She had seen several cats, including a black one, and one of them had growled pretty fiercely at her handyman. After a protracted bout with the police, her story was finally corroborated when an officer personally encountered a puma. Free-ranging pumas also roam elsewhere in England. People started seeing strange cats long before a 1976 Act of Parliament required owners of exotic cats to purchase an expensive license, but afterward the number of sightings soared. Clouded leopards, jungle cats, bobcats, and ocelots are believed to have become naturalized, living on small game and occasional sheep, and on the roe deer that are abundant in some regions. There are so many sightings of large black cats that black leopards are also thought to be on the loose.

The only cat known to be native to Great Britain in historic times is the Scottish wildcat, which was relentlessly persecuted but not quite exterminated. In 1984 a black cat with sparkling white guard hairs, whose head and body length measured twenty-six inches, was shot near a village called Kellas in the Scottish Highlands. Within a year or two several similar cats were shot or snared. Some members of a newly formed group of open-minded scientists and optimistic lay people, called the International Society of Cryptozoology, believed these cats represented a new, unknown species and said there might well be other kinds of cats around the world never previously described by science because of their intensely secretive natures. After all, Iriomote cats were not discovered on their small island south of Japan until the 1960s, and large mammals unknown to taxonomists are still turning up in the rain forests of Southeast Asia. The University of Aberdeen in Scotland performed various tests and concluded that the Kellas cat was a wildcat-domestic cat hybrid. Although this scotched the possibility for formal recognition of a new species, it underlines evolutionary possibilities for the future.

Continental Europe has a remnant, native wildcat species that seems to be experiencing something of a renewal in the Jura Mountains. There are also scattered reports of large pantherlike cats across the continent. Even Australia, where the only native mammals are marsupials and humans, may have pumas. Sightings and livestock killings began in the 1950s. It's rumored that American soldiers stationed there in World War II had captive pumas as mascots. By the 1990s there were thousands of puma reports, some of them combining tawny with black cats, with even less proof than exists for panthers in the eastern United States.

Cats are almost preternaturally adaptable. A clouded leopard, an arboreal native of tropical rain forests, escaped from a zoo into the English countryside in 1975 and was expected to die or be recaptured within days because of the drastically foreign habitat. Nine months later, the sleek, healthy cat was shot by a farmer who was missing rabbits and lambs. Domestic cats gone feral in varied habitats around the world adopt the behavior most advantageous to their situation—males may become solitary or join club-like brotherhoods; females may be territorial or form cooperative sisterhoods. Pumas were versatile enough to colonize many different ecosystems in the Western Hemisphere—they were, after human beings, the most wide-ranging large mammal in the New World—so they may have a reservoir of adaptability that is deep even by cat standards. In recent decades they seem to be adapting to the movements of deer herds by trailing them northward. Though reports of cougars in Saskatchewan and Manitoba date back to the 1800s, none were ever killed in those provinces until 1952 and 1973, respectively. Alaska wasn't even mentioned as part of puma range in Young and Goldman's 1946 classic, *The Puma, Mysterious American Cat.* By the 1960s, however, cougars were being seen in the Yukon Territory, and in 1989 an adult male was shot on Alaska's Wrangell Island. Cougars may also be following on the heels of western coyotes, who traveled north, then east around the Great Lakes (where they may have mixed with remnant wolves in Minnesota), then down the Appalachian ridges. When they reached the East, coyotes grew larger and quieter than they had previously been known to be. Eastern cougars—whether remnant natives, immigrants, escapees, or a mix of all three—would likely be capable of similar and perhaps much more dramatic changes.

Of the various cougars that might be roaming the eastern forests, only the native eastern subspecies, *Felis concolor couguar,* and the Florida panther, *Felis concolor coryi,* are protected by the Endangered Species Act. The problem is distinguishing these from unprotected cougar subspecies on sight. The eastern subspecies was defined by the measurements of seven skulls and the appearance of one skin, typical of the paltry evidence used in the past to make taxonomic decisions.

Revisionist taxonomy is on the rise—witness the recent reclassification of cougars from *Felis* to a separate genus, *Puma,* by the Society of Mammalogists in 1993. At the time of the eastern cougar conference in 1994, the thirty traditional subspecies of cougars were being reassessed. Mammalogist Troy Best at Auburn University in Alabama was measuring every puma skull he could track down in North America and Europe—nearly two thousand—to compare morphological characteristics. At the conference, a petite, raven-haired doctoral student named Melanie Culver explained her more sophisticated method: analysis of molecular data from pumas throughout the Western Hemisphere, as evidence of subspecies designations and population subdivisions. A colleague of hers had just completed similar work on leopards and found significantly less genetic variation than the current list of twenty-seven leopard subspecies implied. Eventually, Culver felt, both the leopard work and her own might result in new taxonomies. Another colleague had determined that the African cheetah and American bobcat and lynx were closely related to the puma. As for the eastern puma subspecies, Culver hoped to obtain dried tissue with still-viable DNA from an 1828 skin in a Quebec museum—the earliest known eastern specimen—to look for any unique genetic markers that might characterize the eastern race.

To the hundred or so people in the audience, this was an interesting but purely academic exercise. All large cats that managed to survive in eastern woodlands were deemed worthy of full legal protection. But no one seemed quite sure how to enter the legal labyrinth of species definitions. And no one seemed ready to begin prodding federal and state agencies to name a recovery team, survey habitats, and—most crucial—open a dialogue with the public about restoration.

Calls for the restoration of cougars in the East had been raised in the 1980s by the Southwest-based radical environmental group Earth First!. In 1990 Earth First! broke up over philosophical differences between advocates of social justice and more focused environmentalists. One of its two founders, Dave Foreman, next inaugurated the Wildlands Project. Foreman is not tall but very muscular, which gives him an impression of bigness, and has thinning, reddish hair and blue eyes like slits in a rugged, open face. A hard drinker and lover of red meat, especially wild meat, he delights in calling himself a hillbilly. Foreman turned to activism after years of working for mainstream environmental organizations left him frustrated with the glacial pace of change. He recognized that existing parks and refuges were too small and isolated to maintain biodiversity, and he applied the ideas of conservation biology on a continental scale to map out the Wildlands Project vision: "the establishment of a connected system of reserves . . . based on the requirements of all native species to flourish within the ebb and flow of ecological processes, rather than within the constraints of what industrial civilization is content to leave alone."

The world would no longer be run solely to suit humans. Land would be managed in a three-tiered system: core reserves based on ecosystem functions, where most human activities would be excluded; buffer zones and undeveloped corridors, where human uses would be strictly defined; and outside, where intensive human uses would continue to dominate. The Wildlands Project did not aim at immediate revolution but hoped that long-term strategies such as educating the public about biodiversity and addressing specific regional needs would change society's values. Roads would have to be closed, dams torn down, people moved out, and all extirpated species restored. My hundred acres of woods at the foot of Cross Mountain, on the border of the George Washington National Forest, would be in a buffer zone, and cougars would call it home.

Foreman didn't attend the eastern cougar conference, and only one or two other Wildlands Project people were there. Without a strong activist presence, there was a certain ambivalence toward restoration. Ted Reed and John Lutz opposed it on the grounds that existing cats ought not to be disturbed in any way, though everyone agreed that any existing cats must be so sparse they couldn't have much of a social structure to disturb. Some people felt that if there were remnant cats of the native subspecies, those genes ought to be preserved in their purity—an approach that failed in Florida. Others argued that a breeding population of eastern cougars must first be found before any further action could be expected from the federal government, even though the federal Eastern Cougar Recovery Plan calls for "three self-sustaining populations [to be] found *or established* [italics added]."

A hulking, bearded man shambled up to the podium. Dr. Ranier Brocke, a biology professor at the State University of New York at Syracuse, traveled with the Downings in the early 1980s, looking for cougars in the Southern Appalachians. He was convinced that none had survived and that the occasional credible sighting was of an escapee. He studied maps and analyzed the possibility of restoring cougars to the Adirondacks. "Most of the East is a huge environmental success story," he told the audience. "Contrary to common perception, many birds and other animals are increasing. There's plenty of deer and cover for cougars. It's not biological factors that would pose problems for the return of eastern cougars."

Brocke had concluded in 1981 that "a potentially reintroduced cougar population cannot survive the high level of man-induced mortality which is probable in Adirondack Park at this writing." Nothing had changed his mind since. By "man-induced mortality" he meant that cougars would be struck by vehicles on the too-many roads in their range, shot and trapped by too many poachers who drive those roads, and killed by too many other people who would feel or actually be menaced by cougars. Brocke's calculation of human density was based on permanent residents and didn't even include summer tourists. There were simply too many people. A population of fifty to one hundred introduced cougars would be extinct within ten years.

"I reached this conclusion with regret," Brocke said, "because the cougar in the Adirondacks is dear to my heart." He had grown up in India, the son of German missionaries, and had come to know tigers and leopards at close range. He thought there was something superlative about big cats, especially the solitary ones. He wanted to make the East safe for cougars. Recognizing that seventy percent of the East is privately owned—the reversal of the public-private landownership ratio in the West—Brocke had mapped out his own wildlands vision: a system of "predator survival spaces." He sketched these on a map as bubbles floating out from a public land core and touching each other across the landscape. Each should be at least four hundred square miles, voluntarily managed by private landowners for long-term timber rotation. It wasn't a map of my region, but I could see how my hundred acres would fit naturally and logically into a bubble. Because I live next to one of the largest chunks of public land in the East, any proposal to restore cougars would put them in my backyard.

In his own way, Brocke was an iconoclast: he championed clearcutting. Clearcuts of one hundred to two hundred acres once a century, with no other entry to those stands during that time except once for thinning out saplings, would give landowners a steady product and predators some privacy. Between cuttings, all roads would be permanently closed. Land-owners who subscribed to this management would lose the continuous access to their woods that other methods offered and should receive tax breaks and other compensatory benefits.

"We have to manage for less risk of death, rather than for any specific habitat conditions," Brocke said. "But we have to do it without changing cultural habits too dramatically, because that's the only thing that will work in the long run. It's all a matter of attitudes."

The rock den where Adam Rudolph hung upside down by his heels in 1850 to shoot his cowering cougar is, as the ravens fly, a few dozen miles from my place. If I walk a little ways up Cross Mountain and into the national forest, I can look up the spines of several Allegheny ridges almost as far as the boulder fields of Paddy Mountain. From a distance Paddy Mountain looks the same to me as it must have to Adam, but the woods are altogether different from Adam's time. The massive oaks so thickly set along Cedar Creek are long gone, smoldered into charcoal to fuel Van Buren's iron furnace. Oaks and hemlocks for miles around were cut over and over for the bark vats at Starr Tannery. Remaining trees were cut again and again for sawtimber and pulpwood. The fabulous chestnuts died from blight. Indians, elk, bison, wolves, and panthers were shot out, but bears still manage to hang on.

Adam's house is surrounded by small fields spiky with pine plantations. The bricks that he shaped from the banks of Cedar Creek are pale red, like faded roses. Sycamores now line the creek banks and stretch ghostly white-barked arms against the bruised blue slope of forest behind them. Adam's grave at St. James Church lies about a mile from his house, on a little rise above Cedar Creek, which still flows by like a vein of molten silver. His tombstone faces the rockslides of Paddy Mountain. His people still climb to the cougar's last den—in fact, they make an annual event of it. One year I joined them.

"I used to go with some of the Rudolph grandkids to the family reunions," Junior McIlwee said, "and I knew that the Rudolph family had marked what they believed to be Adam's route up Paddy Mountain during a reunion in 1940. I wondered if I could retrace their steps." It took him a couple of years, but he finally found the old orange blazes, which he refreshed. The McIlwees go back five generations here, and somewhere back there was a connection with the Rudolph family. Junior McIlwee, a tall, spare, middle-aged man who now teaches school in the Shenandoah Valley, used to sit around the wood stove with other children at the village store, which was run by Hershell Rudolph. Hershell liked to tell stories. Junior grew up hearing the tale of Adam Rudolph's panther.

The mountains that edge Adam's valley are owned by the U.S. Forest Service now, but in the privately owned rolling valley bottom are log cabins on stone foundations and white clapboard houses gone dark gray with age. There are also new houses and mobile homes. Trees are bedecked with orange ties, blue paint stripes, bright yellow *No Hunting* signs. Every yard has stacks of firewood, and the modest McIlwee farmhouse is no exception.

"Every year, that's all they talk about, going up to the panther's den," said Alma, Junior's mother. "It takes all afternoon to get up there and back." She wasn't planning to go along. She looked about seventy, small and quick like a bird, with beautiful hands that belied a lifetime of hard labor. Her only jewelry was a thin gold wedding band. The next day she would celebrate her fifty-second anniversary with the man she had known since they went to school together down the road.

"I saw a panther," she offered. "That was in, let's see, we stopped milking—we had fifty-six cows before we went to beef cattle—we stopped milking in 1977, so probably it was seventy-six. We seen this big thing. It was a-laying down underneath this tree, and he was a brownish looking thing and my son said I'm going down there and see him. He started with a stick in his hand and got halfway and boy that thing jumped up, oh, it was long and he just give a big lunge and had this big tail and out through the woods he went. They've brought them over here and was trying to stock them, and oh, I don't know how many they put out, and every once in a while you'd see one, slinking around. The forest rangers, I guess, that's who stocked them. They used to bring big old black bear, too. It's a good idea to have some of those things around to clean up carcasses, keep out diseases."

Later I asked the national forest ranger, who had also come along for the hike, about state or federal agencies releasing cougars. It's a rumor that floats around the East. The ranger had been in the area for many years and had heard the talk since he first came. He had also heard the government blamed for stocking bears, coyotes, rattlesnakes, and various insects. Some of the rumors were founded on truth. Nuisance black bears live-trapped in Shenandoah National Park were turned loose in the Alleghenies, where they were less likely to raid garbage cans. Some insect species had been released to combat gypsy moths, an exotic pest whose dun-colored egg masses speckled the bark of the trees we hiked past and promised defoliation in the coming summer. As far as cougars go, though—not to mention coyotes and rattlesnakes—the ranger considered the accusations a form of modern folklore. It is hard to imagine that any agency would undertake such a project in secret. Maybe the rumors reflect an underlying mistrust of government, or fulfill some need for a conspiracy theory.

"I wouldn't want panthers in the woods, myself," Alma continued.

"They say they will not bother you as long as they're not hungry. But I read in the papers, why, there's several children killed by them. Course, people don't go and walk after night like they always did. They're usually driving. Now I don't know if they would bother livestock, they could, calves you know, something small, but I don't care to think about it."

Alma's husband Eugene didn't get around too well anymore and wasn't coming with us either. He sat on a tractor and watched the milling crowd of children and grandchildren try to organize for the outing. Like Alma, he wasn't keen on the idea of panthers in the woods. "I don't know, those things would kill your cattle, wouldn't they? They get hungry they'd kill anything, don't you think?" He leaned over to pick up and cradle a barn cat in his arms.

It was March, and there was no snow to make us lift our feet high, as Adam Rudolph had to. Still, it was rough going. The kids clambered ahead searching for orange marks and yelling encouragement back to us when they found one. For a long time, as we followed the youngsters, Junior and his brothers gave the ranger hell for the clearcutting that the Forest Service was promoting in the area. Clearcutting was ugly and destructive, they said. The ranger made a few weak defenses, but he could tell it was hopeless.

Near the top the blazes were easy to see on the gleaming white rocks. The adults picked their way up and looked for comfortable spots to eat a picnic lunch. I sat beside Judy, Junior's wife. She worked as a legal secretary. Every other weekend or so she and Junior and their two children drove up from the Shenandoah Valley to visit Alma and Eugene. They helped with hog butchering, or went hunting for squirrel and deer, or planted the garden, or did whatever the seasonal rhythm of rural life demanded.

"I want my children to understand the simple life, to slow down, to realize that the best things in life are free," Judy said. "I often wonder if people in the old days ever thought about animals becoming extinct or whether they just . . . of course, they ate the meat. I just doubt they ever thought we shouldn't kill animals so heavily off. More people today think about down the road, they want their children to be able to see these animals. I would not have any problems with panthers being here. I'd like to think they wouldn't bother people."

"If they're out there now they're not hurting anything," Junior said. He had hazel eyes and the thoughtful face of a scholar. "Everything has its place. It's no good for one species to exterminate another. That throws everything out of balance. If there were more panthers, of course we'd have to get used to it. But people kill a lot more deer than panthers would. More deer end up in the Dumpster than panthers would ever hurt. I found about a dozen thrown away in plastic garbage bags. Whoever shot them took only the skin and the haunches."

Older kids were holding younger ones by their heels, hanging them down into the den. The commotion was becoming deafening, and we walked over.

"Great God, here's the forked stick they pulled him out with!" somebody yelled, waving a wizened branch.

"I'd have left him in there," someone else replied.

I was standing next to one of the McIlwee grandchildren, a boy of about fifteen. "Why do you think Adam Rudolph took so much trouble, in the snow and all, to get that panther?" I asked him.

He paused for a moment and frowned, wrinkling his smooth young forehead. "Those people," he said finally, "were different from us."

In the end, it doesn't really matter whether eastern cougars are out there or not. What matters is that they should be there. Cougars belong in the East by evolutionary birthright. It is the ripening of this idea that makes our time different from Adam Rudolph's day. Still, it would be difficult to actually turn the idea into reality, to bring cougars back. Unlike bears, which have been teddified for nearly a century, and wolves, whose admirable family life is now well known, cougars offer little on which to hang a notion of kinship. They must be accepted on their own wild terms. To find the humility to atone for past mistakes, to find the greatness of heart to share the woods with a being far beyond our ken—that is the spiritual challenge of the eastern panther.

Ambivalence has long been recognized as fundamental to the human psyche. Sigmund Freud began writing about it in 1912, and many other students of human nature have explored its dimensions. Ambivalence develops through stages that children pass through; perhaps cultures pass through them, too. A child might say on one day she loves her brother and on the next, hates him. With growth comes first the recognition that two opposite emotions might be aroused by one experience or person, then the understanding that those emotions might coexist simultaneously. The final step to maturity is integration: to balance the extremes without denying the complexities.

Sometimes at dusk I sit on my deck and watch sunset-streaked clouds fade away toward Paddy Mountain. I wonder how it would be to know a panther crouches there again, yellow eyes gleaming, muscles taut, utterly focused. How it would be to accept the risks with understanding and respect, in return for the rightness. A dank breeze slides down Cross Mountain and a chill rises up my back. It would feel, I think, like freedom.

BIBLIOGRAPHY

Most of the sources for this book are listed by chapter. Those that were useful in many chapters are listed below.

Barnes, Claude. *The Cougar or Mountain Lion*. Salt Lake City: Ralton Co., 1960.

Hancock, Lynn. "A History of Changing Attitudes to *Felis concolor*." Thesis. Burnaby, British Columbia: Simon Fraser University, 1980.

Hansen, Kevin. *Cougar, the American Lion*. Flagstaff: Northland, 1992.

Tinsley, Jim Bob. *The Puma, Legendary Lion of the Americas*. El Paso: University of Texas, 1987.

Young, Stanley P., and Edward A. Goldman. *The Puma, Mysterious American Cat*. Washington, D.C.: American Wildlife Institute, 1946.

NATIVE AMERICANS AND AMERICAN LIONS

Allen, Craig D. "Changes in the Landscape of the Jemez Mountains, NM." Ph.D. dissertation, University of California, 1989.

Bandelier, Adolph F. A. *Final Report of Investigations among the Indians of the Southwestern U.S.* Papers of the Archaeological Institute of America. American Series III-IV. Cambridge, Massachusetts: John Wilson & Son, 1890-92.

———. *The Delight Makers.* 1890. New York: Harcourt Brace Jovanovich, 1971.

Benson, Elizabeth P., ed. *The Cult of the Feline: A Conference in Pre-Columbian Iconography.* Washington, D.C.: Dumbarton Oaks, 1972.

Billingsley, M. W. *Behind the Scenes in Hopi Land.* [no place]: [no pub.], 1971.

Bradley, James W., and S. Terry Childs. "Basque Earrings and Panther's Tails." MASCA research papers in science, 1991, 7–17.

Brose, David S., James A. Brown, and David W. Penney. *Ancient Art of the American Woodland Indians.* New York: Harry N. Abrams, 1985.

Brown, Joseph Eppes. *Animals of the Soul: Sacred Animals of the Oglala Sioux.* Rockport, Massachusetts: Element, 1992.

Capps, Walter H., ed. *Seeing with a Native Eye: Essays on Native American Religion.* New York: Harper & Row, 1976.

Colton, Harold S. *Hopi Kachina Dolls.* 1959. Albuquerque: University of New Mexico Press, 1964.

Cushing, Frank H. *Zuni Fetishes.* Bureau of Ethnology, 2nd Annual Report. Washington, D.C.: U.S. Government Printing Office; Las Vegas: KC Publications, 1990.

Deloria, Vine. *God Is Red.* New York: Grosset & Dunlap, 1973.

Dobie, J. Frank. "Tales of the Panther." *Saturday Evening Post,* December 11, 1943.

Douglass, William Boone. *Notes on the Shrines of the Tewa and Other Pueblo Indians of New Mexico.* [no place]: [no pub.], [no date].

Eastman, Charles A. *Red Hunters and the Animal People.* New York: Harper & Bros., 1904.

Erdoes, Richard, and Alfonso Ortiz. *American Indian Myths and Legends.* New York: Pantheon Books, 1984.

Gill, Sam D. *Native American Religions: An Introduction.* Belmont, California: Wadsworth Publishing Co., 1982.

Guggisberg, Charles A. W. *Wild Cats of the World.* New York: Taplinger, 1975.

Henderson, Junius, and John P. Harrington. "Ethnozoology of the Tewa Indians." *Bureau of American Ethnology Bulletin,* 1914.

Hewett, Edgar L. *Pajarito Plateau and Its Ancient People.* Albuquerque: University of New Mexico Press, 1938.

Hill, W. W. *The Agricultural and Hunting Methods of the Navaho Indians.* Yale University Publications in Anthropology, No. 18. New Haven: Yale University Press, 1938.

Holloran, Arthur. "A Wildlife Reconnaissance of the Navajo Indian Reservation." September 1961. Unpublished report to the Navajo Nation.

Howard, James H. *The Southeastern Ceremonial Complex and Its Interpretation.* Stillwater: Oklahoma State University, 1968.

———. "When They Worship the Underwater Panther: A Prairie Potawatomi Bundle Ceremony." *Southwest Journal of Anthropology,* 1960.

Hudson, Charles. *Elements of Southeastern Indian Religion.* Leiden: Brill, 1984.

———. *The Southeastern Indians.* University of Tennessee Press, 1976.

Hudson, W. W. *The Naturalist in La Plata.* 3rd ed. New York: D. Appleton & Co., 1895.

Hultkrantz, Ake. *Belief and Worship in Native North America.* Syracuse: Syracuse University Press, 1981.

James, Harry C. *Pages from Hopi History.* Tucson: University of Arizona Press, 1976.

Kluckhohn, Clyde, and Dorothea Leighton. *The Navaho.* Cambridge, Massachusetts: Harvard University Press, 1946.

Luckert, Karl W. *The Navajo Hunter Tradition.* Tucson: University of Arizona, 1975.

Matthiessen, Peter. *Indian Country.* New York: Viking Press, 1979.

Meurger, Michel, and Claude Gagnon. *Lake Monster Traditions: A Cross Cultural Analysis.* 1982. London: Fortean Tomes, 1988.

Newcomb, Franc Johnson, Stanley Fishler, and Mary C. Wheelwright. *A Study of Navajo Symbolism.* Cambridge, Massachusetts: Peabody Museum; New York: Kraus Reprint, 1968.

Parsons, Elsie Clews. *Pueblo Indian Religion.* Chicago: University of Illinois Press; Midway Reprint, 1974.

———. *Taos Pueblo.* General Series in Anthropology, No. 2. Menosha, Wisconsin: George Banta Publishing Co., 1936.

Patterson, Alex. *A Field Guide to Rock Art Symbols of the Greater Southwest.* Boulder: Johnson Books, 1992.

Price, Gene. "Bear Depredation Problems on the Navajo Reservation." Unpublished report to the Navajo Nation prepared for Williams Creek Wildlife Conference, October 13, 1966.

Rethinking Columbus. A Special Edition of Rethinking Schools. Milwaukee: Rethinking Schools, Ltd., 1991.

Riechard, Gladys A. *Navajo Religion, a Study of Symbolism.* Vol. 1. Bollingen Series 18. New York: Pantheon Books, 1950.

Ryan, Pat. "A Status Report: Population Characteristics of Black Bears in the Chuska Mountains of the Navajo Nation." Unpublished report to the Navajo Nation, c. 1984.

Seger, John H., trans. *Tradition of the Cheyenne Indians.* [Colony, Oklahoma]: Arapaho Beeprint, 1905.

Sherard, Priscilla M. *People of the Place of the Fire* [Potawatomie]. Unpublished manuscript.

Sturtevant, William C. *Handbook of the North American Indians.* Vol. 8, California, and volumes 9 and 10, Southwest. Washington, D.C.: Smithsonian Institution, 1983.

Tiller, Veronica. *Discover Indian Reservations USA: A Visitors' Welcome Guide.* Denver: Council Publications, 1992.

Vecsey, Christopher, and Robert W. Venables. *American Indian Environments: Ecological Issues in Native American History.* Syracuse: Syracuse University Press, 1983.

Vega, Garcilaso de la. *Royal Commentaries of the Incas, and General History of Peru.* Translated by Harold V. Livermore. Austin: University of Texas Press, 1970.

Waters, Frank. *Book of the Hopi.* New York: Penguin Books, 1963.

Weir, Bill. *Arizona Traveler's Handbook.* Chico, California: Moon Publications, 1992.

Whiteford, Andrew Hunter. "Fiber Bags of the Great Lakes Indians." *American Indian Art Magazine,* May 1977.

Zuidema, R. Tom. "The Lion in the City: Royal Symbols of Transition in Cuzco." In *Animal Myths and Metaphors in South America.* Edited by Gary Urton. Salt Lake City: University of Utah Press, 1985.

EUROPEAN IMPACT STATEMENT

"[Accounts of Lions]." *Gentleman's Magazine,* 1749, 89.

"[Accounts of Lions]." *Gentleman's Magazine,* 1750,8.

"[Accounts of Lions]." *Gentleman's Magazine,* 1772, 169.

Aristotle. *Aristotle's History of Animals.* Translated by Richard Cresswell. London: Geo. Bell & Sons, 1897.

Audubon, John James, and John Bachman. *Viviparous Quadrupeds of North America.* New York: J.J. Audubon, 1845-48.

Baughman, Ernest W. "A Comparative Study of the Folktales of England and North America." Doctoral dissertation series, Pub. 5855, Indiana University, 1953.

Beverly, Robert. *The History and Present State of Virginia.* 1705. Chapel Hill: University of North Carolina Press, 1947.

Bewick, Thomas. *A General History of Quadrupeds.* Newcastle upon Tyne: 1824.

Bierce, Ambrose. *The Complete Short Stories of Ambrose Bierce.* Edited by Ernest J. Hopkins. Garden City, New York: Doubleday & Co., 1970.

Boorstin, Daniel J. *The Americans: The Colonial Experience.* New York: Random House, 1958.

Bruce, E. C. "A Dish of Capon." *Harper's New Monthly Magazine,* April 1861.

Bryan, Daniel. *The Mountain Muse, Comprising the Adventures of Daniel Boone; and the Power of Virtuous and Refined Beauty.* Harrisonburg, Virginia: Davidson & Bourne, 1813.

Buffon, Georges L. L. *Natural History, General and Particular.* Translated with Notes and Observations by William Smellie. London: T. Cadell & W. Davies, 1812.

Bull, Charles Livingston. "The Puma." *The Century Magazine,* November 1913.

Burrage, Henry S. *Early English and French Voyages, Chiefly from Hakluyt, 1534–1608.* 1906. New York: Barnes & Noble, 1967.

Byrd, William. *William Byrd's Histories of the Dividing Line.* Raleigh: North Carolina Historical Commission, 1929.

Calkins, Franklin W. *My Host the Enemy and Other Tales; Sketches of Life and Adventure on the Border Line of the West.* Freeport, New York: Books for Libraries Press, 1969 (first published in 1901).

————. *The Cougar Tamer and Other Stories of Adventure.* Freeport, New York: Books for Libraries Press, 1971 (first published in 1898).

Cameron, Jenks. *The Bureau of Biological Survey: Its History, Activities, and Organization.* Institute for Government Research. Service Monographs of the U.S. Government No. 54. Baltimore: Johns Hopkins Press, 1929.

Carter, M. H., ed. *Panther Stories Retold from St. Nicholas.* New York: Century, 1904.

Catesby, Mark. *The Natural History of Carolina, Florida, and the Bahama Islands.* Chapel Hill: University of North Carolina Press, 1985. Reprint of the 1771 edition.

"Causes of Discontent in Virginia, 1676." *Virginia Magazine of History and Biography,* 1894–95, 289.

Charlevoix, P. de. *Journal of a Voyage to North America.* Translated from the French. London: Dodsley, 1761.

Clark, Anne. *Beasts and Bawdy.* London: Dent, 1975.

Clayton, John. "Account of Virginia." Philosophical Transactions of the Royal Society of London, no. 210, May 1694.

———. "Virginia Game and Field Sports: Description of Them by the Botanist Clayton in 1739." *Virginia Magazine of History and Biography,* vol. 7, 1899–1900, 172–74.

Cumming, W. P., R. A. Skelton, and D. B. Quinn. *The Discovery of North America.* New York: American Heritage Press, 1972.

Cuvier, Georges, Baron. *The Animal Kingdom Arranged in Conformity. . . .* London: Whittaker, 1827.

DeKay, James. *Anniversary Address of the Progress of the Natural Sciences in the U.S.* New York: G. & C. Carvill, 1826; Arno Press, 1970.

———. *Natural History of New York: Zoology.* New York: Appleton, 1842.

Ewan, Joseph, and Nesta Ewan. *John Banister and His Natural History of Virginia, 1678–1692.* Urbana: University of Chicago Press, 1970.

Ferrell, Dorothy M. *Bear Tales and Panther Tracks,* Books 1, 2, 3. Atlanta: Appalachian Publisher, 1969, 1968.

Flader, Susan. "Leopold on Wilderness." *American Forests,* May–June 1991.

——— *Thinking Like a Mountain: Aldo Leopold and the Evolution of an Ecological Attitude toward Deer, Wolves, and Forests.* Columbia: University of Missouri Press, 1974.

Godman, John. *American Natural History.* Philadelphia: Carey & Lea, 1826.

Goode, B. Browne. "Presidential Address: The Beginnings of Natural History in America." In *Proceedings of the Biological Society of Washington,* Vol. 3. Washington, D.C.: The Society, 1886.

Hamor, Ralph. *A True Discourse of the Present State of Virginia.* Richmond: Virginia State Library, 1957 (first published 1615).

Hariot, Thomas. "A Brief and True Report of the New Found Land of Virginia." In *Explorations, Descriptions, and Attempted Settlements of Carolina, 1584–1590.* Raleigh: State Department of Archives & History, 1953 (first published 1588).

Harlan, Richard. *Fauna Americana*. Philadelphia: Anthony Finley, 1825.

Jefferson, Thomas. "A Memoir on the Discovery of Certain Bones of a Quadruped of the Clawed Kind in the Western Parts of Virginia." *Transactions of the American Philosophical Society* 4, 30 (1797).

————. *Notes on the State of Virginia*. 1784. Chapel Hill: University of North Carolina Press, 1955.

Josselyn, John. *New England's Rarities Discovered in Birds, Beasts, Fishes . . .* London: Printed for G. Widdowes, 1672.

Kastner, Joseph. "How We Invented the Lion." *International Wildlife*, September–October 1990.

Laming, Annette. *Lascaux, Paintings and Engravings*. Translated by E. F. Armstrong. Harmondsworth: Penguin, 1959.

Lawson, John. *Lawson's History of North Carolina*. Edited by F.L. Harriss. Richmond: Garrett & Massie, 1937 (first published in 1709).

Leopold, Aldo. *A Sand County Almanac*. New York: Ballantine Books, 1982 (first published in 1949).

Linzey, Andrew, and Tom Regan, eds. *Animals and Christianity, a Book of Readings*. New York: Crossroad, 1988.

Lopez, Barry H. *Of Wolves and Men*. New York: C. Scribner's Sons, 1978.

McCulloch, Florence. *Medieval Latin and French Bestiaries*. Chapel Hill: University of North Carolina Press, 1962.

Medieval Bestiary. Translated by T. J. Elliott. Boston: Godine, 1971.

Meine, Curt. *Aldo Leopold, His Life and Work*. Madison: University of Wisconsin Press, 1988.

Meisel, Max. *Bibliography of American Natural History*. New York: Hafner Publishing Co., 1967.

Mighetto, Lisa. *Wild Animals and American Environmental Ethics*. Tucson: University of Arizona Press, 1991.

"Minutes of the Council and General Court, 1622–1929." *Virginia Magazine of History & Biography*, vol. 21, 1913, 45–47.

Morton, Thomas. "New English Canaan (London, Charles Green, 1632)." In Force, Peter. Tracts and Other Papers . . . Gloucester, Massachusetts: Peter Smith, 1963.

Old English Physiologus. Translated by Albert S. Cook and James H. Pitman. New Haven: Yale University Press, 1921.

Ord, George. *A Reprint of the North American Zoology by George Ord, Being an Exact Reproduction . . .* 1815. Haddonfield, New Jersey: Samuel N. Rhoads, 1894.

Parker, Gilbert. *A Romany of the Snows; 2nd Series of an Adventure of the North, Being a Continuation f Pierre and His People* . . . 1896. Freeport, New York: Books for Libraries Press, 1969.

Pennant, Thomas. *History of Quadrupeds,* vol. 1. London: B. White, 1781.

———. *Synopsis of Quadrupeds.* Chester: J. Monk, 1771.

"Perfect Description of Virginia [1649]." *Virginia Historical Register,* 1849, 76.

Pliny the Elder. *The Natural History of Pliny.* Translated by John Bostock and H. T. Riley. London: H. G. Bohn, 1855.

Powell, T. G. E. *Prehistoric Art.* New York: F. A. Praeger, 1966.

Priest, Joseph. *Stories of the Revolution.* Albany: Hoffman & White, 1838.

Rafinesque, Constantine S. "On the North American Cougars." *Atlantic Journal and Friend of Knowledge,* 1832–33.

Ray, John. *Synopsis Methodica Animalium Quadrupedum* . . . London: Robert Southwell; New York: Arno Press, 1978 (first published in 1693).

Roosevelt, Theodore. "A Cougar Hunt on the Rim of the Grand Canyon." *The Outlook,* October 4, 1913.

———. "The Cougar." In *The Wilderness Hunter.* 1893. New York: C. Scribner's Sons, 1926.

———. *Theodore Roosevelt, an Autobiography.* 1913. New York: C. Scribner's Sons, 1925.

———. "With the Cougar Hounds." *Scribner's,* October 1901.

Rowland, Beryl. *Animals with Human Faces, a Guide to Animal Symbolism.* University of Tennessee Press, 1973.

Sandars, N. K. *Prehistoric Art in Europe.* Baltimore: Penguin Books, 1968.

Seton, Ernest Thompson. *Lives of Game Animals,* vol. 1. Garden City: Doubleday, Doran & Co., 1929.

Simms, William Gilmore. "The Cub of the Panther, a Mountain Legend." *The Old Guard.* 12 installments. 1869.

Skinner, Charles M. *American Myths and Legends.* Philadelphia: J. B. Lippincott, 1903.

Smith, Seba. *'Way Down East, or Portraitures of Yankee Life.* J. C. Derby; New York: Garrett Press, 1969 (reprinted from the 1854 edition).

Stearns, Raymond P. *Science in the British Colonies of America.* Urbana: University of Illinois Press, 1970.

Strachey, William. *Historie of Travell into Virginia Britannia.* 1612. London: Hakluyt Society, 1953.

Thomas, Roy Edwin, ed. and comp. *Authentic Ozarks Stories, Big Varmints: Bears, Wolves, Panthers.* Little Rock: Dox Books, 1972.

Thwaites, Reuben G. *Early Western Travels, 1748–1846.* Cleveland: Clark, 1907.

Tinling, Marion, ed. *The Correspondence of the Three William Byrds of Westover, Virginia, 1684–1776.* Charlottesville: University of Virginia Press for Virginia Historical Society, 1977.

Topsell, Edward. *Historie of Foure-Footed Beastes, Describing . . . Collected Out of all the Volumes of Conrad Gesner, and All Other Writers . . .* London: Wm. Iaggard, 1607; New York: Theatrum Orbis Terrarum & Da Capo Press, 1973.

True, Frederick W. *Report for 1889.* U.S. National Museum, 1891, 591–608.

Turnbo, Silas Claborn. *Turnbo's Tales of the Ozarks: Panther Stories.* Edited by Desmond Walls Allen. Conway: Arkansas Research, 1989.

Virginia Writers' Project. *Folklore Collection by Workers of the Writers' Program of the Public Works Administration, 1936–43.* Manuscript collection 1547, University of Virginia Library.

Whitaker, Alexander. *Good Newes from Virginia.* London: Wm. Welby, 1613.

Wood, William. *New England's Prospect.* London: 1634; Amsterdam: Da Capo Press, 1968.

Worster, Donald. *Nature's Economy: A History of Ecological Ideas.* Cambridge: Cambridge University Press, 1977.

LION HUNTING IN AMERICA

Barnhurst, Dan, and Frederick G. Lindzey. "Detecting Female Mountain Lions with Kittens." *Northwest Science* 63, 1 (1989).

———. *Vulnerability of Cougars to Hunting.* Utah Division of Wildlife Resources, 1986.

Bond, Jim. *The Mountain Lion.* Portland: published by author, 1977.

Bruce, Jay. "The Problem of Mountain Lion Control in California." *California Fish and Game* 11,1 (January 1925).

———. "The Why and How of Mountain Lion Hunting in California." *California Fish and Game,* vol. 8 (April 1922).

Calder, William A. "Man and the Mountain Lion in the Early 1900s; Perspectives from a Wildcat Dump." *Journal of the Southwest,* Summer 1990, 150–72.

Carmony, Neil B., and David E. Brown, eds. "First Jaguars in Sinaloa." In *Mexican Game Trails: Americans Afield in Old Mexico, 1866–1940.* Norman: University of Oklahoma Press, [no date].

"Colorado Lion Hunt." *Forest and Stream* 63 (December 3, 1904).

Dobie, J. Frank. "Mister Ben Lilly—Bear Hunter East and West." *Saturday Review of Literature,* May 16, 1942.

———. *The Ben Lilly Legend.* 1950. Austin: University of Texas Press, 1990.

———. "The Greatest Tracker of the West." *Saturday Evening Post,* March 4, 1950.

———. "The Man Who Thought Like a Panther." *True West,* November-December 1963.

Graham, Gid. *Animal Outlaws.* 2nd ed. Collinsville, Oklahoma: Gidean Graham, 1938.

Grey, Zane. *Roping Lions in the Grand Canyon.* New York: Grosset & Dunlap, 1922.

———. *Tales of Lonely Trails.* Flagstaff: Northland Press, 1986.

Hall, Del. *Island Gold, a History of Cougar Hunting on Vancouver Island.* Victoria: Cougar Press Ltd., 1990.

Hemker, Thomas, et al. "Population Characteristics and Movement Patterns of Cougars in Southern Utah." *Journal of Wildlife Management* 48, 4 (October 1984): 1275-84.

Hibben, Frank C. *Hunting American Lions.* New York: Thomas Crowell Co., 1948.

Hofer, T. Elwood. "Hunting with a Camera." *Forest and Stream* 30 (May 31, 1888): 370-71.

"Interview with Karen LeCount." *Full Cry,* June 1985.

Journey, Bud. "Chasing Cats." *Outdoor Life,* 23, December 1988.

Kennedy, Bess, *The Lady and the Lions.* New York: Whittlesey House, McGraw-Hill Book Co., 1942.

Lackner, W. S. "Hounds and Horses on a Cat Trail." *Outdoor Life,* July 1936.

LeCount, Karen. "A Track in the Snow." *Arizona Hunter,* August 1984.

Lindzey, Frederick G. *Boulder-Escalante Cougar Project, Final Report.* Utah Division of Wildlife Resources. 1989.

Logan, Kenneth A., et al. "Characteristics of a Hunted Mountain Lion Population in Wyoming." *Journal of Wildlife Management* 50, 4 (October 1986): 648–54.

McCurdy, Robert L. *Life of the Greatest Guide: Hound Stories and Others of Dale Lee.* Phoenix: Blue River Graphics, 1979.

"Mountain Lion Hunting." *Outdoor Life,* 1991.

Nesbit, William H., and Jack Reneau, eds. *Records of North American Big Game.* 9th ed. Dumfries, Virginia: Boone & Crockett Clug, 1988.

Newell, David M. *Cougars and Cowboys.* New York: Century Co., 1927.

O'Connor, Jack. "A Lee for a Lion." *Outdoor Life,* May 1939.

Pringle, Henry F. *Theodore Roosevelt, a Biography.* New York: Harcourt, Brace, 1931.

Putnam, Carlton. *Theodore Roosevelt, vol. 1: The Formative Years, 1858–1886.* New York: C. Scribner's Sons, 1959.

Schueren, Arnold C. *Foxy's Lion Tales.* [no place]: published by author, 1943.

Trefethen, James B. *An American Crusade for Wildlife.* Alexandria, Virginia: Boone & Crockett Club, 1975.

Vosburgh, John R. *Texas Lion Hunter.* San Antonio: Naylor Co, 1949.

Young, Stanley. "Hints on Mountain Lion Trapping." USDA leaflet no. 94, April 1933.

LION SCIENCE, A PAPER

Bass, Rick. "Grizzlies: Are They Out There?" *Audubon,* September–October 1993, 66-78, 110-11.

Cahalane, Victor H. "The Evolution of Predator Control Policy in the National Parks." *Journal of Wildlife Management* 3, 3 (July 1930).

Franklin, William L. "Patagonia Puma: The Lord of Land's End." *National Geographic,* January 1991, 104–12.

Guggisberg, Charles A. W. *Wild Cats of the World.* New York: Taplinger Publishing Co., 1975.

Haines, Aubrey L. *The Yellowstone Story: A History of Our First National Park.* Yellowstone Library & Museum with Colorado Associated University Press, 1977.

Hemker, Thomas P., Frederick G. Lindzey, and Bruce B. Ackerman. "Population Characteristics and Movement Patterns of Cougars in Southern Utah." *Journal of Wildlife Management* 48, 4 (1984): 1275–84.

Hibben, Frank C. *A Preliminary Study of the Mountain Lion.* The University of New Mexico Bulletin, no. 318, Biological Series vol. 5, no. 3. University of New Mexico Press, 1937.

Iriarte, J. Augustin, William L. Franklin, Warren E. Johnson, and Kent H. Redford. "Biogeographic Variation of Food Habits and Body Size of the American Puma." *Oecologia* 85, 2 (1990): 185–90.

Koehler, Gary M., and Maurice G. Hornocker. *A Preliminary Survey of Mountain Lions in Yellowstone National Park.* 1986. Moscow, Idaho: Wildlife Research Institute.

Laing, Steven P., and Frederick G. Lindzey. "Patterns of Replacement of Resident Cougars in Southern Utah." *Journal of Mammology* 74, 4 (1993): 1056–1058.

Lindzey, Frederick G., et al. *Boulder-Escalante Cougar Project, Final Report.* Utah Division of Wildlife Resources, 1989.

————. et al. "Cougar Population Response to Manipulation in Southern Utah." *Wildlife Society Bulletin* 20, 2 (1992): 224–27.

Logan, Kenneth A., and Linda L. Sweanor. *Ecology of an Unexploited Mountain Lion Population in a Desert Environment: Annual Reports.* Moscow, Idaho: Wildlife Research Institute. 1990,1992.

Meagher, M. *Cougar and Wolverine in Yellowstone National Park.* Yellowstone National Park. 1986.

Murphy, Kerry M., Gregory S. Felzien, and Scott Relyea. *Ecology of the Mountain Lion in Yellowstone: Cumulative Progress Report No. 5, November 1987–June 1992.* Moscow, Idaho: Hornocker Wildlife Institute.

————. *Predation Dynamics of Mountain Lions.* (Felis Concolor Missoulensis) *in the Northern Yellowstone Ecosystem: Progress Report, June 1992–1993.* Moscow, Idaho: Wildlife Research Institute.

Murphy, Kerry M. *Relationships Between a Mountain Lion Population and Hunting Pressure in Western Montana.* Statewide wildlife research: big game research, mountain lion ecology studies, July 1981–March 1983.

Orr, Phil C. "Felis Trumani: A New Radiocarbon Dated Cat Skull from Crypt Cave, Nevada." Santa Barbara: Museum of Natural History, 1969, bulletin no. 2, Department of Geology.

Ruth, Toni K., et al. *Evaluating Mountain Lion Translocation, Final Report.* U.S. Fish & Wildlife Service and Hornocker Wildlife Research Institute. 1993.

Seidensticker, IV., John C., et al. "Mountain Lion Social Organization in the Idaho Primitive Area." Wildlife Monographs 35 (December 1973): 3–61.

Shaw, Harley G., et al. *Factors Affecting Mountain Lion Densities and Cattle Depredation in Arizona, Final Report.* Arizona Game and Fish Department, 1988.

Shaw, Harley G. *Soul Among Lions.* Boulder: Johnson Books, 1989.

Sweanor, Linda L., and Kenneth A. Logan. "Life among Desert Cougars." *New Mexico Wildlife,* November-December 1992, 2–26.

————. "Mountain Lion Social Organization in a Desert Environment." Thesis. Moscow, Idaho: University of Idaho, 1990.

Tennesen, Michael. "Reining in a Runaway Herd." *National Wildlife,* October–November 1992, 22-25.

Turner, John W., Michael L. Wolfe, and Jay F. Kirkpatrick. "Seasonal Mountain Lion Predation on a Feral Horse Population." *Canadian Journal of Zoology* 70 (1992): 929-34.

Van Dyke, Fred G., et al. "Reactions of Mountain Lions to Logging and Human Activity." *Journal of Wildlife Management* 50, 1 (1986): 102–09.

White, Paula A., and Diane K. Boyd. "A Cougar, *Felis Concolor,* Kitten Killed and Eaten by Gray Wolves, *Canis Lupus,* in Glacier National Park, Montana." *Canadian Field-Naturalist* 103, 3 (1989): 408–09.

Yellowstone Park Scrapbook: Roosevelt's Visit. 1903. Scrapbook, Acc. no. 941, Yellowstone National Park Library.

TEXAS VARMINTS AND CALIFORNIA DREAMERS

Acuff, David S. "Perceptions of the Mountain Lion, 1825–1986, with Emphasis on *Felis concolor california.*" Thesis. Davis: University of California at Davis, 1988.

Beier, Paul. "Determining Minimum Habitat Areas and Habitat Corridors for Cougars." *Conservation Biology* 7, 1 (March 1993): 94–108.

————. "Cougar Attacks on Humans: An Update and Some Further Reflections." Proceedings of the 15th Vertebrate Pest Conference. Edited by J. E. Borrecco and R. E. Marsh. Davis: University of California at Davis, 1992, 365-67.

————. "Cougar Attacks on Humans in the United States and Canada." *Wildlife Society Bulletin* 19 (1991): 403-12.

Bigony, Mary-Love. "Cat of Controversy." *Texas Parks & Wildlife,* April 1993, 4–11.

Braun, Clait E., ed. *Mountain Lion–Human Interaction: Symposium and Workshop,* April 24-26, Denver: Colorado Division of Wildlife, 1991.

Bruce, Jay. "The Problem of Mountain Lion Control in California." *California Fish and Game:* 11, 1 (January 1925): 1–17.

———. "The Why and How of Mountain Lion Hunting in California." *California Fish and Game:* 8 (April 1922): 108–14.

Bruce, Jay C. *Cougar Killer.* New York: Comet Press Books, 1953.

Campos, Art. "Fund for Kin Grows in Killing by Cougar." *Sacramento Bee,* July 8, 1994.

Carroll, Christine. "Cat Fight." *Texas Monthly,* June 1993, 50–61.

Cooke, Jerry L. *Effects of Predator Control on Desert Mule Deer Numbers.* Performance Reports, 1984-1988. Austin: Texas Parks and Wildlife Department, 1988.

Creamer, Anita. "From Misinformation Grow Hurt and Anger." *Sacramento Bee,* July 9, 1994.

Engstrom, Mark, and Terry C. Maxwell. "Records of Mountain Lions (*Felis Concolor*) from the Western Edwards Plateau of Texas." *Texas Journal of Science* 40, 4 (1988): 450-52.

Fleming, Carl M. "Lion-Human Interactions in Big Bend National Park." Unpublished. 1988.

Grinnell, Joseph, and Joseph Dixon. "The Systematic Status of the Mountain Lion of California." *University of California Publications in Zoology* 21 (1923): 325-33.

Harvey and Stanley Associates, Inc. *Mountain Lions* (Felis Concolor) *in the Vicinity of Carlsbad Caverns National Park, New Mexico and Guadalupe Mountains National Park, Texas: An Ecological Study, Final Report.* Santa Fe: U.S. National Park Service, 1986.

Hopkins, Rickey Alan. "Ecology of the Puma in the Diablo Range, CA." Ph.D. dissertation, University of California, 1989.

Koford, Carl B. *Status and Welfare of the Puma* (Felis Concolor) *in California, 1973–1976.* Final report to the Defenders of Wildlife and the National Audubon Society, 1977.

Laycock, George. "Cougars in Conflict." *Audubon,* March 1988, 88–95.

Mansfield, Terry M. "The Status of Mountain Lions in California." *Transactions of the Western Section of The Wildlife Society* 25 (1989): 72–76.

McBride, Roy T. "The Status and Ecology of the Mountain Lion (*Felis Concolor Stanleyana*) of the Texas-Mexico Border." Thesis. Alpine, Texas: Sul Ross University, 1976.

McKeown, Michael Sean. "An Analysis of Protective Attitudes Concerning the Puma (*Felis Concolor*) in California." Thesis. Chico: California State University, 1973.

"Mountain Lions in Texas: Staff Briefing Report." Texas Parks and Wildlife Department, January 16, 1992.

Neal, Donald L., George N. Steger, and Ronald C. Bertram. *Mountain Lions: Preliminary Findings on Home-Range Use and Density in the Central Sierra Nevada.* Berkeley: U.S. Forest Service, 1987.

Owings, Margaret W. "The Story of the Southern Sea Otter." *Update on Law-Related Education* 17, 3 (Fall 1993).

Padley, Wayne D., "Home Ranges and Social Interaction of Mountain Lions in the Santa Ana Mountains, California." Thesis. Pomona: California State Polytechnic University, 1990.

Payton, Ken, and Gary Sandy. "Death Warrant for the North Kings Lions?" *Defenders,* March–April 1986, 4-9.

Pence, Danny B., et al. *Aspects of the Ecology of Mountain Lions* (Felis Concolor) *in Big Bend National Park: Final Report.* Santa Fe: U.S. National Park Service, 1985.

Perry, Tony. "Park Officials Urged to Move, Not Kill, Cougar." *Los Angeles Times,* September 9, 1993. A1.

———. "Rangers Kill Cougar After Girl Is Attacked." *Los Angeles Times,* September 19, 1993, A1.

Quinn, Michelle. "Mountain Lion's Cub Gets More Aid Than Victim's Children." *New York Times,* May 27, 1994.

Rauber, Paul. "When Nature Turns Nasty." *Sierra,* November–December 1993, 46-52.

Riess, Suzanne and Ann Lage. *Margaret Wentworth Owings, Artist and Wildlife and Environmental Defender.* Berkeley: University of California, 1991.

———. "Margaret Wentworth Owings Oral History." *Bancroftiana* no. 105 (December 1992): 1-3.

Russ, William. *Mountain Lion Status Survey* (Job No. 69, Federal Aid Project No W-103-19, Nongame Wildlife Investigations). Austin: Texas Parks and Wildlife Department, 1989.

————. *Mountain Lion Status Survey* (Job No. 69, Federal Aid Project No. W-125-4, Wildlife Research and Surveys). Austin: Texas Parks and Wildlife Department, 1993.

Ruth, Toni Karen. "Mountain Lion Use of an Area of High Recreational Development in Big Bend National Park, Texas." Thesis. College Station: Texas A&M University, 1991.

Schoenherr, Allan A. *A Natural History of California.* Berkeley: University of California, 1992.

Scrivner, Jerry H., et al. "Sheep Losses to Predators on a California Range, 1973–1983." *Journal of Range Management* 38, 5 (September 1985): 418–21.

Seidensticker, John. "Mountain Lions Don't Stalk People. True or False?" *Smithsonian,* February 1992, 113-22.

Shults, Regina Barbara. "Gods, Humans, and Mountain Lions in the Pecos Pictographs." Thesis. Austin: University of Texas, 1985.

Sitton, Larry W. *California Mountain Lion Investigations with Recommendations for Management.* Sacramento: California Department of Fish and Game, 1977.

————. *Mountain Lion Predation on Livestock in California.* Sacramento: California Department of Fish and Game, 1978.

Sitton, Larry W., and Sue Wallen. *California Mountain Lion Study.* Sacramento: California Department of Fish and Game, 1976.

Stilwell, Hallie C. *I'll Gather My Geese.* College Station: Texas A&M University Press, 1991.

Tischendorf, Jay, et al. "A Sighting of a Large Group of Pumas." Submitted to *Southwestern Naturalist,* 1994.

Vermeulen, Terri. "Cougars May Stall Project." *Anaheim Bulletin,* February 27, 1992.

Waid, Douglas D. "Movements, Food Habits, and Helminth Parasites of Mountain Lions in Southwestern Texas." Ph.D. dissertation, Texas Tech University, 1990.

Ward, Geoffrey C. "India's Intensifying Dilemma: Can Tigers and People Coexist?" *Smithsonian,* November 1987.

Weaver, Richard A. *Status of the Mountain Lion in California with Recommendations for Management.* Sacramento: California Department of Fish and Game, 1982.

THE FLORIDA PANTHER PEOPLE

Alvarez, Ken. *Twilight of the Panther.* Sarasota: Myakka River Publishers, 1993.

Belden, Robert C. "The Florida Panther." *Audubon Wildlife Report,* 1989, 515–32.

Belden, Robert C., Bruce W. Hagedorn, and William B. Frankenberger. *Florida Panther Captive Breeding/Reintroduction Feasibility.* Tallahassee: Florida Game and Fresh Water Fish Commission, 1987, 1989, 1990. Study no. 7507, Federal no. E-1-II-E-7.

Belden, Robert C., et al. "Panther Habitat Use in Southern Florida." *Journal of Wildlife Management* 52 (October 1988): 660–63.

Brana, William V., ed. *Conference Proceedings: Survival of the Florida Panther, a Discussion of Issues and Accomplishments.* Tallahassee: The Conference, 1986.

Dubost, Gerard, and Jean-Yves Royere. "Hybridization Between Ocelot (*Felis Pardalis*) and Puma (*Felis Concolor*)." *Zoo Biology* 12 (1993): 277–83.

Fergus, Chuck. "The Florida Panther Verges on Extinction." *Science* 251 (March 8, 1991): 1178–80.

Florida Panther Interagency Committee. *Florida Panther* (Felis Concolor coryi) *Revised Recovery Plan.* U.S. Fish and Wildlife Service, 1987.

———. *Status Report: Mercury Contamination in Florida Panthers.* 1989.

Flowers, Charles. "Searching for the One True Cat." *National Wildlife,* October–November 1989, 24–28.

Genetic Management Strategies and Population Viability of the Florida Panther: Report of a Workshop, White Oak Plantation Conservation Center, Yulee, Florida, October 1992.

Jordan, Dennis B. *Final Environmental Assessment: A Proposal to Issue Endangered Species Permits to Capture Select Florida Panthers and Establish a Captive Population.* Gainesville: U.S. Fish and Wildlife Service, 1990.

———. *Preliminary Analysis of Potential Florida Panther Reintroduction Sites.* Gainesville: U.S. Fish and Wildlife Service, 1993.

Lebelson, Harry, and Bette Rush. "Take Two Panther Claws . . ." *Science* 84, 5 (October 1984): 82.

Logan, Todd, et al. *Florida Panther Habitat Preservation Plan (South Florida Population).* U.S. Fish and Wildlife Service, November 1993.

Maehr, David S. "The Florida Panther and Private Lands." *Conservation Biology* 4, 2 (June 1990): 167–70.

———. *Florida Panther Movements, Social Organization, and Habitat Utilization.* Tallahassee: Florida Game and Fresh Water Fish Commission, 1989, 1990. Study no. 7502, Federal no. E-1-II-2.

Maehr, David S., E. Darrell Land, and Jayde C. Roof. "Florida Panthers: Social Ecology." *National Geographic Research & Exploration* 7, 4 (1991): 414–31.

Maehr, David S., E. Darrell Land, and Melody E. Roelke. "Mortality Patterns of Panthers in Southwest Florida." *Proceedings of the Annual Conference of the Southeastern Association of Fish and Wildlife Agencies* 45 (1991): 201–07.

Maehr, David S., et al. "Day Beds, Natal Dens, and Activity of Florida Panthers." *Proceedings of the Annual Conference of the Southeastern Fish and Wildlife Agencies* 44 (1990): 310–18.

Maehr, David S., et al. "Early Maternal Behavior in the Florida Panther." *American Midland Naturalist* 122 (1989): 34–43.

Maehr, David S., et al. "Food Habits of Panthers in Southwest Florida." *Journal of Wildlife Management* 54, 3 (1990): 420–23.

McMullen, James P. *Cry of the Panther: Quest of a Species.* Englewood, Florida: Pineapple Press, 1984.

Morin, Tina L. "Indians, Non-Indians, and the Endangered Panther: Will the Indian Non-Indian Conflict Be Resolved before the Panther Disappears?" *Public Land Law Review* 13 (1992): 168–78.

North Florida Panther Reintroduction Study: Progress Report. Florida Game and Fresh Water Fish Commission, February 1993.

O'Brien, Stephen J., et al. "Genetic Introgression within the Florida Panther *Felis concolor coryi.*" *National Geographic Research* 6, 4 (1990): 485–94.

Patterson, Patricia E. "Ecosystem Level Research Planning and Use in the National Park Service: The Case of the Florida Panther." Thesis. Georgia Institute of Technology, 1991.

Pritchard, Peter C. H., ed. *Proceedings of the Florida Panther Conference, Sponsored by the Florida Audubon Society, and Held in Orlando, March 17–18, 1976.* Florida Game and Fresh Water Fish Commission.

Radetsky, Peter. "Cat Fight." *Discover,* July 1992.

Roelke, Melody E. *Florida Panther Biomedical Investigation.* Tallahassee: Florida Game and Fresh Water Fish Commission, 1990. Study no. 7506, Federal no. E-1- II-E-6.

———. "Researchers Report Breakthrough: In Vitro Fertilization." *Coryi: Official Newsletter of the Florida Panther Interagency Committee,* November 1988, 1.

Roelke, Melody E., Janice S. Martenson, and Stephen J. O'Brien. "The Consequences of Demographic Reduction and Genetic Depletion in the Endangered Florida Panther." *Current Biology* 3, 6 (1993): 340–50.

Schortemeyer, James L., et al. "Prey Management for the Florida Panther: A Unique Role for Wildlife Managers." In *Transactions of the 56th North American Wildlife & Natural Resources Conference, March 17–22, 1991, Edmonton, Alberta.* Edited by Richard E. McCabe. Washington, D.C.: Wildlife Management Institute, 1991.

Seal, U. S., et al. *Florida Panther Viability Analysis and Species Survival Plan.* Based upon a workshop held October 31-November 2, 1989 at Gainesville.

Shomer, Enid. *Stalking the Florida Panther.* Washington, D.C.: Word Works, 1987.

Tinsley, Jim Bob. *The Florida Panther.* St. Petersburg: Great Outdoors Publishing Co., 1970.

Ward, Mary. "Florida Panther—Reality or Myth?" *Florida Agriculture,* December 1, 1993, 10–11.

Weisman, Brent Richards. *Like Beads on a String: A Culture History of the Seminole Indians in Northern Peninsular Florida.* Tuscaloosa: University of Alabama Press, 1989.

THE SPIRITUAL CHALLENGE
OF THE EASTERN PANTHER

Altherr, Thomas. "Pantherites Redivivus: The Catamount in Vermont Culture." Unpublished. 1994.

Bodo, Pete. "Ghost of Supposedly Extinct Cat Leaves a Real Devil of a Void." *New York Times,* September 12, 1993, 13.

Boehm, Christopher. "Ambivalence and Compromise in Human Nature." *American Anthropologist* 91 (1989): 921–36.

Brocke, Ranier H. *Reintroduction of the Cougar* Felis Concolor *in Adirondack Park: A Problem Analysis and Recommendations.* Albany: New York State Department of Environmental Conservation, 1981.

Brocke, Ranier, et al. "Restoration of Large Predators: Potentials and Problems." In *Challenges in the Conservation of Biological Resources: A Practitioner's Guide.* Edited by D. J. Decker et al. Boulder: Westview Press, 1991.

Cahalane, Victor H. *A Preliminary Study of Distribution and Numbers of Cougar, Grizzly and Wolf in North America.* New York: New York Zoological Society, 1964.

Coleman, Loren. *Mysterious America.* London: Faber & Faber, 1983.

Culbertson, Nicole. *Status and History of the Mountain Lion in the Great Smoky Mountains National Park.* Gatlinburg, Tennessee: National Park Service, 1976.

Dahne, Bob. "The Truth about Black Panthers." *Florida Wildlife* 12, 6 (November 1958): 26–27, 48–49.

Downing, Robert L. "The Current Status of the Cougar in the Southern Appalachian [sic]." In *Proceedings of Nongame and Endangered Wildlife Symposium,* Athens, Georgia, August 13–14, 1981.

———. *Eastern Cougar Recovery Plan.* Atlanta: U.S. Fish and Wildlife Service, 1982.

———. "The Search for Cougars in the Eastern United States." *Cryptozoology,* 1984, 31–49.

Dunstone, N., and M. L. Gorman, eds. *Mammals as Predators.* Oxford: Clarendon Press for The Zoological Society of London, 1993.

"Eagle, Peregrine, Red-Cockade, and Cougar Among Protected Species in Virginia." *Endangered Species Technical Bulletin* 4, 2 (February 1979): 3, 6.

"The Eastern Puma: Evidence Continues to Build." *International Society of Cryptozoology Newsletter* 8, 3 (Autumn 1989): 1–8.

Fair, Jeff. "The Wolf Test." *Appalachia* (December 15, 1992): 9–23.

Foreman, Dave. *Confessions of an Eco–Warrior.* New York: Harmony Books, 1991.

Foreman, Dave, et al. "The Wildlands Project Mission Statement." *Wild Earth Special Issue* (1992): 3–4.

Francis, Di. *Cat Country: The Quest for the British Big Cat.* Newton Abbot, U.K.: David & Charles, 1983.

Frome, Michael. "Panthers Wanted—Alive, Back East, Where They Belong." In *Conscience of a Conservationist*. Knoxville: University of Tennessee Press, 1989.

Garrison, Bill. "Cougar: Dead or Alive?" *Country,* December 1980, 34–36.

Guynn, David C., Robert L. Downing, and George R. Askew. "Estimating the Probability of Non-Detection of Low Density Populations." *Cryptozoology* 4 (1985): 55–60.

Hugo, Nancy. "A Catamount Tale." *Virginia Wildlife,* February 1987, 9–13.

Huyghe, Patrick. "Maine Event." *Audubon* (May–June 1994): 18, 20.

Lee, David S. "Unscrambling Rumors: The Status of the Panther in North Carolina." *Wildlife in North Carolina,* July 1977, 6–9.

Lutz, John, and Linda Lutz, eds. *Easter Puma Network News.* Baltimore: July 1989–1994.

Nowak, Ronald M. *The Cougar in the United States and Canada.* New York Zoological Society and U.S. Fish and Wildlife Service, 1976.

Reed, Ted, ed. *Panther Prints, the Official Newsletter of the Friends of the Eastern Panther.* Exeter, New Hampshire, 1990–1994.

Regan, Timothy W., and David S. Maehr. "Melanistic Bobcats in Florida." *Florida Field Naturalist* 18, 4 (1990): 84–87.

Sass, Herbert R. "The Panther Prowls the East Again!" *Saturday Evening Post,* March 13, 1954, vol. 31, 133–136.

Shore, Bradd. "Human Ambivalence and the Structuring of Moral Values." *Ethos* 18, 2 (June 1990): 165–79.

Shuker, Karl P. N. *Mystery Cats of the World: From Blue Tigers to Exmoor Beasts.* London: Robert Hale, 1989.

Sincoff, Julie B. "The Psychological Characteristics of Ambivalent People." *Clinical Psychology Review* 10 (1990): 43–68.

Spargo, John. *The Catamount in Vermont.* Bennington, Vermont, 1950.

Taylor, Kenny. "The Cats of the Baskervilles." *BBC Wildlife,* November 1993.

Thomas, Elizabeth Marshall. *The Tribe of Tiger: Cats and Their Culture.* New York: Simon & Schuster, 1994.

Tischendorf, Jay. "The Eastern Panther on Film? Results of an Investigation." *Cryptozoology* 9 (1990): 74–78.

———. "The Puma in the Central Mountains and Plains." Unpublished. 1993.

Tischendorf, Jay, ed. *Eastern Panther Update.* Fort Collins: 1992–1994.

Tischendorf, Jay, and Donald F. McAlpine. "Melanism in Bobcats: An Addendum." Submitted to *Florida Field Naturalist,* 1994.

Turner, Dennis C., and Patrick Bateson, eds. *The Domestic Cat, the Biology of Its Behavior.* New York: Cambridge University Press, 1990.

Ulmer, Jr., Fred A. "Melanism in the Felidae, with Special Reference to the Genus Lynx." *Journal of Mammalogy* 22 (1941): 285–88.

Van Dyke, Fred Gerald. "A Western Study of Cougar Track Surveys and Environmental Disturbances Affecting Cougars Related to the Status of the Eastern Cougar." Ph.D. dissertation, State University of New York, 1983.

Wallace, Joseph. "Has the Big Cat Come Back?" *Sierra,* May–June 1986, 20–21.

Wilson, D.E., and D. M. Reeder, eds. *Mammal Species of the World.* Washington, D.C.: Smithsonian Institution Press, 1993.

Wright, Bruce S. *The Eastern Panther, a Question of Survival.* Toronto: Clarke, Irwin &Co. Ltd., 1972.

———. *The Ghost of North America.* New York: Vantage Press, 1959.

Wrigley, Robert E., and Robert W. Nero. *Manitoba's Big Cat: The Story of the Cougar in Manitoba.* Winnipeg: Manitoba Museum of Man and Nature, 1982.

PERMISSIONS

Excerpts from *Theodore Roosevelt, An Autobiography* by Theodore Roosevelt reprinted with permission of Scribner, an imprint of Simon & Schuster (Charles Scribner's Sons, New York, 1926).

Excerpt from *Tales of Lonely Trails* by Zane Grey reprinted with permission of Northland Publishing (1986).

Excerpts from *The Yellowstone Story: A History of Our First National Park* by Aubrey L. Haines reprinted with permission of University Press of Colorado (1977).

Excerpt from *Soul among Lions, The Cougar as Peaceful Adversary* by Harley Shaw reprinted with permission of Johnson Books (1989).

Excerpt from "Cat Fight" by Christine Carroll reprinted with permission from the June 1993 issue of *Texas Monthly*.

Excerpts from "Margaret Owings, Artist and Wildlife Defender," an oral history conducted 1986–1988 by Suzanne Riess and Ann Lage, Regional Oral History Office, University of California, Berkeley, (1991) used with permission of The Bancroft Library.

Excerpt from "The Problem of Mountain Lion Control in California" by Jay Bruce, *California Fish and Game,* v. II, no. 1, January 1925, reprinted with permission of *California Fish and Game.*

Excerpt from *Stalking the Florida Panther* by Enid Shomer reprinted with permission of Word Works (1987).

Excerpt from *Twilight of the Panther* by Ken Alvarez reprinted with permission of Myakka River Publishing (1993).

Excerpt from *Walking the Dead Diamond River* by Edward Hoagland reprinted with permission of Random House (1973).

Excerpt from *Wild Earth Magazine,* Special Issue on the Wildlands Project, reprinted with permission of *Wild Earth Magazine* (1992).

Excerpts from *Lives of Game Animals* by Ernest Thompson Seton reprinted with permission of Doubleday, Doran, & Company (1929).

Excerpt from "Wilderness" in Susan L. Flader and J. Baird Calicott, eds., *The River of the Mother of God and Other Essays by Aldo Leopold* © 1991 The Aldo Leopold Shack Foundation. Reprinted with permission of the University of Wisconsin Press.

Excerpt from *John Banister and His Natural History of Virginia, 1678–1692* by Joseph Ewan and Nesta Ewan reprinted with permission of the University of Illinois Press (1970).

Excerpt from *I'll Gather My Geese* by Hallie L. Stillwell reprinted with permission of Texas A&M University Press (1991).

Excerpts from *Friends of the Eastern Panther Newsletter* (winter 1990–91) used with permission.

Excerpts from *Roping Lions in the Grand Canyon* by Zane Grey, published by Grosset & Dunlap (1924) reprinted with permission of Loren Grey.